SECRETS

OF THE

SILK ROAD

SECRETS
OF THE
SILK ROAD

Finding the Lost Sacred Books of the Gobi

⟋

LARRY ANDREWS

st. lynn's
press

St. Lynn's Press
www.stlynnspress.com

Library of Congress Control Number 2005927481
CIP data available upon request
ISBN 0-9767631-2-5

The information presented herein is for general
cultural information only and is not intended to act
as advice for any medical or psychological purposes.

Neither the author nor the publisher recommends traveling
to Central Asia without consulting one's State
Department and without consulting with an experienced
travel guide to the region.

First Edition: 2006

Printed in the United States of America
Printed on recycled paper

0 9 8 7 6 5 4 3 2 1

Dedicated to
those who would see through the clouds

CONTENTS

PREFACE

I HAVE BEEN ASKED BY SEVERAL PEOPLE TO JUSTIFY WHY I SHOULD publicly share spiritual teachings and secrets that have long been kept hidden in the remote regions of the Gobi Desert where they originated—information that has only been passed down from teacher to apprentice. So I want to address this concern at the outset.

Gil-Hamesch, the spiritual elder of the Kashi people with whom I stayed, told me that the greatest and truest knowledge could never be bought, sold or stolen. Wise words in the hands of foolish people would only make them more foolish, he said. Furthermore, he directly asked me to share the ancient teachings of his people's *Song of Eternity* with people in the West. I was asked to have faith that there was a higher purpose to his request. To this end, he personally initiated me into the ancient Kashi traditions of the Gobi Desert and provided me with the assistance of an English-speaking guide named Thod.

This is the story of how I came to discover and then study the *Song of Eternity* with the help of three remarkable men. I truly owe them a lifetime of gratitude: Thod, Gil-Hamesch, and "the Cook." I have chosen to refer to them by their nicknames and to change the names and traits of several other people in this book, including the Tibetan monks who escorted me on a clandestine flight across the Himalayas in hopes of meeting the Dalai Lama. This is necessary not only out of respect for their privacy, but from a real concern for their safety.

My Kashi informants dwell within the region of Xinjiang, a semi-autonomous part of China, yet like Tibet, still governed harshly by the Chinese central government. I learned first-hand the fierce determination of the Chinese government to eliminate all forms of religious or cultural expression, which they see as a threat to Eastern China's hold on the untapped gas, oil and water resources. In Xinjiang the only officially permitted religion is Islam, and it is strictly regulated. In spite of this, some native residents along the edge of the Gobi Desert continue a sacred way of life brought to them by their ancestors, the ancient nomadic bards. Secretly, they keep alive the poetic wisdom of the *Song of Eternity*, believing that in the greater cycles of time the foolishness of men has no ultimate reality, and wisdom alone prevails.

If there had initially been an element of objective research to my journey it soon became an expedition into spiritual terrain, a voyage into the roots of all of our stories and myths, whether we were born in the East or the West.

There are a number of individuals I mention only briefly, because I knew little about them at the time this journey took place. After I returned I learned a great deal more about the man I refer to as "the Gardener," as well as Father Franck. Their stories will be told in subsequent books, along with deeper explorations of the self-empowerment techniques that were taught to me during my sojourn in their world.

As for the events described in this book, I have recorded them as accurately as possible. However, my conversations with my hosts were often long and involved—many lasting through the night—as I sought to understand a view of life so different from my own. I have tried to resist interpreting their words or comparing them to other beliefs, except where they themselves made comparisons.

The *Song of Eternity* is ancient, yet its message has never been more relevant. The remarkable heart of its teachings is that there is a little-known and hidden all-pervading source of power that is available to each of us—and more importantly, that it is possible to awaken ourselves to this essential life force and to work with it to bring greater power into our everyday lives.

The Kashi people believe that events do not happen randomly. They would say that if this book has appeared in your hands, it is a gift to you from the hidden mysteries of Spirit. They would say that this is a unique opportunity for new understanding and a new awakening at a deeper level, meant especially for you.

As Thod once said to me: "For those who are ready to wake up, contemplating the verses of the *Song of Eternity* can become a doorway on the journey to the Valley of Miracles."

Larry Andrews

BEFORE

1970. WHEN I WAS A BOY I THOUGHT THE BEST STORIES WERE THE ONES where you had to keep your eyes out for clues, and just when you thought you had the mystery figured out, the ending would be a complete surprise.

I loved books. Perhaps it was an escape from a family life that wasn't always easy, but I think it was more than that. I was hungry to know what the world was about, beyond my nice middle class neighborhood in North Hollywood. Fortunately for me, I was abetted in my quest by a dear family friend, Dorothy. Everyone called her Dorothy, even little children; she wouldn't have it any other way. Dorothy was not my real godmother, but she was the very essence of godmother: warm, nurturing and very much concerned with my spiritual education. I don't think I ever regarded Dorothy as a woman, exactly, she simply *was*. She guided me, taught me, and opened my eyes when they needed opening, which happened with more frequency as I lurched my way through adolescence.

She had the biggest collection of books I had ever seen—whole walls of shelves on archaeology, history and science, and tales of daring explorations in the inner and outer worlds. It was Dorothy who first convinced me that there *were* such things as inner worlds. Her small English cottage in the foothills of Pasadena was to become my refuge for many years.

I can't remember when I first started bicycling on my ten-speed Schwinn to her house on weekends. Dorothy's home was a favorite stopping-off place for people from all over the world. In those days

I didn't fully understand how revered she was as a spiritual teacher and counselor. She was just Dorothy, who seemed to have all the time in the world to sit with me and tell me about the ancient mystery schools and the meaning of the great search stories of mythology. I couldn't get enough. There was such a feeling of comfort and wonder with it all. When she spoke of the existence of an ancient wisdom that lies buried in the heart of every religion it somehow made sense to me, even though I was not especially religious. I had no idea that she was laying down clues for me to follow, testing me in her own way to see if I could be trusted with deeper knowledge.

One chilly March morning when I was seventeen, I arrived at her porch and rapped my usual *long-short-long* on her weathered front door. I had a lot on my mind. My future was a question mark and I needed to talk. I needed to hear again why I should bother applying to college, which at the moment seemed completely irrelevant to me.

Dorothy's voice called to me to let myself in. I found her in her book-lined study where she was sitting with a knitted throw over her legs. More than a month had passed since my last visit and I was surprised to see how frail she looked—how suddenly old. She waved away my worried look with a welcoming smile and patted the seat next to her. "I'm so glad you're here," she said cheerfully as I dropped my lanky frame onto her brown leather sofa. "Lots to talk about, today, I think." I knew that she knew exactly why I had come. She always did.

To this day, I can't remember very well the small details of her appearance. But I do remember her eyes. They were clear and blue, and when she was speaking of profound things I always felt as if someone very powerful—not the everyday Dorothy—was observing me. This morning she listened while I rambled on about my troubles, then she cut short my monologue with a simple question: "What is it you want to do with your life?"

I couldn't answer. I hadn't figured it out. I wanted to do something special, I told her, but I didn't know what that would be. I loved baseball, but my family had already made it clear that that wasn't a worthy goal in life. "Maybe music or languages," I said, "or

I could just take off and hitchhike around the country first, pick up money doing odd jobs . . . see things . . ."

She smiled sympathetically. "So you're telling me—or not telling me—that you need time to grow into yourself." I guess I nodded. "Then my best advice to your restless self would be this: Go to college, do your best to master everything they have to offer you. After that it won't be so hard to sort out your priorities—I promise."

It wasn't the answer I was hoping for. She placed her hand over mine and leaned closer. "There's another reason you came today, dear, and I'm about to tell you what it is. Now, you can think of it as just an interesting story, or you can trust that I have my reasons for revealing it to you." When I looked into her eyes they were *those* eyes, the ones with the power.

"Okay," I said, ready for anything.

"Once upon a time," she began with a wink, "perhaps seven hundred years ago, there was a very learned Jesuit missionary who traveled the ancient Silk Road that extended between Europe and China. His journeys took him deep into Central Asia, where he lived among the nomadic tribes of the great Gobi Desert. After many years he was taken to a remote place with a strange name: the Monastery of the Sacred Tree. It was carved into the side of a cliff and housed both renunciants and lay persons. Yet, curiously, it didn't appear to be a religious establishment in the usual sense of the word. This place existed, he was told, for the study of the higher truths of life. And then he was shown an ancient manuscript. Its origins extended back before anyone's memory—before Christianity or Buddhism, he soon discovered. With the help of the people there he studied the sacred text, which turned out to be nothing less than an instruction manual for the human soul. He had never encountered anything like it, nor had he ever met anyone like the abbot, who was called Gilgamesh. It was said that this Gilgamesh reincarnated through the ages as protector of the manuscript and the wisdom it contained.

"There at the edge of the Gobi Desert the Jesuit priest found what he hadn't realized he'd been searching for all his life. When he finally returned to Europe he was a changed man. He quietly set about forming an order of service, calling it the Order of the Sacred

Tree, and using the teachings of the manuscript as its central principles."

"You're saying this really happened?" I interrupted. I could hear the skepticism in my voice.

"That is for you to decide," she said evenly, and I felt like a child again. "The order that the priest founded was not based on the dogmas of any religion, but on a vision of the unity of all life, and on the power of the individual soul to find its own way towards the Divine. In those days that was a dangerous thing to be involved with. Heresy. You remember what happened to Galileo when he ventured to think outside the Church's vision of the world?" Dorothy looked at me to make sure I was following her.

"So this order had to be secret." I said.

"There was no choice. Fortunately for us, we live in a time when we are free to explore the mysteries of life." She stopped for a moment with her eyes closed, and I thought at first she was in pain. "I'm only resting," she said to my unspoken concern. A new thought crossed my mind: Dorothy could actually *die* one day.

When she spoke again there was more energy in her voice. "In time, this priest drew around him a small group, men and women of great purity and power, who were free of the illusions that fascinate the average person. Their sole purpose was to serve humanity and help it to achieve its noblest potential. I will only say that this group of extraordinary people kept the Order alive through the harshest of times, influencing world affairs in ways that history will never recognize."

"That's pretty incredible," I said. "Whatever became of them?"

Dorothy took a sip from the glass of water on the table next to her. "It's a long story. Why don't we get a nice fire going first? It's a good day for a fire."

As I wadded up the newspapers for kindling and brought in firewood from behind the house I was puzzling about how a secret group of people could possibly change world events if nobody knew about them in the first place. Dorothy's fireplace didn't have gas, so I lit a long matchstick and blew on the first sparks until I finally had a roaring fire going. It felt good to be doing something for her.

"And throw in a handful of the juniper berries from the hearth basket," she said. The berries hit the burning logs with a crackling burst and filled the wood paneled room with a sweet smelling smoke. In my memory of it, the room was always warm with color, from the old Oriental rugs scattered about on the floor, to the tabletops filled with a jumble of things she had brought home from her wide travels—and gifts from her many friends: scarabs from Egypt, a tiny brass oil lamp from India, a seated bronze Buddha from Thailand, fragments of ancient pottery from excavations she had been on, and all those stones she couldn't help picking up from everywhere she went.

We sat in companionable silence watching the fire. "You were wondering what finally happened to the Order of the Sacred Tree," she said after a while. "Well, it depends on whom you ask. I can say with some certainty that the Order still exists."

It suddenly dawned on me. "Are you one of them?"

"No," she said, "but I have been privileged to know of their presence."

I was having trouble guessing what this was all about, what she was really telling me "So these are real people who are alive—on this earth, right now." I looked to her for confirmation.

"Real people," she said, "who have become who they are through the choices they have made. But at the end of the 19th century the Order had grown very small and was almost in danger of dying out, until a man known only as 'the Gardener' traveled to Central Asia to find the Monastery of the Sacred Tree and the manuscript entrusted to its care. From the stories I've heard, the Gardener was a quiet man who loved humanity with a passionate commitment. They say that at the monastery he was initiated into the deepest mysteries of the manuscript before he returned to Europe. It was he who revived the Order as it exists today." She paused. "Yes, they are indeed very real people."

I knew this must all be very important, but I was struggling with it. "But what about the old monastery?" I asked. "How real is that?" At that time in my life I could definitely relate to the idea of a hidden monastery in some mysterious land.

She read the tone in my voice and smiled. "I suppose you'd like nothing better than to skip your education and hitchhike into

Central Asia to find it." She was teasing, but she wasn't far from the truth. I asked if she knew where the monastery was.

"If it still exists—and I believe it does—it would be somewhere on the Silk Road, north of the Himalayan Mountains of Tibet. Now is not the time for you to go. You have so much to learn first. Until it is the right time, you would never be able find such a place anyway. "But," she said, "if you *were* to go, you would have to go to Afghanistan or Pakistan and seek out the Karakoram Caravan Pass through the great Himalayas. At the end of this pass you would find a vast desert and then follow the northern branch of the Silk Road until you reached the Celestial Mountains. No small task for a boy from the suburbs."

I felt as if she had tempted me with something and then taken it back again. "Why did you tell me all this?"

"Because there may come a time when you will choose to seek out the monastery and the one called Gilgamesh, if that is what you wish. My only regret is that I won't be around to see it. Now, I'm going to give you another name to remember: Father Franck. He lives in Switzerland. When you are ready to choose your path in life and you desire to learn more about the Order, he is the one who will help you. Your Aunt Virginia will know how to contact him."

By now I was really uncomfortable with what she was saying, as if she knew she was going to die and she needed to tend to some last details—which for some reason involved *me*.

She asked me to help her up. "I want to show you some things," she said, and walked slowly to a glass display case across the room. She took down a small box that held a piece of white silk, embroidered at its center with a golden figure eight. I recognized it right away from my earliest memories of Dorothy's house. "Do you remember how you used to beg me to tell you what it meant, and I said that it represented the Lord's Prayer?" She began tracing the form of the figure eight with her finger. "The 'Our Father' started here at the top, and the prayer moved around to the bottom as we said 'Give us this day our daily bread,' and then it went up the other side again until we said 'forever and ever.' And I told you that the words of the prayer were just the same as the symbol of the figure itself—from the eternal to the material world and back to the eternal? That was too much for a child's mind, I knew, but you were so interested in it that I had to try to tell you more."

"I think I just enjoyed hearing you talk about it." I said, hoping to lighten things up a little.

"But I've never shown you this before," she said, reaching to the back of the middle shelf and bringing down a small golden statue. It looked like a double figure eight at first, but it was really two entwined serpents, with a sun at the top and a moon at the bottom; like a caduceus, the medical symbol, but more elaborate. I thought it was very beautiful and I said so to Dorothy.

"It is the primary symbol of the Order, a gift to me from Father Franck. He said that it has been handed down for generations, ever since the Gardener brought it to the West from the monastery. When he gave it to me he said I would know who to pass it on to—and I know now that it is you."

She held it out, but I pulled back from it instinctively. Things were getting too strange.

"Take it, dear. There's no one else who should have it." She put it into my hand and closed my fingers over it. It felt cool and hot at the same time, which was *really* strange. "Now pay attention," she said. Her blue eyes were still in power mode. "Someday it is to be returned to the monastery from which it came. Present this to Father Franck when you are ready. Think of it as a key." Almost as an afterthought she said, ". . . and remember, there are many kinds of doors in this world."

That's all I recall of that amazing day at Dorothy's. She gave me a hug and a kiss on the cheek and told me she needed to rest. I got on my ten-speed and pedaled for home with my head spinning and the golden statue tucked deep in my backpack.

~

1996. AND THEN I GREW UP. GRADUALLY, IMPERCEPTIBLY, THE THINGS that Dorothy talked about that day receded into the background of my life, until they were only the stuff of occasional daydreams. But when they did come, my heart would speed up and I would find myself wondering all over again if any of it could possibly be true—

if there really were places on Earth where wisdom was held in trust for the ones who searched.

Because of troubles at home I left early to fend for myself, finishing high school in another part of town and graduating near the top of my class. I never doubted that I would succeed in anything I put my mind to. The only question was *what*. For a while I worked in construction, building houses to earn college tuition money. My college years were always a balancing act of work and study. I drove myself towards accomplishment. I had an easy rapport with philosophy, music and psychology, and believed that my future lay somewhere there. One thing I knew for certain: Whatever I ended up doing with myself I would never become an engineer like my father.

I had lost my mother when I was six, after she fell in love with another man and disappeared from my life to follow her dreams. My father remarried a widow with two children of her own and little affection to spare for my younger brother and me. Dorothy had been the one who filled in as mother—and in some ways as father. Now she too was gone. The feeling of emptiness and irreparable loss buried itself just beyond my awareness and stayed there.

In my earliest daydreams I had fantasized about going to holy places where prayer and meditation were things to study and master, where learning to find inner peace was a worthy goal. As I moved into my twenties I just wanted to stop the sands from shifting beneath my feet.

I began to be seriously attracted to science. Here I found a world of logic and order, a world I could rely upon, where each scientific principle was based on tried and proven precedents. I pursued it with single-mindedness and passion.

In time, the boy who swore he would never become an engineer became one. He married, had children and divorced. He was now a civil engineer, designing municipal projects for cities and working with large private developers. A good citizen, good father, a person people trusted—in most outward ways a success. But the nagging truth was that he had almost lost touch with the boy Dorothy had such hopes for. That, too, was buried just beyond awareness. Except for the daydreams; they never gave up.

I was living in Grass Valley, California, when the invitation from the People's Republic of China arrived on my desk.

I had been thinking about attending a conference for engineers that the Chinese government was organizing to encourage collaborative projects with the U.S. Shortly after learning of the China conference I read in the newspapers about a devastating flood in Urumchi, in the western Chinese province of Xinjiang. Their water treatment plants had been flooded, posing an enormous risk to peoples' health. I knew that this was something I had the skill and experience to help them with. Right away I contacted the appropriate offices in China with a proposal.

The letter on my desk was their response, a cordial invitation for me to meet with engineers and officials in the Urumchi Technology Office. No formal business agreements, just a meeting as soon as I could arrange to be in Western China. I decided to skip the engineering conference in favor of the potential consulting opportunity that had just dropped into my lap.

It was the start of the three-day Labor Day holiday. I set aside thoughts of China and began putting a few things in my overnight bag. Earlier, I had promised to help my friend Christy with a workshop she was conducting for terminally ill people who were seeking help coming to terms with their feelings. Saturday morning I drove out to the Catholic convent in Los Gatos where the non-religious workshop was being held. I thought I was there to help out in practical ways with cleaning, feeding and shopping, but it turned out to be much more than that. Most of the people I was caring for were dying of AIDS and I was forced to deal with the reality of service at a very intimate level. As the weekend progressed I found myself letting go of fears and judgments I didn't even know I had. And I became aware that something was going on with my heart.

The work was exhausting, physically and emotionally. At one point I simply collapsed onto my small wooden bed and immediately fell asleep. I awoke to a dream.

In the dream I was walking through a forest with Father Franck, the man Dorothy had told me about. Though I had never met him in real life, in the dream I knew who he was. He had a message for me, he said, and it was this: *The time has finally come for you to find the Order of the Sacred Tree*. That was all he said. We left the forest and came to the bank of a wide river where I saw an old stone temple and an Indian holy man seated in the lotus position. Then the dream ended abruptly and I was awake. The feeling around it was so powerful that I couldn't shake it off even after sitting up and walking about.

Somehow I knew what Father Franck meant—that some destined time had come for me to do what I was supposed to do. Not in the sense of something of great importance, mind you. More in the way that when certain events in your life happen, even unexpectedly, you just say to yourself, "Oh . . . of course."

I needed to go to Europe and find Father Franck, that seemed clear enough. Dorothy had said that my Aunt Virginia could put me in touch with him. On the drive back to Grass Valley I was mentally figuring flight schedules to Switzerland and trying to recall what Dorothy had said about the Order. I remembered the odd names— Gilgamesh, and the Gardener. And the monastery, especially the monastery, where the ancient manuscript was kept. I hadn't thought of any of this for years. But when I called my Aunt Virginia's house I learned she was away on an extended trip and couldn't be reached.

All my forward motion suddenly had nowhere to go, forcing me to stop and reconsider. Maybe that wasn't what the dream intended. My logical mind took it apart again and analyzed it, setting aside the non-logical gut feeling that I was being summoned to do something.

I couldn't explain the presence of the Indian holy man, but the wide river I assumed was the Ganges, the other side of the world from Europe. And then I remembered the invitation from China that was still sitting on my desk. When I added that to the mix I began to see the shape of a road ahead. I only hoped it was the right road.

I would go to see the engineers in the Urumchi Technology Office, all right, but I would take the long way getting there— starting in India and traveling the old Silk Road into Central Asia and out to the edges of the Gobi Desert, where my imagination had led me so many times before. And if it turned out that there was nothing there for me to find—no mysterious monastery, no pot of wisdom at the end of that particular rainbow—then at least I knew the engineers in Urumchi would be glad to see me. I let that scenario roll around in my head for a while.

I had thought about someday going to India and visiting the ashrams of some of the revered spiritual teachers, but it had never reached this level of serious consideration—any more than I believed I would ever actually find myself in Central Asia, no matter how many times I had wished myself there. Anyway, travel beyond India into the vast remote regions controlled by the People's Republic of China had always been out of the question. Until now, that is. And that was the strangest thing about all this: The Chinese government had only just begun opening its western border areas to a limited number of Western visitors—for the first time in more than half a century—and here I was with a personal invitation. It was starting to seem inevitable.

Two days later I was still on the fence. The more time passed, the more my rational side argued against just taking off into the unknown.

Since my last move, Dorothy's little gold figurine had stayed in a box in my closet, along with a lot of other keepsakes that hadn't found a permanent place yet. I sat down on the closet floor just looking at the beautiful object in my hand, at the entwined serpents, and wondering what the hell I was doing. Hedging my bets, I realized. A big part of me needed to believe in the world that Dorothy had taught me about, while another big part was afraid to know. In a lot of ways it was safer not to know. I could simply remain in my painful state of not knowing and go directly to Urumchi. *But then you would never know, would you?* And finally I got it.

I told my family and friends I'd be gone for a few weeks in India and Central Asia, not mentioning the part about trying to find a lost monastery or ancient manuscripts. My brother said he would look after my house while I was gone. As far as anyone knew, this was just another one of my treks into remote places. Nothing that unusual, except that this time I would be traveling alone.

In less than a month I had managed to secure visas for all the major Central Asian countries, to my amazement, and an airline ticket to New Delhi, where I would start. I had only a vague idea of where to go after that. As I packed, the thought crossed my mind that I might never be heard from again.

～

AND SO I SET OUT TO FIND SOMETHING. I JUST DIDN'T KNOW WHAT. I had my guide books. I had an around-the-world airline ticket. I had a newly strengthened physical body from working out for a month. I had maps and travelers' medicines. And I had the caduceus tucked deep in my backpack. *Think of it as a key*, Dorothy had said.

PART ONE

In the Footsteps of Pilgrims

1

The Stranger

IN THE WEEKS BEFORE I LEFT FOR INDIA I TRIED HARD TO LET GO OF ANY expectations and just be open to whatever experiences might come my way. I wasn't a blank slate, though, because I had had those wonderful years with Dorothy telling me about India and the gods, and the legends of the great spiritual teachers, the rishis, who dwelt in caves high in the Himalayas. And I had had that dream. I couldn't *not* carry all of that with me as part of my baggage. I knew how important it was for me to hold a steady tone. In fact, that was about the only thing I was certain of.

After a long flight, I got through customs at New Delhi's International Airport and was quickly assaulted on every side by aggressive hawkers, tour guides and beggars. I was fair game and I didn't like it. I wasn't naïve enough to expect that I would be met by holy men waiting to tell me the secrets of the universe; I was just an exhausted traveler at the end of a very long twenty-four hours who wanted to get to a hotel as soon as possible and sleep. I tried not to be bothered by the dirt and noise around me, but by the time I fought my way outside to the chaotic taxi area my stomach was in a knot, my temper was barely under control and—worst of all—I wasn't feeling very good about India.

I was careful to choose a taxi driven by a government licensed tour guide, which was what I always did when I first arrived in a Third World city. These are usually the people you can count on to help you navigate in unfamiliar territory. In retrospect, I should have had my driver take me to the nearest luxury hotel, but I was determined to avoid Western tourist centers and really taste the flavor of India—even on my first night, even at two in the morning after a long flight. "What hotel do you recommend?" I asked. "Where do Indian travelers stay?"

"My friend has a nice place," he said. "Not expensive. Very clean."

I did briefly wonder what his criteria for "clean" might be, judging by the state of his car and the sad appearance of the area of New Delhi we were driving through. He dropped me in front of a crumbling building on a dangerous looking street, told me to mention his name and drove off. The humid October air was heavy with unfamiliar smells, not all of them pleasant. I dragged my luggage inside the rundown lobby and inquired about a room for the night.

The desk clerk named a price that I quickly calculated to be forty dollars. I was sure it was ten times the going rate. I protested but paid the money anyway. At 2 A.M. where else was I going to go? I had booked a flight out to Benares the next morning and I was desperate for sleep. The clerk showed me to my dingy room and left me to face my swaybacked bed and a night with the fleas of New Delhi.

By morning my stomach had shut down completely. I returned to the New Delhi airport with grim determination, praying that everything would be different when I got to Benares, India's great holy city—the place where millions of pilgrims have come for thousands of years to wash their sins away in the waters of the Ganges. The Buddha himself had visited there more than 2600 years ago. On the flight south I tried to lose my dark mood and start over.

⌒

"WELCOME!" THE CHEERFUL YOUNG MAN SAID AGAIN AND AGAIN AS HE dogged my steps through the small Benares airport. His name was Krishna. He was in his twenties, with a quick smile, animated eyes and Nikes on his feet. He was a tourist guide, he said. By now I realized that no matter how I thought of myself, here in India I was just a tourist. I shook off the rest of the clamoring taxi drivers and guides and asked Krishna if he would show me around the city. First, though, I had to be sure I had a decent hotel. Oh, yes, he said, his uncle owned a very nice hotel—very clean and reasonable. After some reassurances about what that really meant, I finally agreed to look at it. I wasn't about to be hustled again.

We got there by three-wheel motorcycle rickshaw, with Krishna, my luggage and me bumping along the pitted main road through frenetic traffic until we reached the hotel, a three-story white building from the colonial days. The very British sign next to the door read: *Boarders will be received after 5:00* P.M. It was a comforting little sign, tidy and discreet, bespeaking order and the basic amenities. Somehow I knew I would be safe here.

I still had some time before I could check in, so I left my luggage with the porter in the lobby and set out into the city with Krishna. He asked if I wanted to shop for souvenirs or rugs, or perhaps jewelry for my wife. I didn't bother to tell him I had no wife. "We are famous for our jewelry, you know. Or perhaps you would like to see a brass factory, where they make the very beautiful bowls and implements for dining. You can buy a small brass pot to fill with water from the Ganges . . ."

I said I wasn't here to shop, that what I wanted most was to be able to feel the spiritual heart of India. After a moment's pause he looked at me with a new expression and said, "I understand." I explained that I had the deepest respect for the culture of India and was here for personal reasons having to do with my own search.

"I understand," he said again. "And how long do you plan to stay?

"I don't know yet. It depends on what I find here. I'd like to visit a Hindu temple, but I don't want to go where all the tourists go."

We left the congested main street and snaked our way through side streets until we came to a building with a cluster of elaborately carved red spires rising from it. "This is a very old shrine to Brahma, Vishnu and Shiva," my guide said.

Perfect, I thought, embracing the beauty of the spires with my eyes and imagining what waited for me inside. I was starting to feel I could relax into the ancient, unchanging truths of the real India. I knew these three gods. They were the great Hindu trinity. It was Brahma who created the world, Vishnu the water god who preserves it, sustains it, dreams its dreams and fills it with beauty—and Shiva the old ascetic who comes to reduce the world's opulence to ashes and then destroys the universe so that Brahma can begin again with a new one. Since beyond memory, the stories of these gods have been told by the masses of ordinary people, and by the priestly caste, the Brahmins, who hold the sacred wisdom in their trust.

"I must ask permission of the head Brahmin for us to enter." I watched through the wrought iron gate as Krishna approached an old man who sat in the courtyard lighting incense sticks at a small fire. He was wearing only a white loincloth. Next to him a small monkey on a chain fidgeted with a betel nut. Krishna dropped a few coins in a bucket and bowed. After a long moment the old man nodded and Krishna was granted his request.

Hindu Temple, Benares, India

We entered a long, low-ceilinged stone building with no windows. Once my eyes adjusted to the candlelight I saw many passageways and shrine rooms filled with statues of various gods. Men sat on the floor facing the statues or making prostrations, while others were feeding food to the mouths of the statues and then washing them with water. The temple was dirty and smelled bad. I was having second thoughts about lingering. As we entered one passageway a man looked at us and began beating the ground with a stick. He said something in a harsh voice and Krishna said, "We must leave now, quickly." He gave the man a few rupee notes and we retreated from the building, with the man following us, shouting and gesturing until we were back in the sunlight of the courtyard.

"What was that all about?" I demanded.

"It was an unfortunate misunderstanding," Krishna said, not convincingly.

"Tell me."

"I am so sorry, but in our caste system there is no place for foreigners, so some persons may consider you the same as an Untouchable. That man believed that you were defiling the Brahmins in the temple and so I paid him to make it good again. It is not supposed to be this way, but old customs still linger. I am very much chagrined." His eyes were filled with embarrassment.

"Small minded men always make the worst of their religions," I said. I didn't want Krishna to see how much it really bothered me, on so many levels.

"Then let me take you to see the famous and ancient University of Benares next," he said. "I have friends there. They will welcome you with open arms, I promise."

"Maybe tomorrow," I said. "Right now I want to see the river." I knew the Ganges was just on the other side of the temple.

"Of course," he said. "You wish to be among the pilgrims and drink from the waters of the holy mother river." I wasn't so sure about the last part, but I really needed to feel something even remotely like serenity and peace. "However, I must tell you that now is not the best time for your first visit to her. You must come before the first light of dawn when she is the most beautiful. I will arrange a boat for you."

"I'd like that very much," I said. "Let's just go back to the hotel."

We cycled away from the temple through narrow, winding alleyways barely wide enough for our three-wheeler, navigating around pushcart stands selling fire-roasted chilis and fried cumin seeds. I was sure I would never forget the pungent smells of India. When we were stopped by a crush of emaciated wandering cows, impatient taxis, pedestrians and oxcarts, I found myself staring at the women around me. Maybe I was just sleep deprived and far from home, but every one of them—young and old, even the street sweepers—appeared exotically beautiful to me. I noticed their thick, black hair, the swaying gold ornaments in their ears, the way the women moved in their sweeping saris of gold and red and indigo, and I felt a stabbing pang of loneliness.

Krishna dropped me at the hotel with more apologies, and a promise to come for me the next morning at 4:30. My room was clean, thank God. It looked out onto an old jacaranda tree and a small walled garden. After a decent shower I dropped onto my bed with a long sigh. I had planned to keep a careful diary, but that was the last thing I felt like doing at the moment. The incident at the temple still rankled my American sensibilities. In a childish way I think my feelings were hurt to be so utterly rejected for simply being who I was—and because I had entered the temple with such respectful intentions. It was my fault for only wanting to see the India of my imagination and not the rest.

Every part of me ached for sleep and equilibrium, but I couldn't let myself fall asleep at this early hour or I'd never get my body clock back in sync. Instead, I listened to the unfamiliar sounds of the city outside my window and sent my thoughts out towards the river. What was it about a river that makes it sacred, I wondered—that makes people come to it in prayer and wash themselves in its waters to purify their souls? In school I was taught that without the great rivers of the world most of the civilizations of mankind would never have arisen. But no teacher ever spoke to me about a river's mysteries. I had to find that out for myself. I've pursued rivers all my life, exploring the upper Amazon, upper Mekong between Burma, Laos and Thailand, and in the future I would be led to the upper Nile. I have always found my way to water. I still find myself in awe of something so fluid and yielding, yet with the power to alter the shape of everything in its path. When I'm in a poetic frame of mind I think of water as a feminine force—strong, subtle, life-sustaining, beautiful, and both driven and peaceful in equal measure. Maybe even sacred.

I couldn't wait for morning, and the river. Things had to get better. I was beginning to feel hungry for the first time since my arrival in India, which I took as a good sign. I roused myself to ask at the desk where I could find a simple meal nearby and was directed to a small family restaurant run by yet another relative of Krishna's. I sat alone near a dusty window and ate my rice and dal, listening to pulsing Indian pop music and trying to keep my thoughts positive. I hadn't done a very good job of it so far. Ever since New Delhi I had been off balance and far from the energies of my dream of the holy man who sat beside the river waiting for me. Right now I had my doubts that any self-respecting holy man would give me the time of day.

The next morning at 4:30 Krishna met me outside the hotel. Sleep had done a lot for my state of mind. Before I left the room I picked up my golden caduceus and stowed it in my pants pocket. I didn't want it to be far from me. The air was brisk and humid, and a fragrant breeze awakened my senses. It was still dark as we walked through a maze of narrow passages, coming at last to an opening between the mass of buildings that crowd the riverbank and hide it from view until you suddenly happen upon it. When I saw the river it stopped my breath. Krishna let me have a moment to absorb the scene that was spread out before me. This was not like any river I had ever come to. This was like something conjured in a dream, an impressionist painting of opaline tones and mist-shrouded temples just barely visible to the eye. "It's amazing," I whispered to Krishna, who smiled at my inadequate word.

We stepped out onto one of the *ghats*, the wide stone platforms and stairways that defined the water's edge for as far as I could see. Krishna led me down to the water and helped me into a small wooden boat that was tied up at the steps. "I will be here when you return," he said.

The boatman, a slight, wiry man, greeted me silently then cast off. I relaxed onto a wood bench crudely covered with carpet as our boat slowly parted a sea of floating candles and flower petals and turned to head upstream. The gentle splash of the river lapped at the sides of our small canoe. A few stars still sparkled through the predawn mist. Seemingly from everywhere around us sounds of chanting drifted repetitiously on the sandalwood breeze. *Om namah shivayah* . . . My senses were enthralled. In that moment I felt transported into a perfect world.

One by one, the first rays of sunrise illuminated the slate steps of the ghats. Fantastic carved stone temples and open shrines loomed out of the dark as we glided slowly past. Here and there Hindu monks sat in the lotus posture in meditation, their bodies wrapped tightly in white cloth, while my eyes searched among them, wondering if one of them could be *him*. Golden monkeys crouched in dark corners of crumbling walls, returning my gaze with bored but knowing eyes.

We stayed close to the shore. The current farther out in the river was too powerful for a frail handmade boat like ours. As the new day touched the river, the hovering mist transformed itself into a shimmery silver veil, floating between the water and the pale sky. I watched a group of dark-skinned women in their own shimmery veils of red silk and gold enter the water to throw yellow marigolds onto the currents.

"They are thanking Mother Ganges for her generosity," my boatman said quietly.

A horde of giggling children followed them into the water, brushing their teeth and playing with skinny dogs. Farther upstream, several monks with shaved heads waded out waist deep to fill their brass pitchers with the sacred water and pray.

My boatman pointed just ahead to where thick black smoke curled up from a crimson fire on one of the broad ghats next to the water. As we drew closer I realized what I was seeing: a cremation— a pyre of flaming logs, with a woman's body tied to it, wrapped in a brilliant orange sari and covered with red chrysanthemums. It startled me and I turned away, but then I looked again, fascinated.

"Those are the burning ghats," the boatman explained, but I had already figured it out. "The ashes of one life return to the river, the mother of life, and nothing is ever lost," he said peacefully. *Nothing is ever lost*. I don't know if I would have had that thought if I weren't here, seeing this. Death wasn't something I liked to think about.

Nearby, a man with long matted hair and wearing a white cotton loincloth waded slowly through the water near the smoldering platform. He had a fine net in his hand and he was carefully combing the water with it, with complete concentration. I asked the boatman what he was doing.

"He makes his living like the vulture," he said. "He is searching for the departure gems of the dead." I had no idea what that meant. "When a person is cremated they are sometimes adorned with a piece of jewelry, a departure gem. It symbolizes that person's life accomplishments. Some of these ornaments are beautiful works of art, made with gold and jewels. And so our vulture makes an excellent living recycling the dreams of the dead."

"That seems very strange to me," I said, and yet as I thought about it, what harm was being done?

"That is our duty, you know, to make a beautiful work of art before we die, something to pass on to the world. Only you had better share it with someone before you die, or else it will only end up in that man's net!"

"Have you made yourself a departure gem?" I asked.

He didn't reply right away and I thought that I had asked something too personal. He turned the boat downstream and we started back. I was still scanning the river landings when he spoke again. "Yes, I have," he said. "It took me a long time, because first I had to figure out just what it was that life wanted from me. Now I know. My departure gem is decorated with the symbols of two families. You see, my father's and mother's families have been feuding for centuries. I am the one that brought our clans back together."

I asked him how he did that, and he began to tell me his story. When he was a young man he grew tired of all the fighting and decided to discover what had caused it. He asked a lot of questions, but most of the family members couldn't even remember why they were feuding. After a long time and many questions he learned that his father's grandfather from five generations ago took some land from his mother's family and never paid for it. "Not only did I finally pay them for it, after saving my money for many years, but also I insisted our families come together and make an agreement to be at peace. I had to teach both my parents how to forgive." He was looking directly into my eyes. I briefly wondered if I was being told this for some reason, but that I was too thick to understand.

"Now that I am older," he said, "I know that is what life wanted from me. I have fulfilled my karma and I am finally at peace." He placed his wrinkled hands together in a gesture of prayer, looked upwards, and returned to his rowing. "Now all I do each day is ask God to show me where to take each pilgrim on the river. I know how to listen. And I know how to surrender my will to the Divine. Every day of my life is delightful now." I noticed that he was gazing at me through half-closed lids. I didn't even know this man's name, but I was pretty sure that he knew a lot about me. Or maybe I was just falling under the spell of the river.

Suddenly, the winds picked up and storm clouds moved in overhead, letting loose a torrent of rain. The boatman rowed strenuously towards the nearest ghat. "This is most unusual," he called through the heavy curtain of rain that drenched us. "We will take shelter until it passes."

We stepped from the boat and ran up the stone steps to a roofed open-air temple. The boatman motioned to me to remove my shoes before we entered. Inside we found three men seated in meditation, motionless. I recognized that they were *sadhus*, the wandering holy men of India who live ascetic lives and make pilgrimages to sacred places. I had not told the boatman that I was looking for a holy man, yet now we found ourselves kneeling and bowing our heads to not one, but three of them.

One wore a pale yellow cotton dhoti with a hood that obscured his face. Another was covered from head to toe in a bright orange cloth from which only his weathered and folded hands emerged. The third sat almost completely naked on the stone floor, gazing into the water. His dark brown hair fell to his shoulders, matted and dirty, but his physique was strong and well conditioned. These did not look like lazy men; they were disciplined practitioners of the ancient art of yoga.

From the moment we entered the temple I found myself plunged into a stunning state of silence so deep that my thoughts echoed in my mind like an annoyingly loud radio. I had the odd perception that the sadhus could easily hear every noisy bit of it and I struggled to quiet my mind.

We seated ourselves on the cold floor near the first man, the one with the pale yellow robe. He sat with his spine arched upright and his palms turned upwards in his lap. After a few moments he took a sudden deep breath and his body began to come to life. He opened his eyes and turned to look at me from beneath the shadows of his hood. "What is it you are seeking?" he said, startling me at first, though his voice had tenderness in it. I didn't trust myself to know if this man was the one I had come to find. But I would be a fool not to explore the possibility.

Ganges River Temple

"I am on a mission to find an old monastery in Central Asia. I was given the name of Father Franck." I said no more than that, just to see what would happen.

"Do you believe your mission is the same as his?" His voice was strong but kind.

"I don't know," I answered. "Can you tell me this?"

"You have to answer this for yourself," he said. "Each of us is given a destiny to fulfill. You will feel restless until you discover what it is, and then fulfill it. But once you have accomplished what life wants from you, you can find the true peace of your deeper self."

I felt disappointed. I was hoping for something more—more personal and specific. Anyone could have given me that kind of answer. Even though I suspected he wasn't the one I was hoping to find, still, I wondered what would lead a person to choose a life like his. "Did you have a destiny to fulfill?" I asked him.

"Of course. You cannot escape from life, even by becoming a sadhu like me, until you have fulfilled your karmic obligations."

I closed my eyes, almost against my will. Instantly I felt a shiver in my spine that rippled throughout my body, and a brilliant, swirling, golden vortex appeared before my mind's eye. I saw a serpent suspended within the spinning vortex. In another instant it was gone. I didn't want it to go.

"Follow this sign of life, wherever you encounter it," the sadhu said, "and you will find what you are looking for. But your mind is clouded with doubts and fears. If you want to succeed, it is imperative that you deepen your inner stillness."

My eyes were still closed. I was hearing his voice as if from a great distance. I felt detached from my body; there seemed to be no limits to my being.

"Right now there is a teacher looking for you," he was saying to me. "Go to the Tree of the Buddha, and wait for a sign. You will find a man who is not your guru, but he will teach you to meditate if you ask him. Only then will you be ready to meet the one who will awaken you." He was silent again, and I felt something, as if he had touched me invisibly. I was back in my body and my eyes were open again. "From this moment on, life will guide you quickly to find your destiny. It is important to graciously accept every gift that life offers you. And if adversity comes, welcome it as the most precious gift of all."

He turned from me and resumed his meditations. The rain stopped abruptly, and almost immediately the clouds blew away. The boatman tugged at my sleeve. We stood, made our bows and returned to the boat. My legs were unsteady. The boatman said that it was rare for a storm to appear and disappear so quickly. "Surely the sadhus must have made it rain." I said nothing. Something had happened to me. I felt in my pocket for my little gold caduceus and wrapped my fingers around the spiraling serpents. I couldn't tell if the heat coming from it was from my own body or from the amulet itself. It didn't really matter.

We returned to the docks and the boatman gave me a warm look of kinship as he tied up the wooden canoe. "You cannot go wrong if you listen first to your heart, my friend." I raised my hands to my chest in a *namaste*, afraid that if I said any words my voice would fail me. I knew he would understand.

⁓

KRISHNA WAS WAITING FOR ME NEAR THE LANDING. "WHERE TO NOW?" he asked. That was not an insignificant question.

"Do you know of a place called the Tree of the Buddha?"

"Of course!" he said excitedly. "It is Bodh Gaya, the place where the Buddha sat under the Bodhi tree. It is the place where he attained *nirvana*. You wish to go there?" I nodded. "Then I will call my uncle from the hotel. He has a car. You can leave today."

2

Bodh Gaya

KRISHNA'S UNCLE WAS AN OLD MAN WITH A SCRAGGLY WHITE BEARD and dark, weather-beaten skin. His car was a black British taxi from the '50s. He stowed my belongings in the trunk in spite of my insistence on doing it. I climbed into the roomy back seat and we set out on the 160-mile drive to Bodh Gaya. "How long will it take?" I asked. He shrugged and smiled vaguely, and I gave up expecting to have lunch in Bodh Gaya.

The driver didn't speak much English, which was fine with me because I didn't feel much like talking. That old feeling of *Oh . . . of course* was with me again: Of course the holy man had been there waiting for me; of course he had given me the next clue for my journey. After this morning at the river I think the left side of my brain was finally convinced that something much bigger than everyday reality was going on here. I could hardly wait to see what would happen next. Now, all I had to do was make it to Bodh Gaya alive.

Our car lurched along a perilous two-lane highway heading east from Benares. Overloaded trucks careened past us with harrowing disregard for oncoming traffic, and quite soon I realized that the sadhu was not just speaking in general philosophical terms when he instructed me not to doubt or be afraid; he might have been seeing my day ahead. The sides of the road were littered with the burned-out hulks of vehicles that had rolled over in what must have been ghastly accidents. And then there were the bandits. Shortly after we crossed the border into the state of Bihar we came to a sudden halt because a gang of barefoot young toughs had slung a rope across the road. My driver motioned for me to get out some money. He rolled the window down a few inches and doled out the rupees, watching the ringleader's face to see when we had given enough. I avoided eye contact as the others peered inside the car. I slid my camera out of sight behind me. When the deal was done the leader motioned us on. "Big problem in Bihar, sir," Krishna's uncle explained. "Everything okay?" I think I surprised him by appearing so calm. If anything, I was impatient to get to our destination. But impatience was futile. There were government checkpoints to be gotten through, and all the many small towns along the highway, each of which brought our progress to a standstill with wandering Brahmin bulls, religious parades, and an endless line of trucks spewing clouds of diesel fumes. Also, Krishna's uncle had a need to stop for curried rice and lentils every two hours. He was a kind and very humble man, and I tried not to begrudge him his small pleasures. He showed me how to eat Indian-style, sitting cross-legged on a small wooden bench using only my hands for utensils. I had the feeling that if I had wanted a personal servant he would have been only too happy to oblige.

It was clear that my destiny couldn't be hurried today, and that I would do better to prepare myself for whatever awaited me in Bodh Gaya. I began to think about the great soul who became known as the Buddha. One of the books that Dorothy gave me to read was a first edition copy of Sir Edwin Arnold's "The Light of Asia," a long narrative poem that recounts the Buddha's life. The power of it had touched my heart so strongly that it stayed in my consciousness long after I had forgotten the lines themselves.

The Buddha, according to legend and some historical confirmation, was born the son of a king about five hundred years before Christ, somewhere in Northern India or Nepal. His name was Prince Siddhartha. At his birth the court diviners read the signs and predicted that he would become a great king, but there came another seer who prophesied that the child's true destiny was to become a great spiritual leader who would bring healing to a suffering world. His father, who longed for a successor, was fearful of the prophesy. He took steps to insulate the prince from the world by keeping him confined to a life of ease and pleasure within the palace grounds.

But one day the prince ventured outside and was shocked to see for the first time disease, poverty, and old age. His heart was on fire to understand the meaning of such suffering, and the meaning of life itself. With great anguish he renounced his royal station and set off alone into the forest in search of truth, leaving behind the beautiful young wife and newborn son he loved with all his heart—but not more than he loved the whole of life.

For four years he studied diligently with Hindu Brahmins, gurus and yogis, but he felt no closer to realizing his true nature and the meaning of suffering. He took another step in his search and became an austere ascetic, shunning food, water and shelter. Over the next three years many followers came around him, impressed by his extreme self denial. Still he felt no closer to his goal. His compassionate heart still felt the suffering of all creatures but he was unable to offer solace. In a final act of will he renounced everything, including his asceticism, and set off wandering through the forests of Northern Bihar, now alone and abandoned by his former followers.

Arriving at a great pipal tree, he sat down in meditation, determined to stay there until he either died or broke through into full understanding. For three days and three nights he meditated. The animals drew close around him, protecting him with their bodies while visions of Mara, the great demon of illusion, came to tempt him to give up his quest. But he would have none of it. And then, in the lonely hours beneath the sheltering tree, vast insights began opening to him, one by one. Until finally, *nirvana*—that pure state of knowing, of being at peace, of surrendering the self to the greater reality, of seeing into the nature of all things and the root causes of suffering.

Prince Siddhartha—who was now the Buddha, the Realized One—continued to meditate for seven weeks more. When at last he knew it was time to begin his work he arose from beneath the tree and traveled to Sarnath, near Benares, where he gave his first sermon and began his years of teaching. The tree would forever after be known as the Bodhi Tree, the tree of wisdom, where Buddhism took its birth.

Here was a man who refused to accept the truth that others imposed on him, but instead sought a greater truth, driven by his inner necessity. He did not claim divine origin or to be anything more or less than a human who had realized his true nature. And the fruits of his search he offered to all who hungered. Through all the many philosophical paths that sprang from his footsteps, there were always the twin themes of compassion for all living creatures and the search within the self to find the ultimate truth.

I have never forgotten the story, even in those dark times in my life when I didn't want to think about things of the spirit. Siddartha's life was like a reminder to me that I still had a long way to go.

We arrived in Bodh Gaya at dusk. I thanked my driver for his good efforts and silently thanked the powers-that-be for my deliverance. In the last ten hours I had endured enough jarring potholes to last a lifetime. I couldn't wait to check into the small, whitewashed tourist hotel on the edge of town that Krishna had recommended. It was a place that catered to Indian pilgrims and it was within walking distance of the grounds of the great temple. The rooms were spartan by anyone's standards, but clean.

I had a simple meal in the hotel restaurant and strolled outside afterwards, looking towards the temple whose silhouette I could see looming above everything else in the distance. Tomorrow I would sit beneath the tree where the Buddha sat to receive his great enlightenment. I would walk in the forest where he contemplated the meaning of life. It had rained earlier in the day and the balmy night air was sweet with spicy fragrances. My senses were alert for signs. I wanted the sadhu to be right—that there was a teacher here, waiting to find me. Because I wasn't the most patient person in the world I was half expecting someone to emerge from the shadows that very moment and say, "Follow me." But it didn't happen. I returned to the hotel and went to bed, too keyed up to sleep. I had to trust that tomorrow would unfold as it was supposed to. The anticipation was almost more than I could bear.

Early the next morning I downed a quick power bar on my way out the door and hired a horse-drawn rickshaw to take me to the temple. We clip-clopped towards it with excruciating slowness, passing a row of souvenir shops and food stands that hadn't opened yet because of the early hour. I couldn't take my eyes off the great domed and spired building ahead of us. It was huge, this temple that the venerable King Asoka built 2200 years ago in sincere devotion to the sublime teachings of salvation. The vast temple grounds were ringed all around with a white stuccoed wall, yet there appeared to be just one entrance. The rickshaw driver left me at the front gate beneath an ancient Shinto arch. I presented myself to an elderly, shaven-headed monk who stood at the entrance and seemed to be the gatekeeper.

"Closed," he said with a shake of his head and a raised hand. "Come another time. Three or four weeks." I think he also said something about special ceremonies going on inside. "But I *have* to go inside," I insisted. "I've come a very long way." He made no move to step aside. I pulled out my wallet. "I know there is a way for you to let me inside," I cajoled. "Someone is waiting for me. It's extremely important." I held out a handful of rupee notes but he just shook his head again. I stared at him helplessly, groping for the magic words that would make him step aside and let me in. I needed to go to the Tree of the Buddha, and the tree was inside these walls, behind this gate. Worse yet, he was letting other people inside as I stood there. Heat was rising in my neck and face. I could hear my heartbeat pounding in my ears. Finally I turned away, frustrated beyond reason that I had come this far for nothing. I walked along next to the high wall surrounding the temple grounds, hoping to find another entrance somewhere, maybe for gardeners or deliveries, but I didn't see one. I even had a thought to scale the wall, but that idea died a quick death. I was embarrassing myself.

It took a long time for my anger and disappointment to subside even a little. I didn't want to feel this way. Not here. I found a small park with tame deer and peacocks, and tried to meditate on letting go of expectations, with little success. I spent the rest of the day wandering around the village of Bodh Gaya, always in sight of the forbidden temple. At least I could enjoy being in the midst of Buddhist monks and nuns who were here from every part of the world. There was a palpable feeling of happiness in the way they moved and spoke with one another. I didn't see any frowning faces among them, no one who seemed rushed or anything other than peaceful and centered. I felt like an alien life form, with my grinding solar plexus and tense neck. I snacked at one of the busy food stands and picked up a few souvenirs—sandalwood beads and post cards with pictures of the temple and the Bodhi Tree. The irony of having to settle for a photograph was not lost on me.

I returned to the hotel without the slightest idea what to do next, where to go, who to get advice from. For a start I took a couple of aspirins. Then I reached into the file folders at the bottom of my duffelbag and pulled out my engineering proposal for the Urumchi government office. Plan B had always been to end up there in Western China doing something useful for a large number of people. That was the one skill I knew I had—flood control systems and water treatment facilities. It was my real value to the world, and that wasn't such a bad thing. How many American engineers ever got to go where I was going? I had nothing to complain about, really. I was just fine with Plan B. The best thing would be to return to New Delhi and find a travel agency that could get me to Urumchi by the shortest way, probably through Tashkent, if I'd read my maps correctly. I'd figure all that out tomorrow. I was still suffering from jet lag and hadn't yet had a good night's sleep. At that moment that was all I cared about.

⌒

I WOKE IN THE MORNING NOT THINKING ABOUT URUMCHI AT ALL. No, I was obsessively replaying what had happened at the temple gate. It just didn't make sense and I wasn't satisfied with the way I'd handled it. I recalled the sadhu's advice, that I should accept adversity as a gift. That was a nice idea, but I'd had a lot of adversity in my life and I was having trouble seeing some it as a gift. As I was brushing my teeth I leaned close to the tiny washstand mirror and took a good long look at my haggard face. A new thought dropped into my head.

I was careful to dress simply. I left my watch and camera in the hotel safe. I carried my shoes in my hand. Instead of taking a rickshaw, I walked barefoot all the way to the front gate of the temple, stilling my mind as much as I was able—no great expectations this time.

It was a somewhat humbler me who presented himself to the old monk at the temple gate. He said nothing, but stood aside for me to enter.

Bodh Gaya

Inside, scores of Buddhist pilgrims were circumambulating the sacred grounds, chanting and praying. The great temple complex of Bodh Gaya appeared to be the size of a small town. I didn't go into the main temple at first, but walked around behind it, past many smaller temples, shrines and arches until I could see the tree, towering over the manicured gardens with its great presence. I knew it wasn't the original Bodhi Tree—that would have made it more than 2500 years old—but it was believed to be a direct descendant, the child of many generations of cuttings. Its peace reached out to me from across oceans of time and I drew near to sit under its benevolent canopy. I was hardly alone here in the midst of all the pilgrims, but I immediately felt an intimate connection with the energies of the tree. With each stirring of the breeze, millions of its tiny heart-shaped leaves shimmered in a dance of light and shadow. In that moment I could believe that the whisper of the leaves was the voice of the Buddha, speaking of love and selflessness and compassion. There was no sense of finite time, only expansion.

I sat there, eyes closed for I don't know how long, bathing in the freedom I was experiencing, when my body finally grew restless and dragged my mind along with it. Here I am, at the Tree of the Buddha, I thought. If someone wants to meet me I'm pretty easy to spot in this crowd. I glanced around to see if anyone was looking in my direction, but all of the pilgrims around me were deep in their own meditations. After a while I stood and bowed to the tree with sincere reverence and respect. I would go into the main temple.

I merged with a sea of monks and nuns robed in gold, red, brown and black, from all over the Buddhist world, speaking many different languages. Inside the temple, in its center, was a larger than lifesize seated Buddha, golden and glowing in the light of puddling candles and swirling incense. I wasn't as moved by the ancient statue, as beautiful as it was, as I had been by the tree. That felt like my true point of connection here. I tried to stay visible in the crowd, standing aside as much as possible, but pretty soon I was feeling the need to explore the rest of the great compound.

Outside again, I couldn't help watching a young monk in a brown robe prostrating himself, walking a few feet, then prostrating himself again as he progressed in that way around the inner perimeter of the temple enclosure. I was in awe of his devotion, and maybe a little envious.

Oddly, I didn't feel especially disappointed that there was no one here to meet me. Not seriously let down, anyway—not like yesterday. I loved being among the monks and nuns, loved the easy smiles when our eyes met. There was a feeling of kindness in the air, a sweetness. Most of the pilgrims I saw had come from far places. There were few Indian pilgrims to be seen. I was aware that India was not a Buddhist country and hadn't been for many centuries, despite being the birthplace of the Buddha. India is now primarily Hindu, with a large population of Sikhs and Muslims. Bodh Gaya is an island of Buddhist sacred space within a far larger non-Buddhist culture. I walked among the temples and shrines from Thailand, Viet Nam, China, Burma, Japan, Cambodia, and many other lands, listening to the soft chanting of monks and the chiming of bells from every direction.

Then my attention was caught by a bright, cheerful temple painted in deep red, tangerine orange and golden yellow. Blue and gold awnings with long white tassels hung over the windows beneath a gilded roof. It was Tibetan. I entered through a pair of red carved doors twelve feet high. When my eyes adjusted to the dim light I could see that the walls were painted in soft pastels depicting scenes from the life of the Buddha. Above me was an intricately carved wood ceiling in natural tones.

With the exception of a monk at prayer I was alone to explore. Down the hall I found a small, low ceilinged room illuminated with ghee butter candles. A large horizontal prayer wheel stood in the middle of the room, maybe five feet in diameter, anchored by a heavy post that ran through its center from floor to ceiling. I grasped the wooden handle and turned the wheel while I walked several times around it. I knew that each turn of the wheel was sending out prayers for peace and compassion into the world. I really didn't want to stop making the prayer wheel move, it was such a beautiful feeling. When other people entered the room I moved on, returning to the main room of the temple to sit for a while by an open window and simply feel the benevolent energies around me. In all earnestness and humility, I asked for the wisdom of the Buddha to guide me and bless my life.

I looked up and noticed a painting on the wall next to me. It depicted a Tibetan geometric figure, finely detailed in gold and red. I knew it was a *dorje* because I had come across this image in some of Dorothy's books, but I had never really paid attention to it, other than to be intrigued by its name, which means "the thunderbolt that destroys ignorance and is indestructible."

I stood up to have a closer look at it. If I squinted my eyes, the dorje looked a lot like the golden vortex I had seen with the sadhu— not the same thing, but close enough that my nerves were buzzing from it all over again. The dorje had a small ball in the middle with four stems arching out from the top and bottom, making a three dimensional figure eight with a shaft running end to end through the center. Not only was it similar to the whirling vortex I saw with the sadhu, it was similar to the caduceus figure in my pocket. If I could still believe the sadhu's predictions—and I wasn't entirely sure I could, or if it even mattered anymore—I was supposed to be looking for signs. So now I seemed to have three, and they all seemed to be related . . . but not exactly. Someone was going to have to tell me what it meant, because I hadn't the slightest idea.

Tibetan Dorje

I left the temple and wandered through an area called the Heavenly Garden. As a group of young Buddhist nuns chattered by I noticed a seated bronze Buddha statue in the center of a pool of white lotuses and golden leaves. His body was encircled by an enormous cobra, from the crown of his head to his waist. I couldn't ignore the fact that I was encountering an unusual number of serpents and serpentine shapes lately.

After a few minutes I was approached by three bareheaded Tibetan monks, one young, one middle-aged, and one old, wearing the typical Tibetan scarlet robes over saffron colored shirts. The youngest one, probably eighteen, offered me a banana. The old monk greeted me with a disarming smile, as if he recognized me. The third, more Chinese looking than Tibetan, introduced himself as Tamding. They all spoke pretty good English and had a gentle, cheerful demeanor. They invited me to join them for tea at the chai stand outside the temple complex. I gladly accepted, happy for the companionship. Soon we were sipping steaming cups of chai, the Tibetan tea made with cardamom and yak butter, and sharing sour white Tibetan bread.

Tamding told me he had secretly arranged to smuggle his aging master and the master's young assistant out of Communist China to see the Dalai Lama. They had been traveling for several months since leaving Amdo, in the northern area of what was once part of the free nation of Tibet. They had crossed the Himalayas by jeep. Near the border of Ladakh they had to hike for a day through hot, barren countryside to the Indian border and bribe the local police inspector. "It was very difficult for my master," Tamding said. They had made it this far and were about to go to Dharamshala where His Holiness lived. I asked about "papers," and Tamding said he had some, but not for his master or the assistant—meaning they would be in big trouble if the authorities questioned them, and much bigger trouble back in China if they were reported. "In China, even to say I own a picture of His Holiness means I will be arrested."

I said I was amazed at their devotion to make such a journey, and he just smiled and said it was not a matter of courage, but of necessity. "Certain things are of such great importance that there is no choice. Now I must ask you, what is the gift or message that you have for my master?" He poured more chai into my cup. I didn't know how to answer him. I wondered if there was some etiquette I didn't understand. I told him I would pay for the tea and bread. They all spoke rapidly in Tibetan for a minute, and then Tamding explained. "My master says that his own master knew you in a prior lifetime. His master also predicted that my master would meet you in Bodh Gaya. You match all the signs he gave us to find you. The reason for this meeting is so that you can share with us part of the key to turning the Wheel of Time."

That caught me completely by surprise. I shook my head vigorously. "I think you must have the wrong person. I'm really sorry." I really was. They were so very sincere. "I wish I did have something for you," I said.

The old man simply smiled at my protests. My insistence that I came from America and that I knew almost nothing about Tibetan Buddhism only seemed to further confirm their beliefs. After more deliberation in Tibetan the master invited me to return to the temple compound and join them for meditation under the Bodhi Tree. I was baffled by the way this was unfolding. If he was the one I was supposed to meet in Bodh Gaya, who would teach me to meditate, then I was certainly grateful for the help. But how could I be expected to have something for *him*—and apparently something very important?

We found a bench directly facing the enormous trunk. The branches extended graciously over our heads, shading us from the noon sun. "Let me show you breathing and calmness," the old teacher instructed as he observed my first attempts at meditation. He demonstrated by taking a long, slow breath and letting his eyes melt into deep peace. I followed his example. As my mind relaxed, he told me to imagine that my peacefulness stood like an island in a storm. He spoke quietly. "Root yourself firmly to that island, and the waves of unrest and emotion cannot flood it. Let your thoughts dissolve into the waves of your breath, in . . . and out. And then return your awareness to your center, to your island."

Under his guidance, I began to go into a state of inner peace that I hadn't been able to find before.

I must have stayed with the meditation for an hour or so. I didn't know, because I'd left my watch back at the hotel. When I emerged from my peaceful island I heard his voice again. "Meditate whenever you become distracted by strong feelings of either happiness or sadness," he said, "so that you will remember your calm nature at your center."

"Then I would be meditating all the time!" I laughed. I was a walking catalog of strong feelings.

He saw the humor in my perplexity. "Meditate not to avoid these things, but so that you can live life in the fullest way possible. Without both pain and suffering, and happiness and joy, we would miss some of life's best gifts."

He was a wonderful man. While he couldn't turn me around completely in one lesson, he did give me a sense that it was possible for me to gain better control of my emotions. All I had to do was be aware enough to catch them and seek my calm center—no small order. We stood and made our bows towards the tree and what it represented, and the old monk led me to a place in the garden where there were large carved stone footprints on the ground. He told me that this marked the place where the Buddha paced back and forth after the moment of his enlightenment under the Bodhi Tree, while he debated with himself what to do with his great gift of understanding. "The Buddha realized that his profound message was not only for himself. It was meant to be shared with all sentient beings," he said, with the sweetest expression of love in his eyes. "It is still true that the message of the Buddha is more important to us than Buddha the man."

"I believe that," I said.

"And so it is with the deep inner story of each one of us. Do you imagine that you dream for yourself alone? No! When you dream, you dream for the whole world!" He leaned closer to me, searching into my eyes for something. "Our paths have not crossed by accident," he said. "Maybe we will meet again. Maybe many times. And each time we will share our stories with each other."

I didn't want to disappoint the good monk with my own opinion that he still had the wrong man. I returned his affectionate smile, realizing that each of us was searching for some kind of a sign that would be a clue to our unfolding life stories—something we each thought the other one had. He hadn't said anything more about the Wheel of Time or the key that he thought I possessed, so I left it at that.

Tamding and the master's young assistant had been staying a little apart from us until now. I could see that they were concerned with the old monk's wellbeing. They spoke again in Tibetan, then Tamding said that the master needed his rest for the long journey ahead. We said our goodbyes and parted at the gate of the compound. I took the old man's hand in both of mine. "Thank you for your great kindness," I said. "I wish you success in your journey. Perhaps we will meet again someday, as you say."

Krishna's uncle was waiting for me back at the hotel. He had slept in the car these past two nights and had refused to accept my offer to pay for a room for him. I wanted to return to Benares as soon as I could get my things together. I was sure he would be happy to hear that. I took advantage of my newfound serenity and slept most of the way to the Benares airport. The bandits must have been sleeping, too, because we were able to pass through the most dangerous parts of Bihar state without trouble. I saw that as a good sign.

3

The First Door

As I passed through the boarding gate for my flight out of
Benares bound for New Delhi, I was surprised to see my three monks
in line directly in front of me. Not only that, my seat assignment put
me directly in front of them on the plane, a happy coincidence. They
were going to be staying in the Tibetan Refugee Camp in New
Delhi, which they assured me was much nicer than the name
implied. I asked if I could stay there for a day or two until I could
arrange my itinerary to Urumchi. My around-the-world airline
ticket allowed me to make or change any travel plans without charge,
so long as I was generally heading east to west. Any smaller, in-
country trips I would have to buy on the spot.

We got into New Delhi International late at night. This time I
was in a much better state of mind. Even the dirt and noise didn't
bother me. And best of all, because I was with my robed companions
and not just a tourist, I had the luxury of feeling sorry for all those
poor Westerners around me who were running the gauntlet of
hawkers and guides.

A driver was waiting to take the monks (and now me) to the
refugee camp. It was a large walled-off city block in an outlying
industrial section of New Delhi. The Indian government had
granted it to the Tibetan refugees who had fled from the Communist
takeover of Tibet in the 1950s. I found a comfortable room in one of
several guest hotels there for three dollars a night. The next morning
I could see that within these walls the Tibetans had built a small
village for themselves, complete with a brightly painted temple,

several restaurants, a school, library, travel agency and residential apartments. Inside the guarded entrance the atmosphere was very peaceful, with traditional music everywhere in the air. I especially loved hearing the chanting of the monks accompanied by their strange bells, gongs, horns and flutes.

I was having breakfast in the tiny dining room of my hotel when Tamding dropped by, followed a few minutes later by the master and his assistant. We had tea together and I told them I was about to go to the travel agency. With luck I hoped to get out of New Delhi by tomorrow and be on my way to Tashkent, northwest of here. And then, somehow, to Urumchi.

The old monk smiled. "And again we say goodbye."

"There's something I meant to ask you in Bodh Gaya," I said. "It's about the dorje . . . I saw a beautiful one in the Tibetan temple there, but I don't really know its significance." After a long discussion among them in Tibetan Tamding said, "It is very clear to our master. He says that this is a sign that you should join us on our journey to see His Holiness the Dalai Lama. We will hire a car to leave this morning for Dharamshala."

I accepted their offer on the spot. Not that I liked the idea of another long car ride, but I could see that a last minute reprieve had just been granted for my faltering quest. However, I had a better idea about how to get there.

We walked over to the travel agency where I asked about plane flights from New Delhi to Dharamshala. I was ready to pay for all of us. The young man at the desk said there was only one flight out today. Unfortunately, it was the last flight of the year before the service stops for the winter, and that flight was already full because the Dalai Lama would be on it, along with his retinue.

And so we hired a driver and started out for Dharmshala—my treat. Our car this time was a white, immaculately restored 1945 Ambassador, a roomy thing that gave off the aura of a patient old workhorse with fresh tack. "We will be arriving on the same day as His Holiness," the old monk said contentedly, as he settled in beside me in the back seat. "That is a good omen." The trip took us northwest through the flat green pastureland of Sikh country, punctuated with golden spires and white domed temples. Our driver was good and the monks slept and dozed, as did I, with the old monk's head resting on my shoulder much of the way.

As we left the flatlands and started into the low rolling countryside that gradually rose into the Himalayan foothills, we stopped for a light lunch, rice and vegetables mostly, and lots and lots of chai. The monks—my guys now—were in a talkative mood. They were fascinated by anything I could tell them about America, computers, cell phones. I promised to be their guide if they ever came to my part of the world.

Tamding then brought up the Wheel of Time again. He wanted to explain it to me, he said, since it was probably a new concept for a Westerner. "We believe that there are two kinds of teachings, the outward teachings that are given directly from master to student—and the hidden teachings. Have you ever heard of a *terma*?" I said I hadn't. "It is an ancient teaching that has been hidden in a secret place," he said. "It is not a thing, but an energy, and it has been hidden by the minds of the ancient record keepers, the ones who could see deeply into the cycles of time. The termas were hidden in caves and mountains and rocks, waiting for the correct moment to be awakened."

"You mean psychically hidden?" I asked.

"I think that is the proper word," he said. "And so a terma stays quietly in its place until someone comes whose destiny it is to receive it. And then the terma will manifest itself completely in that person's mind, in perfect detail. Thus the teachings are passed into the future."

I didn't want to appear too interested, but I was fascinated by the idea. "So, if a person was just walking past a rock that had a terma in it, he wouldn't notice any change of energy unless he was the one who was supposed to find it?" I said.

The old man smiled at my question. "If he was born with the key inside his heart, then he will find it," he said. "If he has this key he will not be at peace in his life until he searches for the terma that waits for him to open it."

I knew he was speaking about me. I tried for a more practical explanation of the concept. I wondered if perhaps these termas were just another word for the deep inner stories that pass from generation to generation, waiting for the time and person who will resurrect and resolve them. Like what my boatman had done to heal his family's intractable feud. Five generations had to pass before one person came along who saw how to bring peace again. I was rolling that around in my mind, thinking of how healing it can be to resolve a painful past, what powerful medicine it was for whole villages and cultures—when the old monk gently interrupted my thoughts.

"You know of the one called Padmashambhava?" he asked. I knew the name, that was all. "Twelve centuries ago he, our great and revered teacher, brought Buddhism to Tibet and concealed many termas for the future, including one called the Wheel of Time. Many of us are seeking to open the old termas to try to understand why our culture is being destroyed by the Chinese authorities. The old masters must have foreseen these times and left us some clues." His usually cheerful face was shadowed as he looked expectantly at me.

"I wish I could help you," I said lamely. I decided to be more open about my reason for being in India. I said it was not just for a business trip to Urumchi, but part of a quest for an ancient monastery on the edge of the Gobi Desert. I also mentioned the name Gilgamesh, in case it might mean something. But they could shed no light on any of it, only offering sincere wishes for my success.

It was twilight when we got into Dharamshala. Our car had been climbing in altitude for some time. The air was crisper and less humid as the snowy peaks in the far distance gradually came into sharp view. Deep shadows defined the valleys that fell away on either side of us into rushing rivers. We drove through the city and into the suburb called Macleod Ganj, where the Dalai Lama resides.

We checked into a simple, small inn. Its interior was made of handcarved wood and it smelled pleasantly of some kind of piney resin. I had a room separate from the monks, who right away left to arrange for an audience with His Holiness. They returned within the hour with news that His Holiness had indeed arrived at his residence, but had immediately begun a fifteen-day silent retreat. He had just completed a world tour and would see no visitors until the end of his retreat. That was not a problem for my monks, who would stay as long as necessary to see him. But I didn't have the luxury of waiting. I had told everyone at home that I'd only be gone a month or so, and here I was still in India, with a long way to go. Anyway, what was *I* going to ask the Dalai Lama? My concerns were certainly too small to waste his time.

That night as I lay on the thin mattress of my too-short single bed, I was aware of a kind of clarity energizing the atmosphere of this place, a purposefulness. When I woke the next morning I felt restless to do something, to get out of myself and into the real world. I took a walk around the town. The first thing I noticed was the cleanliness, the next was the ever-present Dalai Lama's face smiling out from behind his glasses. His picture was everywhere. The town was nestled safely in the steep foothills, surrounded by 15,000-foot Himalayan peaks. I knew that there was a significant Indian military encampment nearby that protected this Tibetan homeland-in-exile from China's glaring eyes. It was a place of bustling activity—schoolchildren, monks and nuns, foreign visitors and cafes that catered to their tastes, busy shops and artisan centers—a general feeling of industriousness and at the same time cheer and optimism. And everywhere stood brightly painted buildings with prayer flags flapping in the alpine breeze.

I came upon a makeshift medical relief center for Tibetan refugees run by Doctors Without Borders and introduced myself to the Tibetan woman at the receiving desk. I told her I was in town for a day or two and would love to be of help if there was anything I could do. "My goodness, yes!" she said. "You can sit here and answer the phone while I go to help my poor neighbor. Her sheep have gotten out and wandered down to the river." And off she went.

It was a general clinic, mostly mothers with small children on the morning I was there. One of the doctors, a recent graduate from Sweden, told me that a typical day will bring them children and older adults who have traveled for months out of China, much of it on foot, to find their dream of living here in "Little Lhasa." "It's very sad," she said during a tea break between patients. "Everyone speaks of the eventual return to their homeland, especially the older generation who were born there. They have complete faith that the Chinese Communists will someday fall from power, just as the Soviet empire fell. Then, they believe, Tibet will return to its former glory. But I don't see it that way," she said, lowering her voice "Given the economic and political realities of China, the old ways of Tibet definitely appear at risk of becoming lost forever. It's hard for me to see such hope, day after day, in the face of all that."

The office manager returned, having rounded up the sheep, and I set out to explore the rest of Little Lhasa. I ran into Tamding on the street. He was on his way to visit a school for children who had fled Tibet to escape their "unfavored minority" status in China. The policy essentially denies Tibetan children the same educational and economic opportunities as the ethnic Han Chinese, he told me. Escape to a neighboring country is the only hope for many Tibetans who want to get ahead in life.

Tamding introduced me to a young student from his hometown, a bright looking boy of fourteen with an engaging smile. Tamding had brought a message from the boy's family saying that their rice harvest had been poor and they could send him no money this year. I thought about my own son. After conferring with Tamding, I offered to sponsor the boy's studies until he could finish school. That became the start of a warm friendship and continuing correspondence with a delightful young man named Tenzin.

"If you are staying another day," Tamding said afterwards, "you really should visit the Namgyal Monastery. It is His Holiness' personal monastery, but it is also a world center for the study of Tibetan Buddhism." We arranged to meet the next morning. I occupied myself for the rest of the day in town, easily falling into conversations with other Western travelers, many of them here to study at Namgyal's Institute of Buddhist Studies. I spent my time shopping for gifts for my family and friends back home. For myself, I found a bronze dorje that the shopkeeper said had been brought over the mountains from Tibet and had come from one of the destroyed monasteries.

The next day, I joined Tamding, his master and the assistant at Namgyal Monastery near the Dalai Lama's residence. In the courtyard outside I watched a group of monks debating in the traditional Tibetan style, clapping their hands and waving their arms dramatically to emphasize their philosophical arguments. Inside, the walls and ceilings had been elaborately painted with bright reds, deep blues, and gold. The art depicted the mythology of Tibet. Here too, the omnipresent photograph of the Dalai Lama smiled down upon us.

Tibetan monks in exhibition debates

My friends led me into a small library, not the monastery's main library, but a place that looked like a museum, filled with statues and art. Several dark wooden cabinets with glass doors protected ancient manuscripts that had escaped the Chinese destruction. There was a singular presence in the room, in the form of a life-sized golden statue of Padmashambhava, who sat looking out at us with a fierce stare. This was the Indian saint and Tantric master who had brought Buddhism to Tibet in the 8th century. In his right hand he held a golden dorje like the one I had seen in Bodh Gaya. The monks bowed to him and prayed for his guidance. Then we seated ourselves on cushions facing the statue and were quiet for several minutes.

Tamding leaned close to me. "If you wish to learn the ancient art form of conscious dreaming," he said, "we will teach you." I agreed. Tamding said I could learn to "dream my way into the library." I was supposed to relax to the point of almost falling asleep, while keeping my mind alert. As soon as visual images appeared in my awareness, this was a signal for me to watch what was being shown to me.

I found it difficult at first. This was a very different kind of meditation from the one I had learned at the Bodhi Tree. Following his instructions, I closed my eyes and, instead of emptying my mind, I only quieted it and waited for something to appear. Finally, dream-like images began moving across the window of my mind. I saw a man guarding a path, and I described him to Tamding. After a few moments of this I stopped to complain that it seemed like my own imagination, but Tamding urged me to keep going.

"Ask the guardian for permission to enter," he said quietly, "and make a promise that any information you receive will only be used for the enlightenment of all beings." I did this. Suddenly my mind was swimming in a sea of images that I could not comprehend. I complained again. "I'm sorry, but there's too much noise in my mind to see anything clearly." I simply didn't have the kind of concentration that could keep my focus.

"There is a hidden current inside you that will trigger the information we are looking for. Now, ask about the Wheel of Time," he whispered, ignoring my complaints.

I tried again, and quickly realized that trying wasn't what I should be doing. I needed to purposely *not* try—just let the pictures move. After a few minutes, I saw the image of a man in my mind. He held a dorje and a bell in his hands. A brilliant white light surrounded him in a rainbow of colors. He was neither young nor old. I watched him, transfixed by his presence. It was like those rare moments when you partially awaken in the night and a dream is going on, and you are observing it with a separate part of your mind.

He looked directly at me. I had the feeling it was either Padmashambhava or some great saint. I didn't hear his voice, but rather, the words simply appeared vividly in my mind, as if he were communicating something directly, soul to soul. At first I thought, *this is ridiculous, I'm just imagining it.* But I really wanted to help the monks if I could, so I made a strong effort to put aside my doubts and say what was being said to me in the vision. The words flowed out of me unedited by my conscious mind. Here is what I said:

Long ago, when I brought the Buddha's robe and bowl to the Tibetan shepherds, I also gave them two more gifts: the dorje and the bell. These were gifts from the masters of wisdom in the Northern Desert. The dorje contains the key to the Language of Life. The bell awakens the soul to the vibrating waves of the First Primordial Sound.

When the time comes that the religion and culture of the Tibetan people are under siege, and they are forced to leave their homeland, it will be a turning point for the whole world. The wisdom of the most ancient seers of the Northern Desert will be reawakened. The old teachings will be revived once again, and the people to the east, south, and west will begin to awaken from a thousand years' sleep.

It will be time to open a dialogue with the immortal living force that gave birth to our people's dreams. And it will be a sign to renew your alliance with the people of the desert.

At that, the message stopped, but I could still see the face of the speaker, his eyes locked with mine. I made an effort to reconnect with the flow of thought, to rein in the curiosity of my mind that wanted to think about what was being said. I worried that maybe I had missed something. When I managed to relax into a receptive state again, the words began anew:

When this terma you are hearing is opened by a person from far away, know that the Wheel of Time has already begun a great new cycle. Return to your roots, because the leaves will be shaken by a violent storm. You will reemerge, stronger than ever. Help will come from an unexpected quarter, so have faith.

Ask the Tibetan Keepers of the Way to preserve all of their knowledge before it is lost. Do not waste time. Ask the people of the Snowy Peaks to embrace the teachings. It will be their only safe refuge through the impending chaos. Water the roots, trim the dead branches, and nourish new growth. The rest will be revealed with the next turning of the Wheel.

A cool breeze touched my cheeks. I opened my eyes. The fierce statue of Padmashambhava now seemed to be smiling as if lost in a state of ecstasy. I was still half in the dream. "You see, you did have the key," the old monk said softly next to me. "Now I must contemplate the meaning of the message." My friends bowed to the statue of the saint, touched their foreheads to the floor, and then escorted me from the room. I was a little lightheaded, but it cleared as soon as we walked outside. The monks appeared to be as puzzled as I was about the words I had "dreamed" in the library. Much of it made no sense to me and some of it pertained to details of Tibetan Buddhist culture that I had no previous knowledge of. What I really wanted to do at the moment was get back to my hotel and write down the words while they were still vivid in my memory. I had the strongest feeling that I had just taken a step closer to something I couldn't yet name.

And so we parted for the day, the monks to contemplate the message, and I to spend time writing all of this in my journal. As I sat in my small hotel room remembering the words, I wondered if I had given the monks what they had come so far to find out. But I also started to think that perhaps the monks were also giving me a gift—that the message was not just for them, but for me . . . that through the magic of some ancient Tibetan psychic techniques they were opening a door for me. Not that I would probably ever know for certain.

Looking back on it, I should have felt how truly, extraordinarily strange this event had been. Maybe not strange for a Tibetan Buddhist, but certainly strange for an Anglo Saxon guy from Grass Valley. Instead, I was having that old feeling again of *Oh . . . of course*. It all felt so natural. As an outsider I could open up something in their world for them while they guided me to find my own way forward.

⌒

THE FOLLOWING MORNING I FELT AMBIVALENT ABOUT LEAVING Dharamshala. I wasn't sure where to go next, but I had to go somewhere. I still hadn't booked the flights that would take me directly into Western China. A big part of me didn't want to give up on my search, especially since yesterday's experience. I stayed in my room for several hours trying to settle my thoughts. I was so far from being centered, it was laughable.

The time had come to say goodbye to my monk friends once and for all. We met in the garden of the main temple and exchanged addresses and gifts. They presented me with a long white silk scarf that I still have to this day. The master wrote a prayer on the back of the photo I carried of my children, as a blessing for them. I gave them some small American Indian artifacts I had brought with me. Then the master took both my hands in his and chanted a special blessing for my journey, and another one for my family. Tamding explained that the master was blessing me with two invisible "wish-fulfilling jewels." One would help Padmashambhava guide me in my search. The other would bring good fortune to my family, who he could tell were dear to me.

"May you find what you are seeking without hard work! And may you find the faith you need!" the master added.

Tamding continued walking with me as I left the temple. I asked him what a wish-fulfilling jewel was, and he squatted down on the dirt path to trace the outline of an egg with a stick. It had a small spiral on the fat end, similar to figures I had seen on the walls of the Dalai Lama's monastery. "That is the Tibetan symbol for the jewel. Many Americans come here wanting to meet the Dalai Lama," he said. "They always want a private blessing. Nevertheless, you are receiving his blessing without even meeting him. That is because you dropped your self-absorption when you offered to help that boy. We say that when you give selflessly, and in harmony with the earth, life responds by blessing you with invisible jewels that fulfill your deepest wishes."

Tamding stood and faced me. "The master has contemplated both the terma and your quest, which he now believes are related. You should know that the path of Buddhism traveled along the Silk Road from India to China and on to Japan. Eventually it also made its way into Tibet through the grace of Master Padmashambhava. In the distant past, even before Tibet became a Buddhist country, the first Buddhist monasteries near Tibet were located on the Silk Road, in a kingdom called Kashim. Your message spoke of the elder teachings that came from the Northern Desert. That is the Gobi Desert, and that is the home of the Kashi people. The terma spoke of renewing an old alliance. If you find this place, the master wishes you to tell their abbot that there are signs of a renewed alliance with the province of Amdo."

That was the first time I had heard of a kingdom on the Silk Road called Kashim. If that was where my monastery was, it was probably already destroyed by the Chinese. I had an awful feeling that even if I went to this place there would no longer be a Monastery of the Sacred Tree.

Tamding offered a new thought. "If anyone knows of the existence of your monastery it would have to be the Islamic Sufis. They have maintained a secret unbroken spiritual presence in Central Asia—even through decades of Soviet and Chinese rule when the government outlawed all religions. I will take you to a shop that I saw yesterday. It is owned by an Afghan Sufi who has traveled throughout Central Asia. I believe he can help you."

Tamding led me to the Macleod Ganj Craft Market to find the Afghan. Then he bowed his head, placed his hands in prayer position at his chest, and said a final *"Namaste"* before he departed, leaving me outside one of the shops.

⁓

"FINEST SILKS ANYWHERE IN THE WORLD!" PROCLAIMED A DARK-skinned man with a wide, flared Afghan nose and a thick mustache. He stood taller than the Tibetans. His dark skin contrasted sharply with his white silk shirt, which had a buttoned Nehru collar. His brown wool overcoat had been tied with a strong leather belt, which, together with his high black boots gave him the look of an 18th century noble cavalryman.

"Please, come inside," he said, bowing and smiling as he opened the door to his shop. I quickly realized that he was a very clever trader. Despite my resistance, he easily managed to sell me several pieces of woven silk. Spun by hand in deep colors of burgundy, purple, white, and gold, their beauty made it clear why these fine Asian silks have been sought after for countless centuries. This man could have sold used cars in the U.S. with the best of them. I couldn't help but like him. His name was Mahmood Sahar. After several cups of chai I learned that he had traveled in every part of the Himalayas.

He in turn plied me for stories about life in America and seemed especially curious about what I did for a living. "And so you have come here to Macleod Ganj," he said with a wave of an arm, "and I am asking myself why? Not only for my excellent silks, I venture to say. You are not a pilgrim, you are not a movie star like those who want to be close to the Dalai Lama. You tell me you are a businessman on your way to China. But there are far more direct routes to go there from your homeland. And so I ask myself why are you here?" He looked at me with a piercing directness that I couldn't refuse.

I told him everything—about Dorothy and Father Franck and the caduceus and the monastery, and about the mysterious man I knew only by the name of Gilgamesh. When I was finished, I showed him the amulet. He took it into his hand and gazed at it with great intensity. "I see," he said in a tight whisper, then stood abruptly and closed the wooden blinds on the store window and locked the front door with a thud. He muttered something under his breath and reached into his pocket. He gave me back almost a third of my money, stopping after a moment's consideration to return some to his pocket.

"You are an innocent boy," he said, but without any tone of condescension. "Innocence is a rare and special gift these days. It can take you far. It cannot profit me to tell you this, but I have heard tales of a man named Gilgamesh." He pronounced the name *Gil-Hamesch* in a guttural way, as a German or Hebrew speaker might say *Cha-mesch*. From his hushed tone I gathered he had a great deal of respect for this man.

"He is a good man. His people only want peace. He lowered his voice further, even though no one else was in the shop. "You should know that there is a large price on his head from a radical militant Muslim group who wish to discover his whereabouts. So do not tell others what you have told me. If you find him, you can reward me if we meet again. You must leave for due north immediately—and not stop until you meet him. Even if it means your life." His words and urgency stopped me in my tracks. *Hold everything!* I wasn't a soldier in some war, I was just a volunteer, and not all that committed when it came right down to it. Images of holy warriors jumped into my brain, and worse—images of my fatherless children. He must have seen me go pale because he put a reassuring hand on my shoulder. "If you use your wits you will have no troubles at all, I promise."

"It's not that important to me," I backpedaled. *Grass Valley engineer taken hostage by armed militants . . .*

"No harm will come to you if you put yourselves in the hands of the right people," he said. "I am only here to help. I know people."

Why on earth was I even listening to this man? "I was planning to go to Tashkent first," I said through a haze of misgivings, ready to walk out the door the next moment.

"Excellent!" he said, and gazed over my shoulder as if he could see all the way to Central Asia. "Don't waste your time in Tashkent. I want you to look for a man named Abduvakhid. He runs a small inn in Samarkand, which is not too far from Tashkent."

"Abduvakhid," he repeated. "He is not hard to find, and he speaks English. You can trust him. If you give him my name and show him your talisman, he will do anything for you." The Afghan's young son cleared away the chai cups and brought in a large water pipe for his father.

"Don't assume you can trust anyone just because he calls himself a Sufi, or appears religious. There are many in the Islamic faith who do not believe in peace. That makes your mission a dangerous one." There it was again. "But if it is Allah's will, you will succeed. *Salaam.* Go in peace."

Mahmood unlocked the rear door of the shop and nearly pushed me out. As I walked down the narrow alley, almost tripping on the tail of a sleeping Tibetan Mastiff, he shouted out one final admonition, "Don't give up. This is more important than you think!"

My eyes blinked against the brilliant sunlight once I came out onto the street. People were bustling past me on their way to wherever, but I could only stand there in the human tide paralyzed by cold, get-me-out-of-here fear. What the hell was I doing? Trying to do the right thing, that's what . . . trying to figure out what the right thing was. If the powers-that-be wanted me to succeed so badly, then why did they put me in this situation—tease me with the possibilities, then tell me what's really at stake after I've come this far? How was I supposed to know? My chest was so tight it hurt. I wanted to open my mouth and let out something primal, but I couldn't. I couldn't even think. Everything that had brought me here—all the signs and dreams and voices—crowded into my head at once, clamoring at me to make my choice. I just stood there, feeling the passage of time around me like a wind. Finally, I opened my mouth: "All right," I said out loud, ". . . all right! Whatever it is, I'll do it." I felt tears running down my face. People were looking at me.

I had an overwhelming need to call my children and tell them where I was and where I was about to go. Nobody had heard from me since I left. There was a phone center across the street from where I was standing. The operator asked me how much time I could wait for my call to go through, because he was having trouble with the lines today. Best to try again tomorrow or the day after, he said. I just shook my head and walked out. I knew I was at the point of no return.

4

Samarkand

THE MORNING BUS FROM DHARAMSHALA TO NEW DELHI DIDN'T LOOK very promising. It was so old and battered, I knew the driver's prayer beads must be worn to nubs. I couldn't see myself packed in with a noisy crowd, the curry smells, babies and assorted animals, so I hired a private car to take me back to New Delhi, to the Tibetan Refugee Camp where I'd stayed before. I checked into the same small inn and went immediately to the travel office nearby.

By the time I had my airline tickets in hand I was actually looking forward to the next stage of the journey—at least not dreading it. It helped that my travel agent, Kalsang, arranged for me to be met at the Tashkent airport by an English speaking guide he knew personally and could vouch for. That lowered my anxiety quotient considerably. I would never again underestimate the importance of personal connections in this part of the world. Who else had any reason to care if I lived or died? It was a chilling thought, but as Mahmood Sahar made it clear, I couldn't afford to be an innocent.

From the streaked window of my India Air 767 I looked down on the dense cloud cover below me. Here and there a jagged white mountaintop thrust itself up, brilliant in the sunlight. In my imagination I could see the Karakoram Pass down there, snaking its way through the high ranges of the Himalayas, with long caravans loaded with trading goods from the far ends of the world. And I could hear Dorothy's voice telling me how to find the monastery: *If you were to go,* she said, *you would have to seek out the Karakoram Caravan Pass through the great mountains. At the end of this pass, you would find a vast desert and then follow the northern branch of the Silk Road until you reached the Celestial Mountains. No small task for a boy from the suburbs.*

I wished she could see the boy now. Knowing Dorothy, she probably could. It was a comforting thought as I sat here suspended between earth and sky, feeling terribly alone.

⁓

TASHKENT WAS A SHOCK. I FELT LIKE I HAD BEEN PLUCKED BY A STARSHIP from one universe and dropped light years away. If there was a color to this place it would be gray. I was now in the nation of Uzbekistan, a land of restricted access and Soviet post-Cold War nervous tics. But I had my official travel papers and I was met at the gate by my guide, a tough looking man in his 30s named Viktor, short and muscle bound, with close cropped hair. I felt secure having him by my side as I went through the passport control checks.

Viktor took me directly to his home. We drove through Tashkent's tree-lined boulevards, past hundreds of rows of sullen high rise collective apartments. It was all so *Soviet*, the epitome of the suburban communist dream, except the dream was over and everywhere the stores were boarded up and boys were standing on street corners selling gasoline from 50-gallon drums for old Russian-made cars. Viktor was a realist. He didn't try to put a partisan spin on what I was seeing. "The government is broke," he said. "Work is not easy to find, so I drive a taxi. When I'm lucky I get work as a security guard, but every day is a worry for me and my family. I used to be KGB. Things were better then." Viktor had a resigned sadness about him. "Not many tourists come here, only people on business with oil companies."

His wife met me at the door of their apartment in one of the drab high rises, eager to please the American guest. Our first meal together was boiled cabbage and noodles—and meat, which they rarely ate, except when there was a special occasion. They gave me their teenage son's bedroom, but before he left to spend the night with a friend he pumped me for information about American rock stars, not my field of expertise. After dinner I sat in the living room with Viktor and his doting wife and watched the news in Russian. I thought, what a miracle: Here I had grown up in the Cold War, when not even a spy could make it to Tashkent, and now I was sitting in a living room in the heart of the former "evil empire" with a man who had been a KGB agent. And he was asking me what I wanted to see while I was in town.

The next day Viktor took me out to visit an equestrian stable where a friend, another former KGB officer, kept several of the legendary Uzbek horses. The friend had once been among the elite, like Viktor, but now he was struggling to survive by giving riding lessons to children. On our way back into town we passed the city's main park. Viktor pointed out a statue of Tamarlane, the 14th century Mongol conqueror of Central Asia. Until recently, a statue of Lenin had stood in the same spot. "There was much debate about this," he said. "We—all of us—are asking questions. Who are we, really? Here we have Russians who have come recently, and we have Uzbeks who have been here from ancient times, so who should be our heroes? Do we want to be like Americans now, wearing American style clothes, or do we try to remember another time long ago? How do we make our hearts come alive again with hope?"

We walked through the farmer's market where the stalls were filled with pomegranates and apples, handmade furniture, and even nails handmade by enterprising families. Some of the vendors went out of their way to engage me in conversation, curious to see an American after a lifetime of propaganda about the degenerate West. They were frank about the situation they found themselves in. Many of them were well educated, but they were feeling isolated and depressed. It was if the whole country was down on its luck, hoping for something, they didn't know what, to make it better.

I wanted to see the museums, thinking that I could find out something about the old cultures of Central Asia, meet someone there, maybe a curator who would recognize what I was searching for. But I left disappointed because so little of the old culture had been valued enough to be preserved by the Soviets. I wanted Viktor to take me to the oldest part of the city, from before the Soviet era. He was reluctant, since that part was mostly Muslim, and Viktor didn't feel comfortable there. He had once been charged with keeping these people under control—I gathered not gently. In our brief walk down one of the narrow, overhung streets I got some bad looks and words for being with the Russian KGB agent. The tension wasn't worth it and we returned to our car. My guide wasn't exactly a cultural deep well. If there were any messages for me here in Tashkent I wasn't going to find them with Viktor.

Vicktor at the farmer's market

He wanted to show me a good time, so he took me out for vodka at a pool hall with mostly Russians. A fight broke out and Viktor thought it was all part of the fun. "They come back friends tomorrow," he laughed. But things got wilder and my drinking buddy realized he could get in trouble if anything happened to me, and we left. The whole way home he sang to the Russian pop songs on the car radio. *Das Vadanya* was his favorite . . . over and over . . . *goodbye, my love.* Later, after the vodka wore off, I thought about the song and how it epitomized the feeling of sadness and loss of times that once were great.

After two days in Tashkent, I was eager to leave for Samarkand, 180 miles to the southwest. That involved flying in an old Russian

Aeroflot prop plane with a paneled wood interior and upholstered wood and steel seats bolted to the floor. I was uneasy at the prospect of arriving in Samarkand alone, yet I could barely contain my curiosity about finding this man Abduvakhid. He was the slender thread I was grasping, the only one I had.

⁓

WITH NO ONE TO MEET ME AT THE AIRPORT, I HIRED A TAXI TO TAKE ME to a tourist hotel twenty minutes away. That was all the time I needed to fall under the spell of Samarkand. Now *this* was a city of dreams. My guidebook had called this place "holy ground," and no wonder. Minarets and domes were everywhere, mosques of breathtaking architecture in the process of being restored. My eyes could hardly take it all in. Every surface of every ancient wall was brilliant with fantastic geometric patterns of inlaid tile. I passed crews of artisans installing new floral lapis blue tiles, while others brushed fresh coats of whitewash onto the towering domes. There was energy here, new life trying to wake again after the long, drab Soviet years. So different from Tashkent. This ancient capital of Tamarlane's empire simply oozed history and culture from every crumbling clay brick and worn out cobblestone. I saw signs of traditional culture and religions in the way the women wore their red and gold headscarves and in the military guard that rode on horseback and carried spears. And I knew that there was something here for me.

Now all I had to do was find Abduvakhid. After some inquiries at the tourist hotel I found his telephone number. An energetic voice answered my hello in English. I introduced myself and mentioned Mahmood Sahar's name. The voice on the other end barked a friendly laugh. "If you are a friend of Mahmood, you must come to my home at once. Where are you? I will send a car."

His house was outside of town, in a better area of the suburbs. It was surrounded by a high wall, but once I passed through the gates I was in a garden courtyard with birds flitting about in the trees, and flowers spilling over from brilliantly glazed pots. My host greeted me with a smile and an outstretched hand. "Welcome to my home!"

Any apprehensions I had felt were immediately banished.

Abduvakhid was a man of about fifty, thin with short curly hair and a bushy but neatly trimmed gray mustache. He was dressed in close fitting black cotton trousers and shirt. He ushered me into his formal receiving room where I sat on a cushioned divan while a servant brought us tea. "First, you must tell me about my old friend Mahmood. I haven't heard from the Afghan in many years, not since he lived here in Samarkand." I said I had met him in Dharamshala, where he had a shop, and that he looked well and prosperous.

"*Hamdilallah*," he said, pressing his hands together.

"He told me to find you. He believed you could help me."

"I will do what I can," he said while he fingered his prayer beads in a continuous motion of his thumb and forefinger. "Tell me . . ."

"I am searching for something, an old monastery near the Gobi Desert. I want to find someone who knows about the northern branch of the Silk Road and its history—especially about a kingdom called Kashim in the Northern Desert. I am interested in old manuscripts, in particular." I watched his eyes for signs of recognition and waited while he considered what I had said.

"That is not my specialty, my friend, but there is a man in the city of Bukhara who knows these things. He is a Sufi named Hazrat— very private and not easy to find. There is another man, also Sufi, who may be able to take you to him." He wrote something on a business card and handed it to me. "This is his name and the address of a café. Ask any taxi driver in Bukhara. For now, I wish you to be my guest in my home while you are in my city." I was delighted. After the humble accommodations of the past week, this was a palace. White French windows covered with lace and red velvet curtains looked out onto an orange tiled inner courtyard where a caged canary sang amid exotic red and yellow flowers. The rugs on the tile floors belonged in a museum, the furnishings were carved and gilded and sweet fragrances filled the air—spices that promised delicious foods being prepared in some unseen part of the house.

Abduvakhid had business that afternoon in the city and urged me to join him. "My driver will leave me at my appointment and come for me after four hours. Until then he is at your pleasure. I will tell him where to take you so that you may taste the flavors of Samarkand."

The driver took me into the oldest part of the city where the streets were narrow and uneven. In places it was almost hushed, with none of the usual street sounds, and when I looked up, there would be the dome of one of the old mosques. I asked him to stop so I could enter two of the mosques. In each one I stood to the side as inconspicuously as I could, wondering at the artistry that had been lavished on the walls and floors and pillars. There was something, some energy, alive in the empty space beneath the domes, something in the architecture itself that was of the spirit. I didn't know how it came to be, but I knew it was there. I knew that there had once been people who understood how to tap deeply into the human soul with shape and form and emptiness.

Samarkand

Abduvakhid's driver then took me to a busy marketplace where I wandered among the fruit stalls, the sellers of birds, the basket weavers, the flower vendors and rug merchants, feeling completely and improbably at home—not a stranger. I had no explanation for why this should be. Tamding would probably say it was because I had had a life here before, but I don't think so. Something was changing inside of me, and that was making all the difference.

Abduvakhid and I returned to his home in late afternoon. I was calling him Abdu now, at his request. He showed me to my guest room so that I could rest before dinner. I had to smile, comparing my Spartan quarters at the refugee camp to where I was now, with chandeliers illuminating the Persians rugs and antique cherry wood furniture.

Dinner that evening was a lavish feast served by his wife and daughter, though they stayed apart and didn't join us. Several small children ran in and out, curious about the stranger. Our meal was rich in meats and fats. Lamb shish kebab, soup made of carrots, onions and chickpeas, fresh baked bread with butter, rice pilaf, dumplings with yogurt, and local wine from a friend's vineyard.

Abdu owned an inn for many years, and was now retired. From the looks of things he had invested wisely. He was an intelligent conversationalist and a good listener. His interests were in the art forms of Central Asia, particularly textiles and metal work, and his home reflected that. After dinner we went into his study where he made a small fire in the cast iron stove and motioned to me to be seated on one of the tapestry floor pillows. I thought it would be a good time to show him my gold talisman.

He looked at it, then at me with a questioning smile. "How did this come into your possession?" I said it was from the monastery and had gone through many hands before it came to me, and that I didn't know what it signified. He brought out a magnifying glass and studied it the way an artisan might, with his fingers carefully tracing the pattern of the entwined serpents, paying close attention to the ornate gold chase-work on the surface.

"It is almost certainly a caravan insignia from the early days of the Silk Road . . . and a very fine one," he said. "I wouldn't expect you to know about these things. For thousands of years traders carried such symbols for communication—as a common language in a part of the world where people spoke in so many different tongues. One's insignia identified one's place of origin and one's business. You could be killed or your life spared, just from the talisman you carried."

This was a completely new idea for me. I had just assumed it was a religious symbol. "Do you have any idea what this one means?" I asked.

"I would guess that it was used by traveling shamans. The symbol of the caduceus would have been a universally recognized symbol of their status as healers, even predating its use by the ancient Greek physicians. It was also the sign of the Greek god Hermes, the messenger between the gods and the humans, so there would be a sense of mystery about it—secret knowledge. I once studied these things, but have forgotten too much." He shrugged apologetically. "There is secret knowledge in all the great religions, I think you know."

"Mahmood mentioned the Sufis," I ventured, trying to recall what else he'd talked about in his shop, other than armed Islamic extremists.

"There is a connection with the insignias," he said. "It is the same thing with the Sufis. Each of the Sufi orders within Islam has its own sign with its secret meanings. They have existed in relative secrecy for over a thousand years in Central Asia, which has only fed the suspicions and fears of traditional Muslim leaders. Under the Soviets, of course, there was no religion allowed, and so the Sufis took even greater pains to hide their symbols from public view. I do not blame them."

I had only met one Sufi in my life, and that was a man named Pir Vilayat Inayat Khan, who called on Dorothy whenever he visited Los Angeles. He projected a vibrant warmth that seemed to come from a completely peaceful center, and that had fascinated me. I was still in my teens then, unable to imagine myself ever achieving such a state within my own self. He must have seen that, because he once gave me a book of traditional Sufi stories about the adventures and misadventures of a wise fool named Nasruddin, a famous character in Sufi literature.

"The Sufis are a small group within the larger Islamic family," Abdu was saying. "Some of the greatest of the Muslim poets have been Sufis. They write about yearning for a mystical union with God. Yet their words speak in veiled metaphors about the everyday beauties of earthly life . . . flowers, stars, lovers."

I remembered how Pir Vilayat would talk about creating a path to the Supreme with each moment of one's daily life, no matter how small and ordinary.

"In theory, Muslims believe in a personal and loving relationship with God," Abdu said. "All Muslims follow the teachings of the holy Koran. We are a religion of peace and tolerance. That is what the prophet Mohammed (peace be upon him) brought to the world over twelve centuries ago."

"And yet there is not always peace," I said as delicately as I could.

He sighed. "There are large sects in Afghanistan, Chechnya and other parts of Central Asia that promote bloody violence in the name of Allah. There are even some here in Uzbekistan. I do not consider them good Muslims. They rush to fill the void left by the collapse of the Soviet empire. They distort Islam with their ideas of a new world order." He looked thoughtfully at me. "Do not judge us by the few with darkness in their hearts and blind eyes. All of the great religions of mankind spring from the heart of God—that I believe. What men choose to do with the gifts, that is another thing entirely."

Two of his young sons ran in to whisper something in his ear and he sent them off with a kiss and an embrace. "I tell them to have sweet dreams," he smiled, and I felt a sudden flood of homesickness, missing my own son and two daughters.

"Now," he said, "let me tell you something about Bukhara, where you will find the Sufi man Hazrat. You should be prepared. You are embarking upon the ancient Silk Road now, my friend, and you need to know what that means."

He asked me to picture the world as it once was, with vast distances separating the great cultures—like a body with many beautiful parts, he said, but none of them connected with the other. Over time, the body began to create arteries to bind its parts together and enrich the whole. Men made perilous journeys through high mountain passes and barren deserts, carrying the fruits of their cultures and religions from one end of the earth to the other. Abdu's hands gestured broadly as he painted the images for me. "When I look at a map of the Silk Road I am not seeing small lines scribbled on paper, I am seeing the blood flow of life moving through the body of a world that is no more."

He reached over to a bookshelf and pulled out a large atlas, opening it onto a low table between us. "This is what I mean." With his finger he drew a slow, meandering line from China all the way to the Mediterranean. "That is only one of the routes, one among many."

I repeated that I was especially interested in the northern branch of the Silk Road. "I know," he said patiently, "but I wish you to understand the totality of it. At this moment you are in Samarkand, one of the most important meeting points of the many branches. All of the caravans came through here. But Bukhara . . . Bukhara was once the shining star of the Silk Road."

Later that night I tried to capture his words for my journal, but could only recreate a small part of the wide ranging conversation, which on my part was mostly respectful listening.

I paid special attention to what he had to say about Bukhara, since I was about to go there. The city was unique, and still is, he said, because of the variety of religions that settled there. There was no other place like it in Central Asia. It was still the home of the oldest and most influential of the secret Sufi orders, the Naqshband Order. I had never heard of it. I assumed that Hazrat was a Naqshband Sufi. Bukhara was also once a center for the mystical Manichean Christian Church, he said, but the Christians had departed centuries ago. He spoke of Bukhara's large population of Jews, whose origins are unknown. In the far past they controlled the Asian silk market and owned the caravans that traded from Afghanistan to China. "Somehow," he said, "the Sufis and the Jews have managed to keep their ancient traditions alive, despite the enormous Soviet pressure to banish their faiths." He returned the atlas to its shelf. "You will find Bukhara most interesting, even if you fail to find Hazrat. If you go there early in the morning you can return by evening or by the next day, and then we will speak of what you have seen."

When at last we called it a night he insisted that I stay for several more days in Samarkand. I thanked him for his great generosity, but said that after tomorrow I would be leaving for the east—if not for

Urumchi, then at least in that general direction. It all depended on Hazrat.

"You are a prisoner of your own quest," he said. "No time for pleasures. I understand completely. May you find what you seek, my friend, and may the angels of God be with you."

I didn't go to sleep right away. My long journal entry ended with: *So now I have another name: Hazrat, and another place: Bukhara. I feel myself being drawn deeper and deeper into this world of Central Asia. It surprises me that I have no desire to resist.*

5

The Secret Face of Islam

ABDU ARRANGED FOR ME TO HIRE A CAR AND DRIVER TO TAKE ME TO Bukhara, 160 miles to the west. By now, I had enough faith in whatever was in charge of my odyssey to believe I would quickly and easily find Hazrat, no matter how reclusive he was—and be back at Abdu's house in time for dinner.

It did occur to me that ever since Dharamshala I'd been steadily traveling westward, even though my goal remained far to the east. If the shortest distance between two points was a straight line, I surely wasn't taking it. But maybe the rules were different when it came to matters of destiny. I wasn't an old hand at this kind of thing. The engineer in me kept hoping for clear and simple answers—straight lines; but deep down, I knew it wasn't the engineer who was making this trek, it was the seventeen-year-old boy in Dorothy's study whose heart raced when she told him about the hidden monastery near the Celestial Mountains, and about the mysterious man named Gilgamesh.

My driver was a young man who brought a friend along for the ride. The three of us drove out of Samarkand through the fertile Zarafshan River valley, with high, snow-clad mountain ranges rising on either side. We were on the Silk Road, even though its modern incarnation appeared to be a rutted, paved highway. Last night, Abdu had made sure I appreciated its great antiquity, along with the names of the conquerors whose armies had swept along it, including Alexander the Great and the terrifying Genghis Khan. I was becoming absorbed into the energies of Central Asia, with my senses willing to consider any new experience—except, perhaps, listening to my driver belt out all the words to *I Want My MTV*. The boys had bought bootleg cassettes of Dire Straits and U-2 on the black market in Samarkand, effectively ruining my fantasy of being isolated from Western culture. So it was more than a relief to arrive in the quiet beauty of Bukhara.

Modern Bukhara is a small medieval town of mostly one-story flat-roofed brick buildings, with domes and minarets rising here and there above them. A traveler from the past would probably feel that little had changed, except for the automobiles.

Abdu told me I should go to a part of the city called Labi-huz. That was where I would find the café and the man who could help me find Hazrat. I showed my driver the name and address Abdu had written for me. "Labi-Huz," he said and aimed the car into the labyrinth of meandering lanes where little of the noonday sunlight managed to penetrate the narrow passageways. At first I savored the sight of the brick and stucco walls around me, and the occasional glimpses into courtyards filled with roses, sheep and bicycles. I saw what I thought was an old Jewish temple with a Star of David on its door and some Hebrew writing, but no other signs that the city nurtured a large Jewish population. As we drove, Bukhara's medieval charm began to wear thin because the streets appeared a little too well swept, a little too much like a theater set. On closer scrutiny I thought the whole town seemed to have been recently refurbished with a kind of manufactured antiquity, as if the residents felt required to prepare for an invasion of tourists. Yet I didn't see a single one.

But genuine enchantment was just around the corner at Labi-Huz, an idyllic park with a large reflecting pool and giant, languid mulberry trees that reached out over the pool's edge. Mirrored in the smooth water were the azure blue tiled arches of a nearby domed mosque, and not far away, a life sized bronze statue of a man on a donkey. I recognized him: Nasruddin, the wise fool of the Sufi stories, a comical reminder of the fool in all of us.

We parked near the pool and I left the car. Four old men in dark blue robes and gray skullcaps were sitting cross-legged on a large white square bench by the water's edge sipping tea and gazing towards the great domes of the mosque. My driver motioned in their direction and whispered "Sufis," then walked with me to an outdoor café on the other side of the pool. We took a seat at one of the tables near the grill where food was being prepared. A woman in full black *hijab* emerged from the small kitchen and offered me a menu, which of course, I couldn't read. Uzbek is the official language, but most people speak Tajik, my driver told me. After he said something to her in Tajik she put the menu away and called out to her young son, who had been hiding behind a barrel before scurrying off on his mother's errand.

Labi Huz, Bukhara

While we waited I drank a cup of tea. It was mint, but not like any mint tea I had ever had. My taste buds were instantly overwhelmed by the pungent sweetness of the mint leaves and flowers and sugar.

The woman in the hijab brought me a small plate of chickpeas and flat bread that she had fried on the grill, but before I could take two bites the boy returned, accompanied by a thin man with a broad nose who greeted me first in French, and then in Russian. I introduced myself in English, and he answered, "Sir, I have some fine carpets to show you. Please, come with me."

I looked a question at my driver, who assured me that this was the man whose name was on Abdu's card. He would come for me with the car at sunset, he said, and walked from the café, leaving me alone with the rug merchant.

I gulped down my food and left some money on the table. I accompanied the man through ravines of stucco and brick to an old adobe house, where a middle-aged woman wearing a disheveled indigo dress and a white headscarf glared at me as her husband invited me to tea. The woman, eyeing me with obvious suspicion, brought us overly sweet tea in a long-spouted engraved silver teapot. I was careful to ration my sips for fear of refills, while the old man tried to sell me overpriced rugs and pottery. I pointed out as politely as I could that all of them looked factory made, and of poor quality. Only my host's teapot charmed me somewhat with its simple handmade beauty, but I had no use for one, even if they had offered it for sale.

"This is all we have now," he said with real regret in his voice. "We lost most of our craft traditions when we went to work in the collective cotton factory. We have forgotten how to weave the rugs of our ancestors, so we imitate the Afghan and Turk weaving for the tourists, or resell these directly from the factory."

Then he asked me why I had come to Bukhara. I told them that I had an interest in the old cultures of Asia, and that I was searching for a Sufi named Hazrat. He discussed this at length with his wife in Uzbek, saying finally, "I will drive you to a place."

As I was leaving, I noticed on the wall near the door an ornate painting of a pair of entwined serpents with dragon wings. "What is this?" I asked. The old man grinned. "Elán Puri," he said. "We call on him when someone is sick or dying." Once again, spiraling serpents connected with healing.

We drove out of Bukhara in his white two-door Russian-made car and traveled through a vast expanse of cotton fields until we came to a small rural community that my host called Qasri Orifon. This village is a place of secret pilgrimage, I learned, because it is the birthplace and the location of the tomb of Bakhautdin Naqshband, the 14th century founder of the Naqshband Order of Sufis. There is a humble mosque here, and a *madressa*, an Islamic school. For centuries, Sufis from all over Asia have met in secrecy in the mosque to keep their ancient traditions alive. Under the Soviets it was converted into, of all things, a museum of atheism. "Now it is a mosque again," my host said, "thanks to God."

We walked first to a small stone shrine amid manicured gardens—the tomb of Bakhautdin's mother. Then into the central courtyard of the madressa, through a high brick arch embellished with two large and mysterious wrought iron swastikas spinning in opposite directions from each other. "Look there," he said, pointing to a very old mulberry tree in the courtyard. "The women crawl beneath it if they wish to have babies but cannot. It is a most popular place," he smiled. I was surprised to see that the courtyard also housed a slaughterhouse where people could donate sheep to feed the needy.

Inside the mosque we circumambulated the founder's tomb three times for good luck, along with the local faithful, then sat in a circle as a Sufi *mullah* recited prayers from the. "This mullah will know where to find Hazrat," my friend said.

But the mullah never looked at me and I didn't feel I should go up to him uninvited. I wasn't sure I was welcome there. I asked my friend if he would arrange for a consultation with the mullah. He looked at the mullah, then back at me and shook his head. "It is time to leave now." I didn't know what had just happened.

After we walked from the mosque my attention was drawn to a large rose garden nearby. The devotion and care someone had spent in pruning each of the several hundred roses struck me with wonder. *Where there is beauty, certainly wisdom cannot be far behind*—the phrase came into my mind. I looked up and saw a man staring intently at me from behind a wood shuttered window, but he neither moved nor made a sound. I lingered for as long as possible in the rose garden, but my host became impatient. I reluctantly agreed to leave, vowing to myself to return on my own later, once my driver picked me up again. There was something here for me, I was sure of it.

We returned to the car. I was taking one last look at the faded yellow walls of the madressa when I saw a most remarkable man striding quickly down the street towards the iron gates. He reminded me of Pir Vilayat, the Sufi friend of Dorothy's. He wore a brown hooded robe and sandals. Tall and handsome, he glowed with life, like a man in love. He stopped and looked at me from across the street—really *looked* at me. His eyes brimmed with tenderness and humor.

"Wait!" I cried to my host, and, dashed across the street.

"Please," I blurted out to the brown-robed stranger, "do you know of a man named Gilgamesh, and where I can find him?"

He was not put off by my behavior, but continued to smile at me. I waved frantically to my driver to come translate for me. While I waited, I showed the Sufi the talisman. Hazrat—for my host later confirmed that this was indeed Hazrat—told me that I could find the person I was searching for in Kashgar, in Eastern Turkestan. He instructed me to seek out a certain bookseller in Kashgar who sold handmade copies of the Koran. Then he placed his index finger lightly on my heart and told me to be at peace, and to have more faith.

"You will find what you are seeking soon," he said simply. With that, he bowed deeply and with finality and went on his way, leaving me with far more questions than answers.

6

Gilgamesh

"KASHGAR?" ABDU SAID THAT EVENING. "YOU CAN'T FLY THERE FROM here. First you must fly into China—to Urumchi, in Xinjiang province. Isn't that where you were planning to go for your business in the first place?"

"Yes, but not so soon!" I managed a laugh. I hoped that the fates or the gods or whoever, were laughing with me and not *at* me. I wasn't ready to go to Urumchi, which by now had become a symbol of my giving up. And that wasn't something I was about to do, especially now, after Hazrat had told me I was close to finding what I was seeking.

Abdu smiled. "Trust me. You will not stop in Urumchi for long."

We spent the rest of the evening plotting out a way to get me to Kashgar, which was an ancient trade oasis at the southwestern edge of the Gobi Desert. Today, it is the furthest outpost of the autonomous Chinese province of Xinjiang, with the only access by plane being from within China. And so I would have to fly hundreds of miles east to get to Urumchi, then pick up a flight west again to Kashgar. Apparently, my search wasn't ever going to be about straight lines.

Early the next day, with Abdu's help I booked a flight to Alma-Ata, the capital city of Kazakhstan, planning to fly from there to Urumchi, and then back out to Kashgar. "Take some time in Alma-Ata," he urged. "You will regret it if you are in too much of a rush."

Actually, I wasn't in a rush now. Somewhere in the last twenty-four hours I seem to have stopped thinking about time altogether—

which was funny, because I've always been so aware of time, the lack of it, the speed of it, and the pressures of it.

After warm goodbyes from Abdu and his family, I left for Alma-Ata, where I ended up staying three days. The dry rolling foothills of Kazakhstan were covered in golden grass, with clear blue lakes surrounded by snow covered mountains. I could have been in the Sierra foothills of California, except that I was far, far away in every sense of the word. The thought of phoning home now seemed as remote as it did to *E.T.*

Kazakh guide and his wife in Alma-Ata

While I was in Alma-Ata, being shown the beautiful countryside by a genial Kazakh guide and his pretty Russian wife, I had a strong feeling that there was something waiting for me here, too, something I needed to find. Either I wasn't too good at this business of traveling by intuition, or the scent on the trail was too faint. Sometimes, as I walked on the grassy hillsides with the alpine air cool against my face, I felt the presence of ancient thoughts, ancient peoples, like a veil of memory that I couldn't quite penetrate. I noted this in my journal, not sure what to make of it. Before I left, I vowed I would return one day to this haunted place to try again.

I FLEW OUT OF ALMA-ATA ON A SOVIET AEROFLOT PLANE, HEADING EAST into China. I was now crossing a divide into the farthest reaches of the civilized world. Often I've stared out of airplane windows at vast unnamed areas of the world with sparse roads and few signs of life, and wondered who dared venture into such remote places. Now I looked down and could imagine the microscopic dot of my own small self in that barren remoteness below. My sense of disconnection from the life I knew was almost complete.

At the Urumchi airport I had to check in with the Chinese tourist agency, the CIS. After presenting my travel documents and changing some money for Chinese yuan, I answered a lot of questions about my travels. I told them I was on vacation and that was why I was going to Kashgar. I didn't want to contact the engineers at the Chinese Technology Office yet, just get in and out of Urumchi as neatly as possible. I was finally permitted to board a China Airlines plane bound for Kashgar, where one of the CIS agents had arranged a hotel reservation for me. I had no idea how I would find Hazrat's bookseller.

With Abdu's help, and my guidebook to Central Asia, I had a working knowledge of Kashgar history. In ancient times its location was strategic because it was the only major oasis between the northern base of the Himalayas and the southern tip of Tien Shan, the Celestial Mountains. Today, its location is politically critical because it is just a few hundred kilometers from the borders of Tibet, India, Pakistan, Afghanistan, Uzbekistan, Tajikistan, Kyrgistan, and Kazakhstan. I should have known going in that it would not be a simple place.

For thousands of years, almost every philosophy and religion of Europe and Asia has passed through Kashgar with the trading caravans. It was already an old city when Genghis Khan swept through with his hordes. Marco Polo wrote about it and Alexander the Great found it to be a thriving way station on his march to conquer the world.

The core of the city of Kashgar is still populated by the mysterious Uighers, light-skinned Caucasians with Mediterranean features and language. They may have descended from European Turks or the ancient Scythian and Kushan civilization of the Gobi Desert and the central Asian steppes. Their ancestors traded with the merchants of classical Greece, according to archaeological finds in the area. That much I knew, along with the fact that the biggest population in Kashgar today are the Han Chinese, brought in by the central government of Beijing to settle here.

At the Kashgar airport I found a taxi driver who was eager to practice his English on me. "You are the first American in my car for a long time," he said. The short drive into the city showed me yet another place that was living half in the crumbling past and half in an ungainly industrialized present. The sky was hazy with kerosene smoke in what should have been pristine air. Kashgar's isolated location hadn't protected it against the pollution from Chinese modernization campaigns.

My driver was Chinese. He was proud to be part of the second generation of Chinese immigrants who came here under Mao's rule to modernize the city. I noticed some women wearing dark brown veils and asked who they were. "Uighers," he said. I saw a number of light skinned men, also Uighers I assumed, who wore Muslim skullcaps. I was curious about why the Communist Chinese allowed the practice of Islam when its regime has historically suppressed religious expression. "Times have changed. But they must obey strict rules," the driver explained, "or there are consequences."

He took me directly to my hotel, the SeMan, telling me that foreign travelers all stayed there. The three-story tiled building was at least a hundred years old, with Muslim-style wood arches along the street frontage, and an enormous turquoise blue dome over the entrance. It was built to be the Russian embassy, he told me. It was still a lovely compound, sheltering pleasant gardens, orchards, shops and residences behind its walls. I had no complaints about the accommodations, other than the feeling that I was being monitored by the staff.

Kashgar isn't a big city, so it didn't take me long to locate the bookseller's shop. When I got there it was closed. There was no one nearby to ask when the shop might be open again. Or if it was closed for good. I stood outside for a while and considered what to do next. It didn't make sense to loiter here on the off chance that the shop would suddenly open.

I decided to relax about finding the shop owner and take a little time to explore the city and catch up on my journal. I rented a hefty chrome single-speed bicycle and rode to East Lake Park at the edge of town, a large urban park with a gracefully curving lake, ornamental Chinese bridges and chrysanthemum gardens. Except for some determined fishermen in paddleboats there were few people in the park when I arrived. I chained my bicycle to a willow tree and found a seat on an ornate wrought iron bench facing the lake. The air was pleasantly warm.

As I wrote and contemplated the strange turns of my journey, I began to feel I was being observed. A group of children brought me candies, then ran away, laughing. A young woman came up to me with a flower, smiled shyly and left. I seemed to be an object of great interest. Some people just stood at a respectful distance and watched me. When I looked up from time to time at the graceful purple mountains of Afghanistan on the southern horizon, many pairs of eyes followed the direction of my gaze. At least five families asked to take my picture with them standing by my side. One even brought a video camera to film me sitting in their park. Several serious-looking military men approached and one of them asked me in halting English what I was writing. They left me alone after I told them I was writing poetry and showed my journal.

East Lake Park, Kashgar

At some point I noticed a man with sunglasses reading on a bench nearby, and realized I had seen him several times before, starting at the hotel. If he was following me, I wanted to know what was going on. I walked over to him and said hello.

He looked ill at ease, and it occurred to me that if he *was* following me, I shouldn't be talking to him. He put down his book. "How are you, Mr. Andrews?" he said in perfect English.

"I'm fine, thank you. What is it you want?"

"What is it *you* want?" he parroted back with a calculated smile, then introduced himself as Zeker. He made an exaggerated effort to be pleasant with some small talk about the weather. Then he said he had seen me outside the bookseller's shop. "Are you trying to meet someone here?" he asked.

I didn't trust him at all. I told him I was shopping for a map of Kashgar and I was in this park just to pass the time.

"That store is being watched by the Chinese police. So of course I am suspicious of your interest in that place."

Now I was worried. I had no idea where to find an American consulate, or any Americans at all, if I needed to. I told him I was only sightseeing, and I didn't want any problems related to politics. Just in case it made a difference, I added that I had no intention of going any place where I could run the risk of being kidnapped by terrorists. That brought a genuine smile to his face.

Zeker then confided that he worked as a freelance intelligence agent for cis, the agency of the Chinese government responsible for tracking foreign tourists—the agency that had booked my hotel for me. It was starting to make sense, now. He apologized for making me uncomfortable, but said I had better get used to it. "All foreigners are suspicious here, especially Americans."

I didn't know at that time that all journalists, businesspersons and tourists traveling in Xinjiang are routinely followed. "That's not something I can get used to," I said. I tried to sound civil in spite of my irritation.

"I sympathize," he said unexpectedly. "I am an outsider myself— a Jew, even though my people have been here for thousands of years."

I decided that since I had Zeker for better or worse, I'd try for better. "I'm interested in the ancient legends and present-day cultures and religions of Central Asia," I said. For his benefit I added that when I was in Bukhara recently I had noticed a very old Jewish temple and wondered about it. "I hadn't realized that Jews lived in this part of the world, so far from their homeland."

"Oh, yes," Zeker said, "there are many of us scattered about. Some people believe that this land is actually the oldest part of the Jewish homeland. If you are looking for legends, there are stories I could tell you . . . one in particular, if you are interested." His face had quickly become quite animated.

"It would interest me very much," I replied.

"Mind you," he shook his finger at me, "I have no idea if there is any truth to it, but some people claim that there is an ancient Jewish temple that stands silent and alone among the sand dunes not far from here, even though no one has ever seen it. It was once a place of pilgrimage because this temple is supposed to hold the oldest copy of one of our holy books, the *Sefer Yetsirah*, the Book of Creation, the predecessor of the Holy Kaballah."

I couldn't see his eyes behind his dark glasses, but I could feel the intensity of his gaze.

I told him that I had two American friends who have been students of the Kaballah for years. I knew that the sacred Hebrew science of numbers, letters and sounds had been at the core of Jewish mysticism since the Middle Ages.

"Yes, yes . . ." he said, eager to tell me more. "You see, the Kaballah is actually a poetic description of the ten fruits of the Tree of Life in the biblical Garden of Eden."

"But what about the old temple in the desert?" I prompted. I certainly had my own reasons for being interested.

"It is in great danger. There is a group of Muslim militants who have sworn their lives to the destruction of Israel, and they know of this legend, too. They have threatened to destroy the temple and all of its history—*if* they can find it. Have you heard of a Jewish temple in the Gobi Desert?" he asked, and of course I hadn't, except that the legend was sounding too much like another legend close to my heart. "No," I said, "I only know of that one synagogue I saw in Bukhara."

He shook his head. "They know nothing there. But here, the legend of this temple is well known, even though everyone has a different story about it. And no one can say exactly where to find it. I dream that in my lifetime I will be among those who find it. But that is just a dream." He lowered his voice. "Right now I'm stuck here waiting for a portable biological testing laboratory. That's why I had time to take this assignment watching you."

"Testing for what?" I was having my doubts about Zeker's mental state.

"I shall be traveling to the southeast region of the Gobi Desert. The Chinese used to conduct their atomic tests there, as well as tests of germ warfare. The government shut down the official laboratories, but there are reports of a new black market operation in that region. Maybe I'll find our temple while I'm there."

"So is your job to monitor tourists, or track weapons of mass destruction, or hunt for archeological sites?" I asked, trying to sound respectful and not dubious.

"Everything in Central Asia is related to everything else," Zeker said. "There is a legend that a deadly disease once devastated Central Asia. And the prophecies say that an epidemic will return some day again. Many people believe in this prophecy. There are Muslim radicals from Chechnya to Turkmenistan who want to use this prophecy to justify a massive germ warfare attack. I have even heard that there are radical Arabs who are working on strains of viruses that will target only Jewish people. Can you imagine the fear that such a rumor can cause, let alone the actual existence of such a terrible thing? Kashgar and Alma-Ata are like supermarkets for every kind of weapon you can imagine. They have replaced drugs as the prize market of the wealthy smugglers."

"I don't envy your job," I told him.

"They don't even pay me enough to live on, but there is a great deal at stake here." He grew solemn again. "My superior told me that I am only a small player in a war that has been going on behind the scenes since biblical times. That is why I am not discouraged. Our enemies would gladly die for their cause, so I have to be prepared for the same. Besides," he grinned cannily, "I've been offered an excellent reward if I find that lost Jewish temple before the Arabs do."

I didn't know what to make of Zeker at that time. I suspected he wanted to impress me with his knowledge of clandestine organizations. Only years later did I learn that his stories about terrorists and their trade in exotic weapons were all too true.

"Personally, I think the Germans already got here long ago, and it's too late," he said.

"The Germans?"

"Adolf Hitler sent people to look for the temple, for the same reasons as these Arabs. No one knows if the Germans found it. Some say they did, and destroyed it already. Some people will stop at nothing until every Jew is dead. There is a piece of our history here, and I will not stop asking and looking until I can find the Temple of the Sacred Tree of Heaven. Or until I'm reassigned."

My heart sank. I didn't draw a breath for several beats of time. How could there be two "lost" temples in the Gobi Desert, both with the same name, or nearly the same . . . and both be sources of ancient spiritual manuscripts? Could there really be two, or had there been only one all along, the one that Hitler and the Arabs knew about? Or was this how myths were created, with the deepest hopes of a people needing a story that feeds those hopes—like the story of Camelot. "Maybe none of it has anything to do with reality," I said, finishing my own thought.

"Desert expeditions are not cheap," he said with a wave of his hand, "and they've been going on for years. So someone is convinced it is real."

Zeker became nervous seeing a group of three Chinese military officers milling about nearby. He suggested we go for a walk along the edge of the lake. I was glad to be up and moving again. I needed to clear my head and think about what to do next. This could be the end of my quest—delivered to me on a park bench by a Jewish Chinese spy who thought he was telling me something wonderful. The monastery I hoped to find was either already destroyed, was being sought after by Muslim extremists or never existed in the first place. We strolled down a path lined on each side with white bark aspens that quivered in the autumn breeze and occasionally showered us with heart-shaped golden leaves. I was having a hard time appreciating the beauty of the moment.

"What brings you to our part of the world?" Zeker asked.

I pulled my thoughts together. "Clean water," I said, explaining that China now had the resources to bring its water pollution treatment technology up to modern health standards, and I was a specialist in that field. "So I hope to make some money at the same time as I'm making a valuable contribution to the people and the environment."

Zeker just sighed and looked away. "When I heard you were asking the clerk at your hotel about the water system here in Kashgar, I assumed you were interested in poisoning the city. I am glad to hear there are still a few honest and innocent people like you in the world." He made it sound as if being an engineer was somehow equivalent to sainthood.

"You're the second person in Asia to compliment me for my innocence," I said.

"Only the innocent walk boldly where the wise would not dream to enter," he muttered, shaking his head. I gathered it was an old Jewish saying, like *Fools rush in* . . . I wasn't feeling especially wise at the moment. I told Zeker I had to leave. We shook hands and parted. "Don't worry, I will report that you are a naive but harmless engineer," he said, with what sounded like real sincerity.

As I rode my bicycle out onto the main street at the edge of the park I saw a man start up a small white car and drive slowly behind me all the way back to the hotel. He sat in his car as I went to my room. Not very subtle, but threatening enough to make me very uneasy. I had to assume that someone had been following me from the moment I got off the plane at Urumchi, and not only Zeker. I checked my room for listening devices and hidden cameras in classic B-movie fashion, and spent a wakeful night mulling over my next move. I decided not to return to the bookseller; that would be asking for trouble. But if I didn't, I would be at a dead end. I wanted to find the monastery, if only to do justice to Dorothy's belief in me. After today, I knew I was in way over my head. At the same time I was damned if I was going to be intimidated into changing my plans. I still believed that I had come all this way to find *something*. Maybe it wasn't the monastery—that had been my own assumption.

Have more faith, Hazrat said. I could still feel the touch of his fingertip against my heart. I decided to trust him for the moment and see where it got me—which didn't mean that I would take un-necessary risks. Innocence was hardly a virtue in a land as layered with intrigue as this one.

THE NEXT DAY WAS SUNDAY. ABDU HAD TOLD ME ABOUT THE KASHGAR Sunday Market, the greatest and oldest street market in Central Asia. "Very special," he said, and begged me to take enough time to enjoy it. Traders travel from hundreds of miles by truck, donkey, and horse to buy and sell in this ancient bazaar. Farmers with rickety wooden carts piled high with carrots, grapes, and wheat, and barefoot herders with goats, horses and chickens begin arriving before dawn. I was up early, since I hadn't slept much the night before, and I watched the whole extraordinary procession of people, goods and animals into the city.

Caravans of extended families set up canvas tents on street corners, displaying their raw wool and animal pelts. Some pelts came from Himalayan sheep, and some, I was sorry to see, from endangered species like the Himalayan Snow Leopard. I wandered for hours through endless alleys of exotic spices and strange-looking fruits, like the giant yellow hummi-melon, sampling whatever looked safe.

At mid-afternoon the Muslim call to prayer sounded from the loudspeakers in the nearby mosque. Shops were momentarily locked and shuttered as the men streamed into the mosque for ritual prayers. I was standing on a corner not far from the bookshop. One of the men who emerged from the mosque after prayers walked past me and down the street. I saw him open the door to the shop and disappear inside. I looked around several times. As far as I could tell, I hadn't been followed all morning.

Overcome with curiosity, I strolled towards the bookseller's and went in. It was a small space, filled with Arabic prayer books from floor to ceiling—all of them beautiful, in every size and color, mostly in red and gold, both handmade and mass produced. Over in one corner I found some books in Chinese and other foreign languages. I was browsing among the piles, turning the pages of a Chinese book on the ancient art of Xinjiang, when one of the illustrations stopped me in my tracks: a painting of two entwined snakes, one female and one male, with a sun above and a moon below—similar to my amulet.

I looked around for the shopkeeper who was occupied behind a desk. "Can you tell me about this picture?" I asked, hoping he understood English. He looked at me blankly. I repeated my question and held up the book, but his expression stayed the same. Then he raised one hand and beckoned to someone outside in the market plaza.

As I turned to see who it was, I felt a jolt deep in my abdomen. I couldn't determine if my shock came from fear, or from an eerie feeling that I knew the person who was entering the shop. I could only stare in fascination at the tall man dressed in all-black Western style clothes. "Can I help you?" he asked in clear English with a Russian accent. I wasn't sure if he was one of my shadows from the CIS.

7th century AD painting on silk, portraying Fu Xi and Nu Hua. Note the entwined serpent bodies, with the sun above and the moon beneath. In their hands are a compass and a ruler, symbolizing the twin cosmic principles of circles and straight lines.

Illustration from The Ancient Art of Xinjiang, *China; The Xinjiang Art and Photography Press, China, 1994. (Book acquired by the author in Kashgar)*

"I was just asking about this picture," I said.

He stood a few inches from me and looked at the open book in my hands. "This is from the *Song of Eternity*," he said matter-of-factly. "It depicts the classic male and female forms of Fu Xi and Nu Hua, the creators of the world in Chinese mythology. Does this image mean something to you?"

"Yes, in a way," I hedged.

"If the *Song of Eternity* is of interest to you, there is one man here who can properly tell you about it. If you like, I will see if we can find him."

Overriding any normal caution, I made the decision to trust him. "Actually, I would be grateful to learn anything I can about this," I said. I purchased the book and we set off walking back to the market. He told me I could call him Thod, and I told him my name. He looked Kirgyz, the proud warriors northwest of China. His face was refined and handsome, with Caucasian skin and brown eyes that sometimes darted and sometimes stared with great intensity. He didn't look like one who worked with his hands or spent much time outdoors.

We stopped at a booth in the market and sat down next to an old man with white hair who wore a skullcap and a long black wool coat. He held a burlap bag overflowing with apricots and carrots. I waited patiently, but he didn't look my way. Thod said nothing, so I assumed this wasn't the one he was taking me to meet. The three of us just sat there at the edge of a fruit stand watching shoppers walk past. I had no idea why I was here, but apparently part of it had to do with simply waiting.

After a few minutes, I noticed an even older man watching us from across the street. He turned to walk slowly towards us, pressing his cane into the cobblestone with quiet dignity, parting the bustling street crowd with his presence alone. I felt an immediate affinity with this man in his dark robes and flowing white beard. He looked like a kindly grandfather with his gentle walk and deeply furrowed face, which was quite weathered and had a yellowish tinge, although he too appeared to be Caucasian. If I were to compare him to someone, it would be Gandalf in *The Lord of the Rings*. He came directly up to me and I stood to greet him. After bowing our heads to each other, he took my hands and studied them closely. He smiled into my eyes with the warmth of one who has cared for you your entire life. His gaze had an infinite depth about it, as if he saw everywhere in the universe at once. In that moment I wasn't thinking in words like those. I was enveloped in such a profound sense of comfort and lightness of soul that only much later could I even attempt to describe it. I knew who he was. When I found my voice I heard myself saying to him, "You're Gilgamesh . . ."

He spoke over my shoulder to Thod, who stepped forward to translate for me. "Gil-Hamesch—yes, that is one of his many names. He says that he has been waiting for you for a long time, and asks if you will be staying for a while." Thod looked at me for a reply.

"I don't know," I said, trying not to stare. I wasn't sure what to do next. What I did was reach into my pocket and draw out the serpent amulet. I held it out on my open palm. All three men looked at it, Gil-Hamesch, Thod and the old man with the burlap bag. "It came from someone called the Gardener," I said. "I believe I'm supposed to return it."

Gil-Hamesch didn't move to take it. Instead, he regarded it for a long moment before whispering something to Thod. "He says he knew it would find its way home again. But he says it is not yet time for it to be returned. For now, it belongs in your hands." I closed my fingers around the amulet again. Now what?

"The beginnings . . ." Gil-Hamesch said directly to me in English, and then finished in his own language for Thod to translate.

"He is most grateful for your efforts," Thod said.

"What did he mean about beginnings?"

Thod smirked a smile. "He said you haven't the slightest idea what you are about to find out about yourself. He asks what it is that you wish above all things."

I met Gil-Hamesch's eyes and felt a sudden transfer of energy that nearly lifted me from the ground. There, in the midst of the largest, noisiest market in the whole of Central Asia, with people and animals passing and jostling all around us, I was having a private spiritual experience with a man who probably had the power to clear the streets with his will alone if that was his desire. And yet the power emanating from his being was entirely controlled and benevolent. I didn't have to understand what was happening logically, I simply knew. And I knew that it was no random thing that had brought me to this moment, to this place, with these three men. In answer to Gil-Hamesch's question I said, "I wish above all things to be a good and true man. I wish self-knowledge."

Thod gave me Gil-Hamesch's reply. "He says your goals are very admirable, considering that you are still ignorant of most true things." I looked over at the old man but could not read his expression. I wondered if I had just messed up my one opportunity.

"I suppose I am," I admitted. I was about to ask him about the monastery and the manuscript—or maybe I wouldn't have dared. I'll never know, because at that moment he turned and walked into the crowded street and just vanished, along with the man with the burlap bag of apricots and carrots. I instinctively pressed my palms together in an Indian *namaste* and gazed in the direction of their disappearance.

"Let me see your golden serpents," Thod said, snapping me out of my daze. I unclasped my fingers around it. "This will open doors for you if you let it. I'm not being obtuse, believe me. There are good reasons that Gil-Hamesch wants you to hold onto it."

"I have to ask you something: How in the world did you know I was searching for him?"

Thod grunted a laugh. "You have it backwards. He was looking for *you*. He sent me to stand outside the bookstore. If you hadn't found the book with the page from the *Song of Eternity*, or followed a similar sign of power, I was instructed to stay away and not approach you. It was your decision to make all of this happen." By now I was ready to believe anything, and yet I was wary. I didn't want to be sucked into something out of pure foolishness. But I had to admit, things were happening that I couldn't explain rationally.

"So this came from the Gardener . . ." Thod said, smoothing his fingers over the design of the amulet. "The moment you spoke his name I knew that Gil-Hamesch had not been mistaken about you. I have heard stories about the Gardener all my life. He came to our village a long time ago and changed our lives in ways we could not have imagined. We had not had contact with the West for centuries. If it were not for the ideas that the Gardener planted in the minds of my people, I would never have been allowed to leave our village for a formal education. How do you know of him?"

"I don't," I said, "not really. I was told that he had gone to an ancient monastery near the Gobi Desert, looking for a sacred manuscript."

"The *Song of Eternity* . . . that is what he came to find at the monastery. And, as you already know, he found it. You must come and visit my village—that is, if you are interested in seeing the monastery. It is in the Kashi district. I'm driving back tomorrow, if you wish to come." It took me a moment to comprehend what he was offering me. "It is what Gil-Hamesch wants," Thod added, "as well as myself."

"There might be a problem," I said. "I'm staying at the Se Man, and I've been followed by the security police ever since I came here. I don't think my visa covers the Kashi area."

He waved a dismissive hand. "Meet me at the small restaurant behind your hotel tomorrow morning at six. We can talk about this then. I will make sure nobody follows you."

I returned to the hotel and lay down on my bed, staring up at all the cracks in the old plaster ceiling. My mind wasn't tracking in a logical way. How could it? I hadn't given it anything logical to work with in the last few hours. I should have been writing in my journal, recording everything that happened. Words should have flowed from my ballpoint like liquid poetry—describing Gil-Hamesch's eyes, his energy, how I felt when Thod said that he could take me to the monastery (the monastery!) . . . telling about the strangeness of the day from the moment I woke this morning . . . and then finding the spiral symbols in the book that just happened to be from the *Song of Eternity*, which just happened to be the sacred manuscript that the Gardener went searching for. No, none of that. Not until hours later, after it had grown dark and I turned on the bedside lamp did I finally pick up my pen and write, in simple block lettering:

> DOES GILGAMESH REALLY EXIST? YES
> DOES THE MONASTERY REALLY EXIST? YES
> DOES THE MANUSCRIPT REALLY EXIST? YES
> WOULD I BE CRAZY TO TURN BACK NOW?
> YES . . . CERTIFIABLY

PART TWO

WHOEVER ENTERS NEVER RETURNS

7

The Beginnings

"So, TELL ME, WHY EXACTLY DID YOU COME HERE?" THOD SCOWLED as he took his sunglasses off just long enough to pick the peanuts out of his Muslim-style breakfast of fried rice and boiled eggs.

"I just assumed you already knew." I was only half joking, but he didn't smile. In between bites of my own rice and eggs I gave him the short version of my life up to that moment. "After the dream about Father Franck and the sadhu on the river I finally stopped fighting with myself. So I stepped out of the life I knew, at least for a few weeks."

"You realize that once you step out of a life you will not be the same person when you step inside it again," he said.

"I don't want to be the same person," I said. For some reason I started telling him the story of my pet canary, Hermes. He was one of the dearest things in my life. I thought he was happy, even though some of his long warblings were so plaintive that I was sure he was calling to a mate he would never find. "And then one day a cat got into the house and knocked his cage over and he flew away to his freedom. I was sad for myself because I loved him and I missed his beautiful singing, but I also knew that he was finally free of his cage— free to be himself."

"So you are Hermes . . ." Thod said, finally looking up from his food. "What do you expect to find here, so far from your cage?"

"In a word—answers."

"Answers are everywhere," he said with a flick of his hand. "Be more specific."

"I want to learn about the manuscript that the Gardener found."

"The *Song of Eternity* is not just one manuscript."

"What is it, then?"

"It is the name given to a whole set of sacred teachings. They were written in a very old language that is rarely used any more. Very difficult for someone like you to understand—maybe impossible."

"But you know what they are . . . you've seen them. You know what they say."

"Even if I could translate them for you, the words would have little meaning. For one thing, you have to understand how we see the world, and I know that you don't."

"I'm willing to learn," I said, just a little annoyed with his quick evaluation of me. "I'd be willing to pay you for your help."

"What would you do with these books if I agreed to translate them for you?" he said, chewing loudly.

"Study them, learn from them."

He pushed his plate away and fixed me with a stare. "This is a matter of initiation. Do you know what that entails? Here in our world we do not just read and study spiritual books as if they were textbooks or curiosities. Each book is sacred. It has a sacred voice, many layers of meaning. A teacher initiates his students into each book with great care."

"I would like that for myself. I know I'm capable of grasping the deeper meanings of the texts," I said. Thod rolled his eyes. "I'm interested in learning more about your ancient spiritual beliefs," I persisted. As an afterthought I said, "but I don't want to convert to your religion."

He fired another look at me. "And just what are your own beliefs?" I said that I considered myself a spiritual man, but not necessarily a religious one in the formal sense. I believed in the general unity of all religions. That didn't seem to impress him one bit, so I began to tell him how open minded I was, what a quick learner, how much I admired science and logical inquiry. By now, Thod was looking at me with clear disdain. "I think you don't even realize what a fantasy world you live in."

I wasn't sure I could get along with this man, though Lord knows, I was trying. This just wasn't working.

His mocking expression suddenly relented. "I promise, I won't ever ask you to believe in anything at all. There is only one requirement: that you be willing to open your eyes and take nothing for granted."

"That I can agree to," I said, feeling like I had finally gotten somewhere, though I wasn't sure exactly where. Thod dropped a few Chinese yuan on the table. "That golden statue of yours—keep it close. Now we had better get going. My village is in a small oasis some distance off the road to Urumchi. That is where the monastery is. There's a long drive ahead."

I walked around the corner and back to the hotel, trying not to attract attention by appearing to be in a hurry—hoping no one could read the excitement I was feeling. I was heading out into the Gobi Desert with a very peculiar man, going to the place where the legends started, and all I could think was *Yes!* My pulse was nearly jumping from my skin as I stuffed my things into my duffel and backpack and checked out of the hotel. I had the presence of mind to tell the desk clerk that I was joining a tour group headed south on the Karakoram Highway to Pakistan—the opposite direction to where I was planning to go. I hoped the ruse would sidetrack any CIS shadows.

I met Thod a short distance from the hotel and tied my bags to the roof of his old Land Rover while he checked the tiedowns on a large number of boxes and bulging burlap sacks. I dropped my liter water bottle, and when I bent down to pick it up out of the dirt I noticed two extra pairs of feet standing on the other side of the car. I came around to investigate and saw Gil-Hamesch and the old man from the market, looking like apparitions in the dusty, misty morning. Nobody said anything as Thod helped the old men into the back seat and motioned for me to sit up front next to him. I couldn't quite believe what was happening, it seemed so very ordinary and without fanfare. Gil-Hamesch—the one I had woven dreams around for so many years, the mysterious reincarnating protector of ancient manuscripts—was sitting in the grubby back seat of a well worn Land Rover with his hands folded in his lap and a grin on his face. I was learning my first lesson: Nothing is as it seems.

We drove out of Kashgar in a plume of dust and headed north on a desolate road that snaked its way along the foot of the bleak spires of the Kirgiz Range of the Tien Shan Mountains. Those were the legendary Celestial Mountains towering above us like immense fortress walls, at one moment fully visible and then suddenly engulfed in billowy white clouds. "I've thought about these mountains ever since I was a boy," I said to Thod, who just glanced at me and returned to his driving. There wasn't much conversation for the first hour, except when I asked Thod how long it would take to reach his village, and he said, "Too long for one day's drive."

He left me to ponder what that meant as we bumped and skidded along washed-out lanes and around potholes big enough to swallow our heavily loaded car. The outside air was hot and I was glad I had brought along an extra bottle of Danone, the Chinese analog of Evian water. I was acutely aware of the presence and mental activity of the two men in the back seat, even though no one said anything. In an odd way it felt as if I was being scanned and assessed. It wasn't an intrusion, it was more like an inquiry, and my instinct was to thank them for their kind attention. I turned around in my seat and saw that they were both smiling at me. "I am called the Cook," the old man with Gil-Hamesch said and offered me his hand. It felt leathery and warm—and very kind, if I can use that word to describe a hand.

"I'm happy to be with you," I said to both of them.

"It is a happy time, old one," Gil-Hamesh said to me, still with a gentle smile on his thoroughly wrinkled face.

We pressed along the western edge of the Gobi Desert following the ancient Silk Road, even though it was sometimes just a barely discernable track. The Land Rover's suspension system was tight and I wished I had more fat on my bones to cushion the jolts and lurches. But I wasn't complaining, not with the stunning infinity of the desert all around me, not with Gil-Hamesch in the back seat. He and the Cook were quiet for long stretches of time and then would chatter softly and burst into laughter at something hilarious between them.

We had been on the road for almost four hours and we hadn't passed a single inhabited town, only the crumbling ruins of military outposts that once guarded the borders between the Soviet Union and China. Now they were covered with dunes of yellow sand blown by the rolling dust clouds into high piles along sagging barbed wire fences. The dusty sameness was punctuated occasionally by the sight of abandoned oil and gas wells that glittered brilliantly in the sun because abrasive sandstorms had removed both paint and rust. I could tell that a few brave humans had once tried to live in this desert. Eroding mosques and minarets came into view occasionally, and we passed a few abandoned villages of crumbling yellow adobe. Hardly a livable environment, but for all its bleakness it possessed a seductive, mysterious beauty. Once we saw a small herd of Bactrian camels, a rare sight, since there are so few of the two-humped camels left in the wild. "Their habitat is being lost," Thod commented as we stopped to look at the beautiful creatures that were foraging in the dry grass, tended by a young boy. "The waterholes are being ruined by human activity." The camels looked up at us with wise eyes as we passed, and I had the feeling that Gil-Hamesch was communicating with them.

We stopped along the road at one point to take a break and eat. The sun was intense, but Thod was resourceful. He rigged a tarp out from the roof rack and secured it to the ground below with tent pegs. We all sat down under the small square of shade and passed around handfuls of raisins, dried apricots, almonds and sunflower seeds. Suddenly, everyone was in a talkative mood, especially Thod.

"This part of the Gobi is called the *Taklimaken*," he said. "It means 'Whoever enters never returns'." I asked him if I should be worried, and he threw back his head and barked a laugh. "Who knows? We should never take our lives for granted."

"Is this where you were born . . . this part of the world?" I'd wanted to know more about him because he had such an unusual appearance.

"I was born in the land of the Kyrgyz," he said, "and then I became an orphan when my mother and father were taken away by the Soviets. It is a story for another day. But I will tell you how I got my name," he said and removed his sunglasses. "Look at my nose. My uncle thought I looked like the Egyptian god Thoth—the one with the head of an ibis bird and a long curved beak. I like the name because Thoth was the scribe of the gods, the lord of books, the overseer of all the arts and sciences. Thod is a good name for me."

"I was named for a character in a story that my mother loved," I confessed. "Larry Darrell in *The Razor's Edge*. I rarely saw my mother, but once when I was fifteen we met briefly and I asked her why she gave me that name. She said she didn't know—it was just her sense of who I already was before I was born."

"What is this book?" Thod looked interested.

"It's about a man who goes to India to find spiritual teachers, and to find himself."

"And does he?"

"Yes, he does. By the end of the book he's the only one in the story who is truly happy."

"Then your mother gave you something of great value."

I said nothing and took another drink from my bottle of Danone. But the damage was already done. Just thinking of her had opened up the old, awful emptiness in the center of my being again—the disappointment, the abandonment. It surprised me with its power after all these years. It was all I could do to keep from crying. I felt Gil-Hamesch's eyes on me. "In the desert . . . everything is open," he said quietly, moving his fingers gracefully like a Hindu dancer, as if grasping at unseen lines of energy.

"You might think, looking at him, that he is only a dreamy old fool," Thod said close to my ear. "But trust me—he is a man of great knowledge and power. Miracles follow him wherever he goes. This is because he is in constant communication with the spirit of life."

I looked over at Gil-Hamesch, who was gazing toward the horizon with rapt attention, where there was absolutely nothing to be seen.

"What does his name mean?" I asked. "You said it was just one of many he is called."

"Gil-Hamesch is actually an honorary title, not a proper name. It means, 'The one who voluntarily gives up eternal life to live in this world.' The title belongs to the person who is responsible for keeping alive the vital essence of the *Song of Eternity* so that it doesn't degenerate into dogma."

"When I first heard his name I thought it must be related in some way to the old story of Gilgamesh, the hero in the Mesopotamian epic."

"I know that story," Thod said. "Gilgamesh journeyed to the underworld in search of immortality. But that story is from ancient

Mesopotamia, which is now part of Iraq. We are Kashi people. There are some similarities between the two stories, however. In our story, the Kashi king Gil-Hamesch and all his people lived in a heavenly place called the Valley of Miracles. But this great king was not content with this place of perfection. He wished above all to understand the world of humans. And so he left the Valley of Miracles to come into the human world. His quest was to journey to Earth without forgetting his eternal self through absent-mindedness or laziness. He failed, and therefore he became mortal. But while he lived on earth he met a serpent who taught him the secrets of immortality and the *Song of Eternity*. That is the story that our people have told their children for countless centuries."

"And yet he is still alive and here with you now," I said.

"The Kashi believe that there is and always has been only one Gil-Hamesch, and that he continually reincarnates voluntarily out of compassion for all life." Thod nodded towards his teacher. "He has crossed the Great Desert and he has found the Valley of Miracles. And yet he stays among us out of love."

I did my best with that information, but the heat of the day and the strangeness of the whole situation made it hard to take in fully. I asked Thod if there were stories about where or when the *Song of Eternity* had been first written down.

"The *Song* has always been an oral tradition," Thod said. "It's true that we've written it down and translated it into a few different languages over the centuries, but the real book, the one with the true knowledge, is kept here." He pointed to his heart. "Kashi mythology says that the originator of the *Song* was a mysterious wise woman who came from the West thousands of years ago."

"Like a goddess," I offered.

"If you wish—but some faded paintings in my village show an old man with a long white beard, walking down from a mountain carrying a book in his hand. In any case, it was Gil-Hamesch who first wrote down the *Song of Eternity* a very long time ago in a language that is no longer spoken. That is all I can tell you about its history."

"And now it is the centerpiece of your religion, of your faith," I said.

"No, not at all," he shot back. "It is the song of life itself, out of which both religion and philosophy arise. But it is also the cure for religion and the cure for philosophy."

"The cure?" That was a strange thing to say.

"The *Song of Eternity* is not a philosophy of words or concepts. It is a philosophy of freedom. And it definitely is not a faith. Some of us are Muslim, some are not, and it doesn't matter. This is not a matter of religion."

At a sign from Gil-Hamesch that it was time to be on our way, Thod stood up and started taking down the tarp, while I did what I could to be of help. "Myself, I don't take those old stories so literally," he said after we had packed up and returned to the car, "especially about the *Song of Eternity* being brought to us from some far away place. I think it originated right here with the first shamans, as a kind of mystical medical and musical manual. The way I see it, thousands of years ago the first shamans in Asia learned to open their minds through trances and other altered states of consciousness. Then they learned to keenly observe the life process and the nature of the mind. In their meditations they must have discovered the Supreme Truth—that the true nature of anything can never be known directly by the senses. And they discovered that humans are capable of extraordinary powers. Many geniuses lived back then. They were not as ignorant as we modern people like to think. Their insights were profound."

Then Gil-Hamesch must be a shaman, I thought, even though I didn't know what that really meant, at least not yet. What the Cook was, I couldn't tell. He had spoken very little, but when he did, his deep baritone voice rose and fell in a musical way that expressed an affectionate nature. After we had been back on the road for a while and no one was conversing, he began to sing a melodic chant. His voice sounded rich and full, almost hypnotic, and I fell into a drowsy half sleep that transported me deeper into the mystery of the Taklimaken Desert.

Thod's voice woke me some time later, saying, "Personally, I believe there is only one faith worth worshiping, and that is the religion of Biology. It is not written down anywhere except in the cells of our own bodies."

I opened my eyes and stared straight ahead for a moment. Where did that come from? I had assumed he was a spiritual man. I certainly didn't expect him to hold such a materialistic view of life. Then he added, as if for emphasis, "We are biological creatures. Every subject, whether philosophy or religion or mythology, is merely a fiction we create to entertain ourselves." Thod's piercing directness took some getting used to.

"But what about the *Song of Eternity*?"

"That too is the words of our biology speaking to us. I am a doctor, trained in Western medicine. But I was also trained as a traditional shamanic healer. I have lived in both worlds and I know how the mind and the emotions are connected to the most subtle workings of the body—how the body affects our perceptions of reality." That's all he said for another long period of time. I gazed out the window at the ochre sand dunes on all sides of us. They rose and fell like waves on an endless tawny sea below a brilliant sapphire dome of sky. The *Song of Eternity* wasn't the only ancient sacred text to be born in the desert. The power of the solitude and the naked sun burning through the deep blue sky of the desert had ignited the passionate spiritual fires of Islam, Judaism, the ancient Egyptians, and Christianity. Moses wandered in the desert for forty years before speaking directly to the Creator through a fire that illuminated a tree. And Jesus began his final mission after forty days alone in a barren desert. Many great religious prophets of history, including Mohammed, Abraham, and Elijah, received their most profound inspiration while alone in the solitude of the desert. I was in good company. If there was something to be learned here, so far away from everything that passed for normal in my life, I was willing to try. I was open.

8

On the Nature of Truth

WE STOPPED TO REFUEL IN THE RUNDOWN MUD-BRICK CITY OF AKSU, but didn't linger. I was grateful for even a few minutes to stretch my legs. Gil-Hamesch and the Cook stayed in the car, obviously a lot tougher than the American when it came to endurance. I regretted that the language barrier prevented an easier exchange of thoughts, because my head was brimming with questions. Fortunately, there was Thod. When he wasn't being acerbic he could be wonderfully informative and a willing translator.

I told him about my encounter with Zeker, the Jewish CIS agent in the park in Kashgar, especially the part about the Nazis and the Jewish temple in the desert. "He may have been talking about our monastery," he said. "Or maybe there once was a Jewish temple in the desert. In the old days, people used to come to our village from all over this region. And in the distant past we had visitors from many regions of the world. But now our district is closed to travel except by invitation or special permit. As a result, all sorts of wild stories are told about us. We don't have a Jewish temple, but it wouldn't surprise me if some people say we do."

The day wore on, and I dozed for a while. "How much farther until we reach your village?" I finally asked.

"Have faith," he said.

"I thought you didn't believe in faith."

"I'm speaking of you, not myself."

I wasn't going to ask him where we would be staying the night— I almost didn't want to know. There was nothing on the horizon but the huge sand dunes, endless files of them, sculpted by the winds into a landscape of stunning symmetry and an emptiness that was absolute.

Gil-Hamesch tapped Thod on the shoulder and said something to him, then smiled at me and settled back into his seat. "He wants me to tell you about the *Song of Eternity*," Thod said. "If you are going to be an initiate you will need to know a great deal that you do not."

"Is this the best time for me to learn about it?" I wasn't feeling much like an able student at the moment. I searched through my pack and retrieved my notebook and pen.

Thod ignored my question. "The *Song of Eternity* is a collection of teachings on many different subjects. However, the primary teachings are contained within the first four books, or songs. The first book is called the *Book of Truth*. It is a description of the Supreme Truth, and it is the philosophical foundation for all the books that follow."

The *Book of Truth*, the Supreme Truth, I repeated to myself. I didn't know if I would be tested on this later.

"The second book is called the *Book of Creation*. As you can guess, it is the story of creation, and it is also dedicated to the healing arts. The next two books are the *Book of Correlations*—which explains the nature of human relationships and provides the basis for our sacred dances, and the *Book of Immortality*—which outlines a sort of grand formula for the complete understanding of all aspects of life."

I was still thinking about the concept he called the Supreme Truth. I felt uneasy with it, with the idea that I would be required to believe in some unprovable dogma. That was the problem I'd always had with religions and philosophies. I wasn't sure I wanted to go down this path.

"We only call it the Supreme Truth to keep from becoming too arrogant," Thod explained to my unspoken objection. He apparently intuited my thoughts. "The Supreme Truth is that there is absolutely no ultimate truth at all—only an infinite set of partial truths."

Now I wondered if Thod was joking. How could they seriously believe that nothing at all is true? "Isn't that a truth in itself?" I argued.

"First of all, it is impossible for anyone to understand the Supreme Truth because it isn't a philosophy, or even a concept. What if I said it is a description of 'the way things really are'? Everything has an opposite, an undercurrent: truth and lies, beauty and ugliness, good and bad," he explained. "But when we talk about the Supreme Truth, we are referring to that which has no under-current—or, to put it another way, we are talking about everything that exists, together with its undercurrent."

His statements made no sense to me. And at the moment my brain wasn't working at peak levels. This was too much like one of the logic classes I took in college—another reason I lost interest in traditional Western philosophies.

Thod barked another laugh. "Gil-Hamesch thinks I'm confusing you, I can feel his thoughts. Unfortunately, language is utterly worthless to describe the Supreme Truth. All I can say is that the words of the *Book of Truth* come closer to describing the Supreme Truth than anything I know of."

"I don't know if I'm comfortable with anything that calls itself the ultimate truth," I had to say.

"The book itself begins with the warning that it is only hinting at the actual truth. This book that is so vital to us doesn't once ask for our faith. Instead, it warns us that each individual person can only discover the truth for oneself. That is why we have managed to stay free from the perils of religion for so long. Comfort is the reward of religious faith . . . but the reward of realization of the Supreme Truth is freedom."

"Freedom?" I asked.

"You see, we believe that the Supreme Truth can never be fully grasped by the mind; it can only be experienced directly. Therefore, the experience is different for every person. So it's pointless to make rules about it, or say that there is only one right path to reach an experience of it."

I was fine with that, but the air was too hot and I was too fatigued to wrestle with it right now. I put my head back and closed my eyes. I heard animated conversation from the back seat, and Thod was part of it. "The Cook says to tell you that in one moment you can realize the Supreme Truth and in the next moment you can forget it.

So we are always trying to remember something that the mind cannot grasp in the normal way."

"I can see how that could be," I said and heard more talk back and forth, with some laughter interspersed.

"Gil-Hamesch says to look at yourself in a mirror." Thod held one hand up flat in front of his face to demonstrate. "Without you and your reflection there is no separate reality. You create your reflection and your reflection creates you. The Supreme Truth is the direct experience of awareness, apart from its reflection." I looked back at Gil-Hamesch. He gestured with a graceful motion towards the desert and said in English, "Look . . . see it everywhere!"

For a long time I gazed out the window at the endless windswept horizon of the Taklimaken Desert, which had taken on an iridescent, otherworldly beauty. The Supreme Truth eluded me. All I knew was that I saw something true in the eyes of Gil-Hamesch. I knew, too, that I was close to remembering something that lay just beyond my reach. The feeling persisted, too powerful to ignore and too deep not to fear—as if I had once known something very important but I had forgotten it, and now it was time to find it again.

In the Taklimaken Desert

Eventually we left the desert floor and climbed a long, barren mountain pass. From there we descended into a valley on the other side, where the Aksu River flows into the Tarim Basin from the Celestial Mountains before disappearing forever beneath the golden sands of the Gobi Desert. The sun was low in the sky and I had no idea where I would be sleeping tonight, but I didn't care. I was where I was, and apparently where I was supposed to be. That was good enough.

9

The Moment Between the Winds

"THE CABIN IS JUST AHEAD," THOD SAID. "WE USE IT AS A WAY STATION between the village and the Kashgar market." We had left the main road about an hour earlier and were bumping along a rough, unpaved stretch through small groves of trees and flowering bushes. We were in rolling, burnt-yellow foothills now, with distant snow-capped peaks on one side and purple, yellow and red hued mountains on the other. This was another kind of beauty, with large boulders and rock formations and dramatic cliffs and canyons.

I asked Thod how often they made the trek into Kashgar. He said he made the journey often, but that Gil-Hamesch rarely did, which made me wonder at the incredible piece of luck that had brought me to Kashgar on that particular day. I loved the feeling of being in the flow—where you just manage to show up at the right moment. I hoped it would never end.

The simple adobe cabin sat in the midst of scrub vegetation with no other buildings anywhere in sight. Its windows were covered over with boards. As I stepped from the car I caught my plaid flannel overshirt on the door and ended up flat on the ground, twisting my knee and providing my hosts with a good laugh. Not a very auspicious arrival. I limped along gamely while we unloaded the supplies and inspected the Land Rover's engine and tires. So much for being in the flow. Thod was troubled by a new crack in the windshield.

The first task at the cabin was to take down the boards from the windows. There was no glass in them, only wood shutters and a few iron bars. They had been covered up not against intruders, but against windstorms. Inside, there appeared to be three rooms besides a small sitting room and the kitchen area and a long wooden table for eating. The cabin had been left well supplied with food and kerosene lanterns and fat tallow candles. The walls were built from white stucco, and the ceilings were covered with rushes. I was given a very small, cell-like room with a wooden cot.

Gil-Hamesch and the Cook went for a walk to visit an old shrine in the hills nearby, leaving Thod and me to relax with a cup of tea in front of the cabin. It felt very companionable sitting there cross-legged on a small wooden bench, watching the colors of the afternoon sky change gradually into deep, shimmering tones of evening.

"Whatever happened to your mother and father?" I asked, as we both looked straight ahead at the glowing horizon.

"I don't know," he said without inflection. "One night some men came to our door and took them away. I was hiding when my uncle found me the next day and he took me to live with him. I was very little. We never talked about it after that. Those were bad times under the Soviets."

"I'm sorry. How did you end up studying Western medicine?"

He looked over at me with a quirk of a smile. "One day when I was still very young I was in the marketplace with my uncle and I saw Gil-Hamesch for the first time. I ran up to him and threw my arms around his knees and refused to leave. Gil-Hamesch chose to take responsibility for me and give me an education—with my uncle's permission."

"Do you think Gil-Hamesch recognized something in you that day?"

"Yes, he told me so later. He has always treated me like a son. With Gil-Hamesch and the people at the monastery I had a very large family."

"But how did you get your Western education? It's a long way from a Central Asian village . . ."

"I was always a restless boy. All I could think of was seeing the world. Gil-Hamesch and others trained me to be a traditional shamanic healer, but I was more interested in modern science, especially medicine and biology. Eventually, it became possible for me to leave my Kashi village and study at Moscow University. After Moscow, I lived in Kyrgyzstan for a few years and traveled to the Middle East and to Egypt. I felt at home in Egypt. I saw my namesake on the walls of temples and we compared beaks," he added.

He was quiet for a time and I didn't want to intrude with more questions. After a while he said, "Your thoughts are very noisy. Tell me what is on your mind."

"Everything," I said, "like, what am I supposed to do now? I want to read the *Song of Eternity*, but how is that going to happen? If it means that I have to go through an initiation ceremony, I'm willing to do it."

He fixed me with one of his uncomfortable stares. "I've already told you, merely reading the *Song* or participating in a ceremony is a waste of your time and mine. The Supreme Truth is not something you can learn with your mind. You learn it with your body. I studied the *Song* as part of my training as a shaman, but it wasn't until years later that I was forced to learn it with my body."

"What do you mean, you were forced?"

"In order for me to study in Russia, I had to pay off a KGB agent to get my citizenship papers. A few years later, the agent got into trouble with the authorities for providing an entry for a Chinese man who turned out to be a spy. So, because of that situation, the State threatened to revoke my citizenship. Then word got to the KGB about the results of some of my research into smallpox and the plague, and soon they were monitoring my every move. It wasn't safe in Soviet Russia to know too much. They thought I was a spy for China. It was a tense time for me.

"One afternoon, two KGB men came to my Moscow apartment with an order to deport me to a labor camp in Kazakhstan. One of them pulled his gun out and told me not to bother packing, while the other one searched my house for valuables he could steal. I panicked. I thought I would die that minute. Have you ever been faced with imminent death?"

"I know what it feels like to have a gun pointed at me," I said.

"In that instant, my mind was useless to me, and then I remembered the *Book of Truth*, and something deeper than my mind took over. I yelled at the two men with the sound that our hunters use to stun a wild animal when they have no weapons. It wasn't exactly a scream; it was a menacing yell that came straight from my gut. The men froze in place. Everything around me became dream-like, time slowed down. I felt as if I had become invisible to them. Without effort, I retrieved my wallet and citizenship papers, walked out of my apartment and escaped. In that moment, I experienced the truth that I could alter my normal state of reality, at least while my will exerted itself to an extraordinary level. I had unleashed *schug*, the will-force, and the wind shifted in my favor.

"That's when I say I first experienced the power that lies hidden behind the Supreme Truth. My training as a shaman saved my life."

I let out my breath, realizing that I had held it in suspension while he described the scene. "What do you think really happened to you?"

"I went into a state of *no-wen*. It means 'the moment between— when the wind turns from one direction to another.' In that moment in Moscow I let go of the knowledge and experience in my mind, out of fear, and tapped into the deep power of pure will much greater than my own. The power of the will is normally dormant, but during times of panic our body knows how to use it. I used this power to affect the attention of those agents. I don't know exactly what I did or how I did it. But I did exactly what I needed, without thinking, and that's what saved my life. I was able to be in a state of *no-wen*, from which my will-force could arise."

"*No-wen*," I repeated, liking the sound of it. I told him about the time when a motel owner in Arizona once held a gun on me. When he realized he had mistaken me for someone else, he put the gun down and I left. But I never forgot the moment of panic when my mind went blank and there was only my will to guide me and some- how I knew I would make it.

"In that moment, even though you didn't realize it, you were employing one of the points on the Shield of Power," Thod said.

"That sounds like a martial arts term."

"The Shield of Power is not a style of fighting," he said, "it is the art of handling power. It is an art that involves the body, the mind, and the non-mind. It takes a lifetime to master because, foremost, it is the art of mastering your extraordinary non-mental powers. But look out—it can also destroy you."

I hadn't the slightest intention of using the Shield of Power any time soon.

"Those moments of panic awaken you to a deeper level than your ordinary thoughts or feelings. Both the warrior and the shaman learn to be present in that place of power. The *Book of Truth* and the concept of the Supreme Truth are tools to help you access the non-mind, too. It is only there that you can find your whole being. And it is there that you have the chance to experience the subtle winds of energy that flow through everything that exists."

"So that's the right place to begin," I said. "*No-wen*."

"It is as simple—and as difficult—as learning to surrender your being without reservation to the invisible presence that is hidden behind the Supreme Truth," he answered. "I like to call that presence the Breath of Life and the Heart of Hearts. You don't use your mind to do this. You use your conviction and willpower."

How could I *not* use my mind to contemplate it? I liked the idea of the Breath of Life and the Heart of Hearts as the hidden presence. But it wasn't going to be easy going into a state of non-mind to find it. It all sounded so esoteric—so zen. But it obviously had special meaning for Thod, so I was happy for him.

"Would you say your life had more meaning after that terrifying experience?" I asked.

Surprisingly, he shook his head. "I live my life with conviction. But I can tell you for sure that my life has no purpose or meaning at all, at least in the ordinary way people think of it." He glanced at me accusatorily. "Are you still looking for the grand purpose of your life?"

"Of course. That will never end."

"Then you need to get over the illusion of a purpose as soon as possible. Life has only one purpose, and that is the unavoidable pull towards evolution and greater intelligence. There's only one place you can find your so-called 'meaning' in this life, and that's in the opinions of others. You could spend your entire life trying to live up to the expectations and beliefs of your family and friends. That sort of meaning has no value at all."

I was wishing that Gil-Hamesch and the Cook would return and set me free from Thod's relentless wordplay. He seemed to relish keeping me off balance. "Tell me how I'm supposed to understand myself without feedback from people around me."

"You already know who you are. Maybe you have forgotten."

I gave up. "All right, maybe I have. Now what . . ."

"Until you find your freedom, life will insist on enlisting you in its missions. It will compel you forward to solve its problems. And if you try to ignore these directives from life, it will be at your peril. But this is only true until the day—and the hour—that you re-discover who you truly are. Until you find your freedom you are only a pawn in a game that is eternal. It is a game that never ends. You have to find your True Voice—if you want to be free."

"And how do I do that?" I could hear my own exasperation.

"All you have to do is let go of your judgments about other people. Then let go of your judgments about yourself."

"Is *that* all?" I said. "People spend years overcoming these things. Maybe even a lifetime isn't enough."

"Don't be discouraged," Thod said with an unexpected sympathetic smile. "This desert is an excellent place to begin. Something about the uncluttered openness here makes room for your inner essence to speak to you more clearly. Not only is it possible to free yourself of your habit of judging everyone and everything—it is essential before you can be initiated into the *Book of Truth* and translate it."

I had gone in a circle with Thod's logic, from something I thought I could grasp—*no-wen*—to the idea that I was a prisoner in my own life and all I had to do was give up judging people. And after that, I might be allowed to read the first book of the *Song of Eternity*. And that was just the *first* book.

That night, after the two elders had come back from their prayers at the shrine and we had sat around the kitchen table eating a wonderful vegetable stew that the Cook prepared, I fell onto my cot and pulled my heavy nomad herder's wool blanket over my head. I heard the Cook singing in his own room, some soothing chant, and I wished that life were as simple as that. I was worried about what was coming next. And I wasn't sure Thod was the ideal instructor.

I finally fell asleep to the sound of a strange buzzing insect outside my window.

10

Culling the Past and Beckoning the Future

I WOKE TO THE SMELLS OF SOMETHING BEING FRIED IN HOT CARAMEL butter. The Cook was happy at his work, humming to himself, Gil-Hamesch had already left the cabin for someplace, and Thod greeted my groggy presence with a gift. "You will be more comfortable wearing these," he said, handing me a pair of loose cotton trousers and a homespun shirt that tied in the front. "How is your knee?"

"Better," I said.

"Good. Have some food and then we will walk. It's time to begin your training. I want you to leave your wristwatch behind today." I gathered that we weren't going to be driving to his village just yet. After a breakfast of black tea, hardboiled eggs and fried breadsticks I changed into my training clothes. Thod was waiting for me outside with his daypack and bottles of water.

We set out walking along a trail that led up into the barren foothills. I followed along behind, looking back at the cabin from time to time for a reference point. The cabin disappeared from sight once we entered the rough folds of the hills, and the insane thought crossed my mind that I should be leaving a trail of breadcrumbs to find my way back. I suspected that this was going to be a long day—a walkabout with Thod, only it was taking place in the wilds of Central Asia instead of the Australian Outback. I noticed all sorts of scrub plants that were nearly invisible until I was stepping on them. I asked Thod about the various ones and he was quick to tell me their local names, their botanical names and their medicinal uses. I knew that by the time I wrote in my journal that night I wouldn't remember any of them, but I did pick a few leaves and tiny flowers to press between the pages.

After about an hour of moderately strenuous walking we stopped to rest under a shady circle of trees. Thod told me their names too, but they weren't familiar to me. We sat on the ground facing each other. The gusting wind brushed against us with a pleasant, astringent fragrance. "We are on the path to the old shrine," Thod said. "Every time Gil-Hamesch and the Cook come this way they leave a blessing where their feet have walked. Be still and try to feel it."

I closed my eyes, but my mind was too busy wondering what Thod would do next. After about five minutes, he took several deep breaths and expelled the last one with a loud *ha!* "Now . . ." he said, "we shall begin." I made an effort to calm my mind and be receptive. "In order to be fully initiated into the *Song of Eternity*," he said, "you must undertake the full apprenticeship of a shaman. This process takes seven years. But since time is precious, and you do not intend to be a healer or a musician, I will try to teach you everything you need to know in one year."

"But Thod!" I interrupted. "I only have a month at most . . . not even that!"

He removed his sunglasses for a moment and stared at me. "Then we'll both have to do our best. I will teach you the key elements now. The rest will be up to you."

"So Gil-Hamesch gave his permission?" I needed confirmation that I was actually a candidate for the teachings. By now, Thod had made it pretty clear that I was incompetent in most areas of my life. I truly didn't know what to believe.

"The spiritual progress of humanity is marked by turning points," he began. "Gil-Hamesch has long foreseen that another great turning point is coming."

I wondered if he meant in my life, or in the world. "I can believe it," I agreed. "The world needs a lot of help."

"There are many signs appearing now. To Gil-Hamesch, your return of the statue from the Gardener is further confirmation. He says that we all have a role in the changes that are coming. Your role apparently is to translate the *Song of Eternity*."

"That's incredible," I said, sounding like my seventeen-year-old self when Dorothy first told me there were secret things waiting for me to find when I was ready. "I mean, it really *is* . . ."

Thod smirked a smile and said nothing, while I just sat there letting his words sink in. If I felt fear it was only that I couldn't live up to Gil-Hamesch's expectations. The last thing I wanted was to fail. "You know, Thod," I said, after I'd thought about it, "I may be a beginner, and I may not always know what the hell is going on . . . but I'm a tenacious son of a bitch, and I'll do whatever it takes."

"That was the right answer," he said, and for the first time we actually shared a laugh.

~

AND SO IT STARTED. WE STAYED UNDER THE CIRCLE OF TREES FOR many hours. It seemed like no time at all. That's not where the teaching was taking place.

"The first lesson is called *culling the past and beckoning the future*," he said. "I was taught this when I was in training as a shamanic healer, before I decided to go to the university to study medicine. It's the necessary process of self-examination. As humans, we inhabit two worlds: the past and the future, but we have almost no control over either. If you want to see what is true, you must first become free from your past so that you don't unwittingly fall into the same old traps in the future. Do you think you are free of your past at this moment?" he challenged me.

"Probably not," I replied, and waited for him to tell me why I wasn't a free man.

"The Kashi shamans believe that the value of memory is not to create a comfortable self-validating world in which to live. Rather, memory is a tool at the service of the totality of your being. You can learn to use your memories to take control over your future. I will teach you four techniques that the Kashi practice to enhance the power of the mind and 'clear the inner lenses,' as we call it. These are called *currency*, *relevancy*, *positioning* and *shortening*. They will enable you to cull the past in order to position yourself for the future.

"First, the technique of *currency*: This involves examining each past experience in your memory while asking yourself what its current value is. If it has current value, then position it to help you seize a future opportunity. If the stories you are telling yourself have no more current value, then withdraw the emotional undercurrent and place that liberated energy at your service instead."

"But it's not always obvious if something has current value or if it doesn't."

"It will become clear. This is a practice for the rest of your life. Every night before you go to sleep, examine the events of your day. If you find a lingering emotional charge from any of the day's events, you should make every effort to follow the thread back to its roots, and then resolve, release and forgive before you sleep." He repeated the words several times: resolve, release and forgive. "You have more choice about your feelings than you let yourself believe."

Maybe, I said to myself. I'd have to think about that.

"Now I will speak about *relevancy*. This is the discipline of inquiring into the personal relevancy of all information regardless of its source, whether it comes from the past, present or future. You should always ask the question, 'What does this experience have to do with me?' This is the only way to become free of our perpetual habit of ruining our lives over other peoples' dramas.

"The freedom to choose the currency and relevancy of past information allows us to position ourselves to respond to new events with advantage and intuition. That is what we call *positioning*. Bad events do not happen to us, but unexpected events always occur. We choose to experience them as good or bad because of our expectations and fears. Therefore, the best way to position yourself for future opportunities is to have no expectations and as little judgment as possible."

At this point I was starting to feel overwhelmed. I asked Thod to stop for a moment.

"You are not used to considering so many ideas at once," he said, "but they must be introduced in sequence. You think your mind is tired and therefore you must stop, but in fact your mind has very little to do with what you are able to understand."

And so he went on to the most challenging Kashi concept yet: *shortening*. "The ultimate goal for all humans is continuous realization of the Supreme Truth. Every other goal is either a longer or shorter path to that ultimate goal. The goal of shortening is to forge a stronger link with the subtle energy that is the source of life. In the end, for those who fully realize the Supreme Truth, the future, together with all of its grand plans, dissolves into a state of being rooted only in the present moment.

"You told me in Kashgar that you don't want to be the same person you have been—that was not hard to say—but what is much harder is to objectively view all of your beliefs about yourself and about the world, and learn to be emotionally detached from them."

"But I don't want to lose my ability to feel," I argued.

"Is that what you think you heard me say? You replied from a preconception of yourself, a limited definition of what emotions are. It would be sad to cross the entire world to find a teaching if you aren't willing to make the proper personal effort needed to understand it."

"I'm more than willing," I retorted, stung by his suggestion that I wasn't up to the task. "But I don't think I want to radically change who I am. It's too late for that."

"Who gave you that idea?"

"Nobody . . . it's just the way it is," I said, and started to feel depressed. It was true—in some parts of my life I did feel stuck. I often became trapped by doubt and indecision, or had the feeling that I wasn't doing what I should be doing with my life.

"Who gave you that idea?" Thod repeated, and waited for me to think about it.

Once I stopped resisting his question, I had an immediate re-collection of my school teachers and counselors and my parents, all pleading with me to go to college and become an engineer, when all I really wanted to do was be a musician or a baseball player. I heard my dad's voice telling me to be serious. *Enough with the baseball . . . you have to study . . . you don't want to grow up to be a nobody.* Of course that was before baseball players earned millions of dollars.

As I let myself remember, I could see how I learned to conform, like most children do in one way or another. But I also saw how it left me feeling that I was living in someone else's world. And then I saw how that had led to my problems with making decisions about so many things, including in my profession.

"I've just followed one thread," I told Thod. "There's a lot of pain in it."

"I can see. And that is from only one thread."

"I want to feel more confident. I want to make decisions with no doubts about what I'm doing or what I want."

"The Supreme Truth is the golden doorway to confidence," he said.

He was back to the big abstractions. "But the Supreme Truth says that there's no real truth to anything," I objected, "so how can I have confidence in anything at all?"

"On the contrary. When you understand the power of meaninglessness, you will be able to invest every decision and every action with ultimate power and faith. But first you have to rediscover who you are. You have to find your True Voice. Tell me . . . who is there when you're free from living your life for other people? Everyone who has lost faith in their own life suffers from the same thing: They have lost their True Voice. When you speak and act from your unique authentic self you will abound with confidence, no matter what kind of luck you have. You have to detach from all the other voices in your head."

From out of the blue, I began to feel anger, not at Thod or the Supreme Truth, but at my parents and all those teachers who pushed me into the life they wanted for me. I didn't like the feeling, to say the least. "I'm not doing very well, Thod," I confessed.

"Stop," he said. "Find a point on the horizon and fix your attention on it. Now breathe deeply into your abdomen, very slowly, and hold it until you feel the release of emotion from your belly." I did as he instructed, and was surprised that it seemed to work. "This too will take practice," he said. "Every belief and every emotion carries a hidden undercurrent. That undercurrent holds the key to reclaiming your freedom, if you desire it enough."

"I couldn't stop the anger," I said, trying to reflect on what had just happened. "Even though I know very well that everyone wanted the best for me, and I was the one who made those choices." That was quite a surprise to me, to see that I still carried so much emotion around this.

"When you begin to follow the threads you can't stop halfway," Thod commented, and the next moment I was feeling a welling-up of anger again. This time it was about a woman I had once cared about, who had pushed me even harder than my parents had. She wanted me to be successful and make lots of money. I worked my heart out, trying to be the man she wanted. And then after a year together she left me for a man who had more money than I could ever make. It hurt me very deeply, in a way that wouldn't heal for a long time, though I never admitted it to anyone. I even told her I didn't care, but I did. I couldn't comprehend how she could be so heartless.

"I think it's high time to forgive her."

"But she doesn't deserve it!" I almost yelled.

"So you're going to punish her by not letting yourself love anyone again?"

I didn't know what to say. He spoke the truth, of course. Whether she went on to break the hearts of ten more men or not, didn't matter to me. What mattered for me was to release the energy around her and take back my power to be happy. If that was forgiveness, then I forgave her.

"She gave you a 'Mortal Wound,'" Thod said, lowering his voice. "We are all vulnerable to Mortal Wounds—each and every one of us." Thod explained that humans have something like an Achilles heel, except that it is in the heart, not the foot. "We can defend against almost any attack, but a Mortal Wound does not heal on its own. It is an unavoidable part of the human condition and many people waste away and die from one. Only love, forgiveness, and pure will-force can heal these wounds—and each of these always requires making a difficult choice, and taking difficult action. It is the only way."

Thod urged me to search for more threads to follow. There were more, many more, intimate personal memories and emotions that arose, one after another. I was experiencing a state of receptivity that was completely new to me. I could hear Thod's resonant voice at the perimeter of my senses, quietly asking me to observe this, observe that. Beyond the words themselves however, I felt an energy flowing that I had felt before, but never knew that I could control.

As the hours wore on, it became easier for me to inquire into the currency of each experience. Was it still relevant? If not, then I breathed into my abdomen, forgave people I believed had been unjust to me and let the attached emotions go—or added them to a reservoir of memories to call on when the need arose, like an actor might choose to remember an emotion to call on for a performance.

"Now you can be the one who chooses," Thod said. "It is a matter of practice, using your emotions to empower rather than weaken you."

By now, I was acutely aware that when a memory came forward that made me angry, I would feel it as a surge of energy in my body. What to do with that energy was up to me: I could choose to use it to reinforce some negative idea about myself, or I could just take a deep breath and refocus. Thod kept repeating the point that no one else but myself could make me happy.

Here in the solitude of the desert it felt easier to be impersonal and detached about the past. What importance did past injustices have, viewed against a stark environment where survival is always at the edge of your mind? Here, everything was up for examination. With no friends, families, newspapers or television to reinforce my preconceptions about the way things were, I could look with new eyes. It was easier to strip away the illusion that the world I had placed so much importance in was the only one there is.

I don't know how long we had been sitting under the trees, but I finally came to the end of my ability to absorb anything more. "I don't want to talk about my life anymore," I said.

"Neither do I," he replied and reached out a hand to help me up. I had never sat so long in one position. He was amused by my first stiff, tentative steps down the trail. "You'll get used to it. Tomorrow we will go out again." We spoke very little on the way back. My mind had gone quiet—everything around us seemed to have gone quiet, even the ever-present wind. By the time we reached the cabin the sun had gone behind the mountains and the desert floor was bathed in a soft magenta glow.

Gil-Hamesch greeted me at the door with the most enveloping look of caring on his face. "You are open, dear one," he said then finished his words in his own language for Thod to translate. "He wants me to tell you that the Cook has left some fruit by your bed and that it is best for you to be alone tonight."

On the floor beside my bed I found a bowl of grapes, a small towel, and a tin basin filled with water from the outdoor cistern. I washed away the dust of the day and sat down on the edge of the bed to check on my inner condition. I was exhausted, but felt happy, very happy, it was as simple as that. I hadn't felt like this in a very long time . . . maybe never. I liked it a lot.

11

The Fortress of the Guardians

At dawn I heard Thod's voice outside my door. "We leave in fifteen minutes." I threw on my clothes and hurried outside. There was no one in the cabin, no one by the car. I spotted Thod in the distance, making a series of slow, graceful motions that looked like Tai Chi. He paid no attention to me while I waited for him to finish. Thod never seemed to lose his focus, no matter what he was doing. I couldn't imagine ever coming to that state.

Finally, much longer than fifteen minutes, he stopped what he was doing and joined me. "We're taking a different trail today," he said, gesturing towards the hills in the opposite direction from yesterday's trek. I thought about breakfast, but didn't want to make a point of it. Maybe fasting was part of the training. He handed me a bottle of Danone and we set out. The early morning air was crisp and bone-dry. There were no clouds in the sky, so I expected the day to be hot.

For the first two hours we made a long, gradual climb through the barren hills until we came out into a small sheltered valley ringed all around with huge rock outcroppings. We descended to the center of the valley's bowl which was a marshy oasis with a grove of tall white birches. And there we rested beneath the meager shade, eating figs, delicious black ones with red insides.

There was no one else in our little valley. I couldn't see any animals or even hear the sound of birds. But I definitely felt the presence of the great stone outcroppings looming above us. They surrounded us in an almost perfect circle, some of them over thirty feet in diameter. The whole arrangement looked like a great, crumbling fortress wall, though I couldn't tell if the stone circle was a natural phenomenon or had been made by man. At the far end of the circle stood two towering boulders. I asked Thod if this place had a name. "The Fortress of the Guardians," he said, without elaborating.

We hadn't spoken much so far this morning, which was fine with me, because I was still working on some thoughts of my own after yesterday's session out on the trail. Obviously, I had been weighted down by old scenarios that were not my own—I could see that now. I also saw that many of the people I had encountered on this trip had their own personal mythology or personal inner story that defined them. They had habitual ways of thinking about life and about themselves. But not all of them. And that's what I wanted to ask Thod about.

I told him about my boatman on the Ganges, who had been born into a family with a self-perpetuating story of betrayal and anger, and how he had chosen to defy the story and create a new one that brought blessings to everyone. "Yesterday was a revelation for me," I said. "I saw the stories that I had carried all my life. Last night I couldn't sleep because I was so caught up in this idea—about the things we carry around with us and don't even realize. And I started thinking about all the people who are still haunted by the ghosts of World War II and Vietnam, and all the other wars and injustices. And I asked myself how many unknown or unremembered stories people receive from their parents and their ancestors—stories that shape how they think about life." Thod listened patiently. "It left me with a question," I said. "Do we have an obligation to heal the wounds of the past?"

"I wouldn't put it quite that way," he said. "I would say, rather, that we will be trapped in the wounds of the past until we can see them for what they are and release their power over us. Your personal stories brought you here, too, but now that you have arrived, you can discard your plans. You don't need them anymore."

He looked past me and said, "Now, I want you to concentrate on that circle of stones. I want you to squint your eyes and use your imagination. Yesterday you loosened your attachments to some of your beliefs. But there are still significant beliefs that you have an irrational investment in protecting. They sit like sentinels on the horizon of your world, guarding your kingdom like those two big boulders there, the biggest ones."

I asked Thod what kinds of beliefs he was talking about. After yesterday, I had pretty much looked at them all, I thought.

He fixed me with another one of his stares. "Whom do you admire the most in the world?"

"Jesus," I answered, without much thought. Thod contemplated this for a moment and then pointed to one of the stones on the perimeter, as if to indicate that it represented Jesus.

"He is just a lie! Just like your concept of God!"

"Excuse me?" I said, trying not to sound shocked. Although my religious feelings had wavered and even become a bit cynical over the years, I still took offense. "That's a terrible thing to say!"

"He is only a lie," he repeated, "a fantasy you have created in your mind to defend something you are hiding. Did you know Jesus personally?"

"Of course not."

"Even if you live with someone for ten years, you might not know him. So how can you know anything about someone you have only heard about through hearsay? You must accept the fact that Jesus is no more and no less than a collection of beliefs and stories given to you by other people—beliefs you probably never made a conscious choice to accept."

"What's your point, Thod?" I felt exasperated with him.

"The point has nothing to do with Jesus," he said. "Nor does it have to do with the Christian religion. This is about you and your own personal mythology. The point is that you are still affected by beliefs given to you by others long ago. And you rarely think about them now."

"So, are you saying I have to get rid of everything I ever believed in?"

"No. That's not what we're after. Do you remember when you got your shirt caught in the door of the car? Do you remember how we all laughed at you?"

"Of course." I had tried to be a good sport, but it had bothered me. I had felt like a fool in front of them, Gil-Hamesch especially.

"You still have your shirt, your pants, and even your shoes caught under those rocks there! But you don't have to destroy the boulders to get free. Just gently tug in the right spots."

That one I understood.

"In the same way you are stuck beneath many large rocks. Fix your attention on that rock that we shall call Jesus, until you can tell me in what way you are judging yourself. It's your self-judgment that keeps you trapped."

I gazed at the rock and I reflected on my feelings about Jesus. "All right," I said, "I'm carrying a lot of guilt. I could never be so humble, so filled with faith, so self-sacrificing . . ."

"So the real truth is that you're selfish! How much effort do you put into punishing yourself over this? You are far harder on yourself than anyone else could ever be." His face relented into a smile. "Let me guess—when you can't stand the pain of judging yourself any more, you switch to judging other people, either for being too selfish or too charitable."

"I acknowledge that," I said. "I hold myself to a higher standard sometimes, but I don't think that's necessarily a big fault."

"Ah, the joy of self-righteousness!" Thod smiled again. "It's okay to like yourself just the way you are, you know! Tug yourself free from that boulder!"

Thod was right, of course. I wasn't sure if I could tug myself out from under that particular boulder in that moment, but I knew I had to, and that it was possible. And that he would be relentless with me until I did it.

"You have transformed the figure of Jesus in your mind to represent an unattainable goal. You worship your own interior judge as he eternally condemns you. But that judge has no real power over you. Walk away from the judge in your mind and you will see that most of the world shares your former chains. Then maybe you will even discover another Jesus—a more gentle Jesus who can teach you about not judging others or yourself."

I finally saw what he was getting at—I thought.

"Now tell me about that stone over there," he said, pointing to another in the circle above us.

"Buddha," I said. I had spent a great deal of time reflecting on Buddha's life. My experience with the Tibetan monks at Bodh Gaya had given me a lot to think about.

"And?"

And what? I thought. "And I realize I can never become that perfect, that enlightened and that wise." This time I anticipated Thod's reaction. "All right, I accept that I'm a little stupid, sometimes . . . or maybe a lot. But I don't have to criticize myself about that anymore."

"In fact, it's okay to be plain simple-minded!" he added, slapping his knee.

We continued around the circle as I named the other "immovable stones" in my life: my father, my birth mother, my brother, my professors, Dorothy, and other persons I've judged myself against.

"Let them go," Thod said, quietly this time.

He dug through the sand looking for a pebble. He picked one up and began comically trying to throw it away, but pretending it was glued to his hand. "Now it's time to let go of the judgments people put on *you*," he said. "Believe me, they are much smaller than the judgments you have about yourself, but they still stick to you!"

One by one, I went through a list of people whose opinions mattered to me. And here I was, doing something I couldn't have imagined doing earlier: telling Thod how I believed I could not be a good enough son, a good enough father, a good enough employee, boss, lover, even a good enough engineer. Thod didn't react or judge any of these confessions—for which I am eternally grateful. He kept pushing me to stare at the desert, breathe, and reclaim the emotions these things brought up. It was getting easier. I was making progress.

"Now, look into the face of love," he instructed cryptically. I gazed up into the white branches of the birch trees and closed my eyes, just because it felt good to do. A small breeze rustled the branches and a few leaves floated down slowly over my head. In the next moment I remembered something that happened to me when I was six years old. I was camping with my family in the Sierra

Nevadas. I had wandered off, pretending to hunt squirrels and bears. I found myself under a clear blue sky alone in a pristine alpine meadow. I walked along the edge of a gurgling brook lined with enormous redwood trees. A warm breeze had blown through the trees then, just like here. Facing that beautiful world alone, I was swept up into a profound sense of wonderment. I had never experienced anything like it. And in that moment I no longer cared that my mother had left. I no longer cared that my father and step-mother would fight, and that my brothers and sister were mean to me. I didn't have to justify myself to anybody else. Because I was so young, I didn't understand about God or Nature or ecstasy. In the absence of any such knowledge I had the direct, unclouded experience of life in its most natural state, and I reacted with excited bewilderment at the overwhelming beauty of Nature.

"Who are you now?" Thod asked after I opened my eyes.

"I'm a little boy, and I'm in total awe at the stunning beauty of this world."

Thod clapped his hands in delight. "Finally, you got it! You have found your True Voice!" He sounded relieved. Every other time when he had asked me to tell him who I "truly" was, I had answered "part of God" or "a soul" or "an animal" or "an engineer," or else I had stated that I honestly didn't know.

"To lose one's True Voice is the saddest thing in life," he said. "You have rediscovered your sense of wonder—and that, after all, is our single greatest trait as humans. Even the most jaded scientist must be compelled to reverence in the presence of the sheer wonder of life. Now it is time to challenge your world again. Throw away everything that is not yours and see what is left. If you can return as a grown man to your original innocence, there is hope that you can change the whole of your life."

With eyes closed, I took a long, deep breath of the sweet air, feeling the breeze caress my face, like the touch of a gentle lover. The sun bathed my skin and I felt a heightened sense of pleasure. When I opened my eyes this time I saw the glory that was all around me— the vibrating energy that scintillated at the edges of the great boulders, the crystalline sky . . . everything. The wilderness surrounding me had somehow changed from being silent and lifeless to mysterious and beautiful, and my heart overflowed with appreciation. Instead of drowning in the utter silence, I was swimming on waves of serenity and deep stillness.

"How do you feel?" asked Thod.

Nothing could describe how I felt or what I was thinking. "Words can't do it justice," I said at last.

Thod laughed. "You have been touched by the Supreme Truth! And much sooner than I predicted! Now that you have experienced the challenge of finding words for things that cannot be described, we are almost ready to translate the *Book of Truth*. Still, you have not yet seen the dark side. But you have experienced one important thing—how to find joy even in the barren desert." He picked up a slender birch leaf and held it up to the sunlight. "The Supreme Truth is a message of great joy," he said, "but it is bad news for your ego. I have to warn you that the ego does not surrender so easily."

I figured as much.

12

The Two Sentinels

THERE WAS ONE THING MORE THAT THOD WANTED ME TO SEE BEFORE we left this hidden valley.

It was just after I had the remembrance from my childhood. I was still puzzling over how I could so completely forget what it had felt like—the unquestioning joy and connection with life. If I could feel that at age six, what was keeping me from feeling it now? "What happened to me, Thod?" I asked.

"I was about to ask you the same question. What did you do with that experience you had in the forest?"

"I don't know. I remember that I tried to talk about it, but my brothers and sister made fun of me. It made me very sad for a long time. I wanted people to listen to me—to tell them about this amazing thing that had touched me. Much later, I found Dorothy and she understood. I wanted to be like her, and like those other teachers who were her friends. I even had a brief thought about becoming a priest. There I was, wanting to give this gift . . ."

Thod stopped my words with a wave of his hand. "Now you have come to the second lesson for today. Look up there—at the two tallest boulders in the circle. Those are the Sentinels of the Fortress of the Guardians. They represent the guardians at the threshold of your inner kingdom. They stand there, barring the way to your freedom."

I looked at the two huge boulders towering above us. "The one on the right is your Mortal Wound," he said. "You know that one very well by now. The other one is your Badge of Honor. It is a more subtle hindrance. You defend these two like your life depended on them, while all the time they keep you trapped here. Let us examine your Badge of Honor, because that is the issue of the moment. Tell me, what is it you are hiding behind—what are you defending?"

"I'm not defending anything. What do I have to defend?" He waited for me to figure it out, which I finally did. "I'm defending my faith in God, the simple, innocent faith in God that I once had." I took a deep breath and finished the sentence, "but a long time ago it turned into the feeling that I knew something others did not, and that I was alone in the world." That was a revelation, the first time such a thing had even occurred to me. I didn't know if Thod was putting the thought into my mind or if I was just getting better at dissecting myself. I could suddenly see how I had created a shield around me, my so-called goodness that set me apart all through my life. "I was proud to be that way," I said, more to myself than to Thod.

"Exactly. That is your Badge of Honor. Can you see that your strategy only served your image of yourself—that it didn't bring you power or happiness?"

"What do you mean, 'my strategy'?" That stung.

"How you present yourself to people. Without your realizing it, you decided at some point to be the man who knows more, who aspires higher—the man whose moral judgment is above question. In fact, all of this prevented things from coming towards you. We say we admire a priest, but no one wants to be friends with one, unless they need a constant confessor." He burst into laughter. "Look at you! You don't look as joyful as you should be right now!"

He offered me another fig, but I refused. "I'm appalled, if you want to know the truth. This isn't exactly comfortable."

"Of course not," he barked back. "If you want your freedom you must surrender what you treasure most. That's never comfortable. Surrender is the only way out. Life comes to teach us to surrender through the disguised blessings of bad luck and misfortune. Through banging us on our heads. Through threatening us with death. Through ridicule, disgrace, arrest and poverty. When you surrender what you defend the most, whatever it is, you allow the universe to take away one of your greatest obstacles to happiness and freedom. You allow the cycles of bad luck in your life to be broken.

This is true for every person. We lose our True Voice, and instead we preach our Badge of Honor to the world. You aren't the first and you won't be the last."

"That's not my point," I countered. "It's not pleasant discovering that I've been tiresome and holier-than-thou for a good part of my life."

He gave me a stern look. "Now you're punishing yourself. How selfish. I thought we were finished with that lesson. It's clear that you never really understood the story of the Buddha, even though you say you admire him highly. Do you remember how he gave up being a king in order to understand why people suffer so much. . . how he became a wandering ascetic for years? He became a master of fasting and yoga and meditation and self-denial. This was his Badge of Honor. You could say he became the King of Suffering. But then one day he gave it all up. He surrendered. And that's when he found his True Voice.

"I will tell you another story: I knew a miser once, who also became a great master—a master of watching every coin he had. His thriftiness was his Badge of Honor. But he didn't die a happy or even a wealthy man. His Badge of Honor blinded him to seeing through a business offer that turned out to be too good to be true. We vigorously defend the one thing that can bring about our total downfall."

When he finished, he stared at me until I finally had to respond. "All right. I accept that I have my Badge of Honor," I said. "I accept that I'm defensive about it."

"And . . ." he prompted.

"I accept that it's blocking my progress. But at least I know it's there, and I didn't before."

"Good enough . . . for now," he smiled.

"So, what is *your* Badge of Honor?" I threw back at him.

"I'm a rebel," he replied without hesitation. "I'm a rebel against doing things and seeing things the way they've always been done. Gil-Hamesch has taught me for years about the spiritual life, but I have spent a great part of my life trying to prove that science is supreme. I see the world as sacred, that's true. But I am a scientist at heart. For me the Supreme Truth is not superstition, or religion—it is the philosophical underpinning of the entire scientific system. And I believe that all our ancient books are only poetic descriptions of our biology. So there you have it! You're learning the Kashi shamanic traditions through the lens of my scientific perception, because that is my Badge of Honor."

"But you accept your Badge of Honor. Why is that?" I had to ask.

"The difference between us is that I know this is only my Badge of Honor, and I don't believe in it anymore. It has become an artifice that I use to engage and distract people. You will learn how to do this some day, too."

Thod stood and gave me a hand. We rolled up the red wool carpet we had been sitting on and walked out of the Fortress of the Guardians. I turned for one more look. As we left the protected bowl of the valley we met the winds again. They were circling and gusting, raising columns of sand and dust high into the brilliant blue of the sky.

By nightfall we were back at the cabin and the winds had died down. I asked where Gil-Hamesch was and Thod said that he had gone into retreat to prepare himself for the work ahead and re-energize the atoms of his body. Thod didn't say where the retreat was, or how long it would last, and I didn't press him for details, but I could imagine that it was in a protected place, maybe in another hidden valley or in a cave. I was sorry not to see him.

That evening three of us shared a silent dinner of rice and lentils on a wooden bench on the rear porch. As I gazed out at the stars I could barely make out the familiar constellations, because so many stars were visible in the windswept desert sky. They looked as if they had multiplied threefold since I had last looked at them. After dinner, the Cook entertained us with music played on a *chang-qobuz*, a sort-of Uzbek Jew's harp that sounded like a didgeridoo. It only played one note, but he somehow modulated that one note into a winding series of twanging rhythms that gave voice to both sadness and humor, and left us laughing in delight at his musical skills.

Before I went to my room I thanked Thod for all that he was doing for me. I didn't want him to think I was resisting his training. I was more grateful than I could express.

"I have been through this," he said sympathetically. "It will not get easier, but it will lead you to freedom. Starting from this moment, I have two words of warning for you: Stay alert."

I startled awake in the middle of the night, feeling that I was being watched. The room was filled with the presence of others, except that I wasn't in my room, I was outside the cabin, in the middle of a jostling crowd of people. They were staring at me, yelling, jeering, fawning, and reaching out to touch me. I felt vulnerable and alone and unable to defend myself. I tried to escape but they wouldn't let me. Suddenly, they melted away, and in the distance I saw a beautiful woman who was calling my name. Light was streaming from her sheer, billowing robes, and from her hands and from her eyes. Her breasts were bare, garlanded in blood red flowers. I tried to run to her, but there were obstacles in my way—deserts, rivers, oceans, whole eons of time. I was desperate to reach her but I couldn't. I knew that everything I had ever wanted was there, beckoning me to her. She was singing to me, some ancient, ancient song that made my entire body vibrate. Then the song split into a million pieces and became color, pulsing in the air in front of me, changing with my thoughts, alive to my presence. When she moved, everything moved with her, the green plants, the trees, the birds, the animals, the fish in the waters. Form and sound and light flowed from her and about her in a slow, erotic, indescribably beautiful dance, and somehow I knew that this was the Dance of Life and that she was the one who had created the *Song of Eternity*. She smiled at me and then gathered the flowing forms back into herself until there was only the song, and then it too was gone and I was in my bed again, alone. After a while I heard a man's voice speak softly from the darkness, saying, "She knows your heart, old one . . ." It was Gil-Hamesch's voice, but he was not in the room.

~

SO BEGAN THE STRANGEST PART OF MY JOURNEY YET. I CAN'T HONESTLY say how many days and nights I stayed in the cabin in the desert. I can only attest that my nights were as filled with lessons as were my days, and that Gil-Hamesch, in some way, was guiding the process on the inner levels of my consciousness, while Thod was working on the rest of me with our daily walks out into the wilderness. I was aware that I was losing weight. I was aware of the Cook's music. I was in a state of heightened mental and sensory focus, yet with a kind of stillness that I believe was greatly assisted by the energies of my two teachers. I remember everything with the utmost clarity. What changed for me was the sense of time. I was not operating in normal time, but in some far more expanded definition of time. I was given to understand that the process of my training had to be accelerated because I had to rejoin the world of normal time very soon.

I remember wondering why we (I) choose to focus so much on our past suffering. Why the moments of beauty don't stay with us in the same way. Why we make it all so complicated, so that we finally come to a point where we need to rediscover who we really are. As I peeled away the barnacles that had grown over the clarity of my six-year-old consciousness, I asked other questions: What is it that leads some people to undertake lifelong spiritual quests? Was it any more than a desire to regain the simple happiness of childhood? When you feel awake and alive, when you feel the profound beauty of nature—and you're aware of your place in it—what else is worth seeking, really?

I had come to this desert retreat without a clue about where I would go from here, but one morning I awoke with the thought that I could learn to be a healer or teacher of some kind, and share the insights I was gathering. Only this time I wouldn't do it from the point of view of my Badge of Honor, but from a place within me that was far truer. Maybe I would take people on wilderness treks so that they could find this for themselves, this Truth that can't be found in words. If people discovered the happiness that comes from removing the burden they carry of other people's opinions, and if they could learn to break free of the chains of self-judgment, their lives could radically change . . . the world could radically change.

If my original goal was finding a lost monastery, I was rethinking it. I still didn't know if I had a destiny, much less what it might be. But that didn't seem to matter any more. I was beginning to sense that perhaps this was what Dorothy wanted me to find. Maybe it never *was* about a hidden monastery or a mysterious manuscript.

13

An Ultimatum

Gil-Hamesch is back, I WROTE IN MY JOURNAL ONE EVENING AFTER I HAD retired to my room. I knew it was so, because I had just heard the front door open and close and I felt his presence again in the cabin— his flesh and bones presence. I heard the murmur of voices, his and the Cook's, and then silence.

In the night I had another dream about the woman—the goddess, I didn't know what else to call her. This time I was in a verdant place at the edge of a great sea. It felt like paradise. The air was dense with energy, brilliant birds swooped and called, insects glowed from the light of dazzling flowers as they sucked the nectars. She was there, watching me, but this time she didn't show herself in female form. She was everything, all of it. My eyes couldn't get enough of her, in the sky, in the multitude of creatures, in the vast, lush greenness where I stood. The whole of life around me was singing and I almost couldn't bear its joy. I opened my mouth to sing with it. Words streamed from my lips in a language I had never learned, a language that was pure music. I sang and sang, reveling in my delight, bathing in the sweet sensation of belonging to everything that exists. I thought to myself, I must hold on tightly, because if I let go I may never find this place again. And in that instant the music stopped and the paradise was gone.

I lay in my bed in the darkness, my eyes shut, my heart pounding. I was separate again—just me, alone in the room with the memory of the beautiful words that I had been singing. They made no sense to me now, but moments before, they had *meant* something. I expected to hear Gil-Hamesch's voice commenting on what I had just experienced, but that didn't happen this time. I had to figure it out for myself. I knew only that the vision had been a gift to me, and that I had done something to send it away.

At breakfast I sat with Gil-Hamesch and Thod while we drank black tea and shared our plates of fried vegetables and boiled rice. I told them about my dream. "I didn't want it to stop. I could have stayed there and never come back."

"The *Song of Eternity* can consume you if you are not careful," Thod warned. "If you approach it with humility and respect it can become a powerful ally. In fact, it is even possible to develop a personal relationship with it. But first you must become aware of the dark side of your own nature—more aware than you are."

Gil-Hamesch nodded and smiled at me. I realized how much his approval meant to me, how much I wanted to succeed in this training for his sake, as much as mine. Which was probably the exact wrong reason. I still hadn't figured out what success was supposed to consist of in this remote desert school.

"Now," Thod said, pulling my attention back. He placed his palms flat on the long wooden table where we sat. "Imagine that this is a special table on which rest all your ideas about yourself. You can call this table your ego."

I prepared myself for one of Thod's usual probings. He placed a bowl of apricots at one end of the table. "At this end is happiness." He then piled up our dirty dishes on the other end of the table. "At this end are pain, loneliness, and self-rejection. Most of us stay trapped over here because we don't like ourselves." He held me with a steady look. "But we have the power to shift our awareness to the other end of the table, to the bowl of fruit."

"But I don't dislike myself," I said. "And I don't feel trapped anymore."

"So you say. Just for the sake of this lesson, let's assume that you have not yet achieved full self-awareness."

Now I felt foolish and painfully transparent. Of course I didn't have full self-awareness. "I'm listening," I said.

"First, give up your stupid selfishness," he fired off. "Then overcome your fear of the ghosts in your life. They aren't real anyway. And let go of your constant self-pity. As you do each of these things, your fear of life transforms into a love for life. And with a love for life comes a love for yourself."

I decided not to comment until I could get a better grip on my reactiveness. I really believed that I had made good progress in all these areas. I did love life, I protested silently. Gil-Hamesch's eyes were more inward when I looked at them again, as if he had removed his approval, and it worried me. I didn't know what I was doing wrong.

"When people say they are seeking God," Thod continued, "what they usually mean is they want a way out of misery. They are looking for the way to cross over to the other side of this table—to the side of happiness."

I reached to take a ripe apricot from the bowl. "And happiness is the Supreme Truth," I added, knowing it was the right answer.

"So you say," Thod said once more. "Look again. This is your ego, with suffering and joy at its two poles. Our lives are always ebbing and flowing between these two poles, and experiencing all the other possibilities between." He waved his hands all around the table, as if to indicate that there existed something beyond the ego. "The one who realizes the Supreme Truth sees that there is little difference between joy and sorrow. They are only the two ends of the same table."

"Why would anyone want to see things from that point of view?" I ventured.

"Because the table is not real. Your ego is only an illusion created by your mind to classify and sort your experiences. It's like the fleeting image you see in the mirror, except that this image is alive, and believes it is real. It supports its belief by selecting images that perpetuate its conviction about its reality. However, our true being is not what is reflected in that mirror. Our true being is the light itself. That is the Supreme Truth." He crossed his arms and looked at me as if he had just explained everything, but his explanation sounded once again like an unsolvable riddle.

"We seek to free ourselves from identifying with the false image in the mirror," he reiterated. "We seek to reclaim what we were before the birth of the ego, and to awaken to that which we will be after its death. This requires an enormous act of courage. You have to be willing to truly let go of everything you believe in. That leap can be terrifying, because you cannot return unchanged."

This time, when I looked at Gil-Hamesch his eyes were alight with encouragement, which was something I needed a lot at the moment, because I had just been given some kind of ultimatum by Thod, and I wasn't sure I fully understood it.

That was the end of the lesson. Thod and Gil-Hamesch intended to drive out to a small village some distance away to buy a tire for the Land Rover, leaving me behind with the Cook for most of the day. I hadn't spent much time with him, since I was usually engaged in dialogue with Thod or out on one of our long treks into the desert.

The Cook was a quiet man who hummed and chanted as he worked. He had an entirely loving nature, which I found very soothing as I struggled with the morning's lesson about the table and all the rest of it. I worked alongside him, learning to use the small handmill to grind wheat and barley, sifting some of the cereal into flour for baking, laying out fruit on the drying racks, and gathering small dried branches to feed the clay oven.

The Cook didn't speak much English so I had all day to think about the elusive concept of the Supreme Truth and how it related to Thod's definition of the ego. I had always thought that the ego was the selfish or proud part of me, the thing that stood as a barrier to happiness. Everyone could agree with that. But that wasn't what Thod had said. Ego, as he used the word, meant *everything* I knew about the world and myself. Not only the parts I didn't like about myself. What about generosity, humility, and compassion? I wondered. Did he expect me to give up those things too? And why would anyone want to abandon the self altogether, instead of merely improving it? Why would anyone trade happiness for what I imagined to be a state of apparent mindlessness? The whole idea terrified me. I would be quite content with a little more happiness in my life. Could there be something wrong with me for being satisfied with just being reasonably happy?

I began to seriously question whether Gil-Hamesch and Thod lived in a state of intentionally induced insanity. After all, when Thod implied that not only is it possible to live without suffering, but also to live without happiness, he seemed to declare war on the very meaning of life.

I realized I'd heard these concepts before, but I hadn't gauged their implications until now. Loosening the grip of self-absorption, and shifting suffering into happiness—these are worthy goals that I could understand. But going beyond this to the complete unraveling of the self—is this not the most dangerous deed possible? If this is what the religious teachers and prophets have been telling us, no wonder people ignored or crucified them! Why would anyone follow such a dangerous teacher, once they discovered the truth of their mission? And how could a whole society be expected to ever embrace such a radical concept? The world is built from the ego. It can't afford suicide. The whole thing began to fill me with dread just thinking of the impact on my own life if I were to take such a leap.

The Cook had sent me to sweep the porch. I must have swept it a dozen times, moving back and forth robotically while I grew more and more distressed. Yesterday I had felt happy and centered. I was pleased with how far I had come in my inner work. Now I was plunged into an abyss of the greatest fear and emotional upheaval I had ever known. I can't explain the full depths of this fear. My world felt threatened in a way immeasurably more terrifying than the fear of being hurt or dying.

I excused myself after lunch and retreated to my room to try to make sense of my mounting dread. I forced myself to write about it in my notebook, to do something normal and grounding. But the words came out as a cry of panic: *I'm swimming towards a whirlpool of nothingness in which I could lose everything I have in the world . . . I don't know how to save myself . . . I'm afraid of being abandoned . . .* I had to stop. I needed to engage my mind and go step by step through this.

What did I know about myself? For one thing, I wasn't ready to let go of my attachments and pleasures. I remembered the words of the Buddha who said that our attachment to the things of the world always leads eventually to disappointment and suffering. But I rationalized that for me it would be different. This is what gave my life passion. I admit that my ambition and my desires for love, recognition, and success sometimes trap me and make me unhappy, but those ambitions and desires also give me a reason to live.

In fact, my ambitions and desires helped create who I am today, and I love who I am, I told myself. How could I conceive of giving up everything now, especially when I could see that I stood on the verge of success and happiness with my life? The emptiness of the Gobi Desert would seem like nothing compared to the emptiness of a life without full engagement of my ego. If God waited for me behind that door right now, I knew I would run away, rather than open it.

If life is a game, whether you are winning or losing, you don't just quit in the middle. Where would I go, anyway? What would I do if I were not my old self anymore? I imagined what it would feel like to say goodbye to my family and friends. To let go of my creative dreams. To give up my romantic dreams. Surrendering my life that deeply would be to enter a vast solitude of eternal loneliness, far worse than the loneliness I already knew.

And how would I support myself now, much less in my old age? It meant throwing myself on the generosity of the universe, on faith alone. I pictured myself wandering the streets like a drunken beggar in tattered robes. I wasn't afraid of a simple life, but the thought of poverty terrified me. Perhaps I could wait to surrender my ego until I grew old enough and wealthy enough to retire.

My success in business grew its roots from my passion, my drive, and my love for overcoming challenges. I fed on stress. If I dropped even a single ball, my business could fail. I pictured myself as an engineer attending important business meetings when I returned home. My eyes would shine with bliss and I would break out into laughter at people, the way Gil-Hamesch sometimes did. I would lose my clients the first day. People would think I was crazy. I *would* be crazy.

Ambition, drive, motivation, success, planning, discipline, and risk-taking—I had always believed these were virtues. I had built my life on these principles. They made up the bones and flesh of my ego. That was who I was! No doubt about it.

Just when I thought I had solved the problem, my doubts returned. Perhaps these fears were irrational. Was there a possibility that by putting my total faith in the emptiness of the universe I would be led to a better life, a life I had not yet discovered?

So there I sat, impaled on the horns of the greatest dilemma of my life. Do I say goodbye to this particular spiritual path, with gratefulness for the healing and joy of self-acceptance that I have received? Was it time now to fully embrace a happy life, free to pursue success and pleasure? Or do I give up everything I am familiar with, to serve a God I do not know or understand? My anxiety relented long enough for me to call on more tools of understanding.

I decided to use one of Thod's techniques—the one he called the Council of Inner Voices. When he is faced with a difficult choice, he told me, he calls on his "Council" to discuss the matter. The body has several voices of its own, he explained, as do the mind, the heart and the soul. He asks the same question of each of these voices.

Assuming I had my own Council, for lack of any better advisors at the moment, I began to examine the question of surrendering my ego-centered life. I knew the Cook must be wondering what was taking me so long, but this was something I had to do, right now. I closed my eyes and imagined the separate parts of my being having their own voices. I put the problem to them and just listened to what they said.

First, my body: It answered that it would gladly accept a life of surrender! It didn't appreciate the stress and caffeine that I heaped upon it. It also apparently had no fear of poverty. That was good, because poverty was a distinct outcome of such a path, I imagined. Next, I questioned my heart and soul and had an immediate answer. Both of them thrilled at the possibility of surrender to a spiritual life.

Only my mind rebelled. It cried out loudly and set up such a clamor that I almost couldn't hear another more quiet voice trying to get my attention. This fifth voice urged me forward: "If you do not surrender now, then how long must you continue to live in the illusion of a false dream? You know the Supreme Truth is true. So why do you postpone the inevitable?"

I knew it was now or never. In two days we would be leaving for Turfan. From there I could catch a ride to Urumchi, and return to the life I left behind. Or else I would ask Gil-Hamesch to initiate me into the *Song of Eternity*, an act that I knew would change my life irreversibly.

14

The Leap of No Return

BY THE END OF THE DAY I HAD REACHED MY DECISION. I THOUGHT THAT Dorothy would understand. I had done my best to fulfill her dreams for me, but they had been *her* dreams. Anyway, I wasn't the same person I was twenty-five years ago, when a spiritual quest seemed like a great adventure. I was here to attest that it was anything *but* an adventure. It was pain and agonizing reappraisals, with momentary glimpses of pure joy. Now it was time for me to get a firm grip on myself and abandon this search while I still had my security and sanity. I had done my best. I was grateful to everyone who made efforts to bring me to this point of self-knowledge. I loved them all, and I was ready to take the next step, but it would be into the world that belonged to me and not into an exotic world that I could never really understand. For the first time I let go of my desire to learn anything more about the *Song of Eternity*. I knew that I could leave now and not look back with regret.

All of this was going around in my head while I worked with the Cook, preparing the cabin for our departure for Turfan. We made sure it was well stocked for the next time someone would visit. The last thing we did was bring in the raisins, apricots and nuts that had been laid out to dry in the sun. I couldn't tell if the Cook was aware of the extremes of my emotions throughout the long day. I tried not to let them show. By dinnertime Thod and Gil-Hamesch hadn't returned from their errand to find the new tire, so the Cook and I ate our vegetables and rice without them. A warming fire burned in the hearth and we shared an unspoken feeling of fellowship from our day's work together. My body was tired, but my emotions were truly exhausted. I started thinking about my engineering proposal that I hadn't looked at for weeks. The Urumchi Technical Office was expecting a practical, problem-solving American at their doorstep, not a spiritual pilgrim. I planned to bring myself up to speed again and refocus my mind on business. It was such a relief to finally know what direction I would go from here. I couldn't recall when I had last felt this much in control of my life.

The fire burned down to embers and I was about to call it a night, when the Cook stood up and motioned to me to follow him. It was his habit to disappear every evening to recite his prayers and meditate. We entered a dark chamber in the back of the house with chalky white-stuccoed walls and one small window with iron bars. The floor was covered with old red prayer rugs. A book lay open on a low brass stand. We sat cross-legged on the rugs while the old man bowed his head and began his murmured prayers. Gradually the soft prayers became louder, turning from a monotonous chant into a deep, rich song—powerful singing that vibrated from his throat and shook the air in the room.

At first I resisted the sound because I could feel it drawing me into another waking dream, and I didn't want any more bliss, any more yearning after impossible states of perfection. But this wasn't bliss, it was clarity.

I found myself back twenty years, remembering the first woman I had ever truly loved. Patty. We were so happy together, life was wonderful and promising. And then her world was ripped apart and everything changed. She was hospitalized for schizophrenia. I did all I knew to help her out of her darkness, but our relationship never recovered. That was the first time I realized how much we take life— and our sane interpretation of it—for granted. Our love and our plans had seemed so real. But some disease, some chemical imbalance in the brain, had erased our entire world.

The Cook's melancholy singing grew louder, and my sad memories intensified until I began to weep. I wasn't only crying for Patty. My tears fell for the pain of my whole life—for everyone's life, and for the mortal wounds we all carry inside us. It was not just the pain of the memory itself, it was also the feeling of loss in letting go of the pain. That was such a strange idea, that I would actually miss the pain, that I had become that much attached to the painful memories from my past. Yet, even knowing that I was reluctant to let go of that sorrow, I couldn't do it easily.

The Cook was engrossed in his chanting, the room alive with the energy of his sound. It held me in my state of deep remembrance until I had extracted the last drop of its meaning. I didn't feel embarrassed to be weeping in the Cook's presence. Gradually I felt myself letting go of feeling sorry for Patty, and for myself. It was then that I discovered that some part of me was carrying an irrational personal responsibility for the unhappiness and misery of the entire world. I could see that now, and I set it down.

The Cook's song stopped. The room was still dense with the vibrations of it. He began another song. It too was melancholy, but it affected me differently from the first. This chant had a deeply spiritual feeling of longing and hope for something beyond this world. I didn't resist it. The sound of his chanted prayers carried me further back, to my childhood, to the Saturdays in Dorothy's book-lined study where she had inspired me to imagine a universe of infinite beauty and interconnection and seek out my place in it. I couldn't deny that she saw through to my soul and planted seeds that she hoped would grow and flower. I couldn't deny that the seeds were in me still, and would never go away. Now, in this darkened room, I felt the old, deep longing for union with the divine arising in my heart again. Reluctantly, I acknowledged its irrevocable presence in my life. There was no place in the universe I could go and leave that longing behind, even if I thought it was possible. There was no way I could deny my necessity to take the next step towards that knowledge of the divine. I just couldn't.

The old man ended with a softly mumbled prayer. I opened my eyes and looked at his radiant face, as if seeing him for the first time. I perceived a man with an infinitely deep heart, a man of the utmost humility. If my heart felt like a tender flower starting to open, his felt like an enormous garden of compassion and caring. In that moment, feeling the kindness of this man who wanted nothing from me but shared everything, I knew what I had to do. I would take the leap of no return and ask Gil-Hamesch to initiate me into the *Song of Eternity*.

WE SAT IN SILENCE FOR A WHILE, MEDITATING TOGETHER. I DIDN'T want to leave the energies of this room. I had never known that the human voice had such power to affect the deepest recesses of the soul. I was almost afraid to leave the Cook's room for fear I would lose my resolve once I was outside its compelling force field. I heard the Land Rover drive up and stop in front of the cabin.

When Thod and Gil-Hamesch came inside, the Cook gave them a brief nod and then retired for the night. I told Thod nothing of my day, except my amazement at the Cook's powerful, rich voice. "You are very, very fortunate," Thod told me. "He is famous as one of the last of the great Order of Singing Dervishes. He can accomplish in one hour what would take me a year of talking. His Sufi name means 'Gateway to the Beyond'."

I was dumbstruck to realize that the man I took for a menial cook was a master. No wonder. I just assumed he lived his life as a shepherd or farmer.

"I've made my decision," I said, "It wasn't easy getting there."

"And . . . " he prompted.

"I wish to learn the *Song of Eternity*. I think I'm ready."

Thod stared hard into my eyes. "YOU cannot learn anything," he intoned. "YOU have never known anything. YOU do not know anything now. And YOU will never know anything."

I was stunned by his attack. My mind went blank. In that momentary emptiness of mind I saw into the great emptiness of Thod's mind. There was no anger, he was utterly calm. Rather than succumbing to the fear of my immediate reaction, I chose to simply accept that the emptiness I saw around me is who "I" am. Of course "I" don't know anything—not the real "I."

Thoughts began to arise in my awareness, but they no longer seemed like my thoughts. They appeared as clouds drifting across an empty sky. Clouds of memories, training, emotions. Just thoughts moving, drifting through the brain. I did not identify with them, so they slowly floated away on their own. I didn't feel that I had entered an altered mental state. I felt absolutely present and centered. My point of view had merely shifted at a primary level. I would describe this experience as shifting from listening to the sounds of the world to experiencing the silence that supports the sound and makes the sound possible. The world around me appeared as a constant state of flux, but I remained calm and still. And I knew that everything I had ever believed was a lie—that it had to be a lie—because it came from a limited point of view centered somewhere in that cloudy flux of motion in my mind. I also felt that everything else seemed false by comparison to the truth of this awareness. Yet I could not find a single word that could describe this ineffable state of being, because words are only descriptions of the clouds in the mind.

We walked outside and built a small fire in a rock pit under the bright light of the moon. Thod waved out towards the desert and asked me to tell him what I saw. My mind was still as empty as the sand dunes that paraded into the distance. The desert shimmered with an iridescent beauty.

"The moonlight dances on the sand dunes with joy, because we have shown up to watch its performance," I said aloud. I didn't know where the poetic words had come from. Thod's fierce eyes glowed from under his hood as it flapped in the strong desert breeze. We gazed in silence at the desert night sky. No thoughts arose in me, but the magical perfumes of joy and beauty arose on their own, as if showing me that they alone possessed the true essence of the life that pulses through our veins.

Thod motioned for me to sit by the fire while he went for Gil-Hamesch. "Feel yourself as a vessel, filled with the most powerful force in the world—the emptiness that surrounds us. Be centered in the non-action from which all of your actions spring." I understood what he was saying, but not with my mind.

When they returned, Gil-Hamesch took his place by the fire. This was the moment. He looked at me, then set his gaze into the far distance and began a monotone chant that evolved into a rhythmic song with words of the most serene beauty. And I recognized them. I had sung them in my dream vision the night before. That had been Gil-Hamesch's gift to me, a preview of what might be if I chose to take the leap of no return. I closed my eyes and invited the words deep into my being.

Every few sentences Gil-Hamesch paused while Thod translated them into English for me. "Thus begins *The Book of Truth*," he said:

Salutation to the Universal Teacher who is present here and now!

May these words awaken the experience of the Supreme Truth in me

and in all living beings.

May all who listen to these teachings with an open heart and mind

find their freedom from the trials of the world.

In slow and measured tones, Gil-Hamesch recited the *Book of Truth* to me—verse by verse, in all its elegant simplicity, embodying the ancient wisdom of the Kashi people and pointing the way towards the freedom of the Supreme Truth.

"Don't try to remember everything tonight," Thod told me after Gil-Hamesch's voice ended the recitation and the air was quiet around us again. "These words are not merely words, they carry the accumulated energy of thousands of years of spiritual wisdom, sung from teacher to student, teacher to student—and now to you. Gil-Hamesch wants you to know that you are connected to all of them now, and they with you. That should be a comfort," he added with just a trace of the old Thod in his voice.

PART THREE

The Eight Precious Jewels

15

The Supreme Lie

"Prepare yourself," Thod warned me the next morning. "Initiation by its very definition is only the beginning. If you thought you could now rest safely within the comforts of great knowledge . . . " He left the rest unsaid. I had no illusions. I knew that the verses of the *Book of Truth* were only hints, carefully placed arrows along the path. I didn't for a moment think that I was suddenly wise. I was just here, walking into the wilderness with Thod again, trying to clear my mind of clutter and only be.

Thod had brought along a *dombro*, a double-stringed wooden lute with a narrow stem. But when I asked if he was going to play it for me, he said no, he had a special purpose for bringing it. The scorching heat made it hard to keep up with him as we crossed white sand dunes so precisely formed that not even a leaf marked their perfect smoothness. When I looked up I saw the wind whip sand from the tops of the dunes directly into the blue sky in clouds of fine sand. In the distance, the Tien Shan Mountains rested beneath a clear sky, covered with a permanent blanket of snow.

I had wrapped myself in white linen to protect against the flaming sun. Thod gave me a thin cloth to wrap around my mouth to block the sand that I otherwise inhaled with every breath. He promised we would soon find cool water to bathe in. Here in this unrelentingly arid desert, the natural assumption would be that water was a scarce commodity, but that's not always so. Small springs flow into seasonal creeks and rivers, cutting canyons through the red and yellow sandstone and shale. We were heading for one of those canyons. For centuries, the natives of the foothills adjacent to the desert floor have built literally hundreds of miles of tunnels, called *karez*, to divert these desert creeks to their meager vineyards and homes.

By the time we reached the canyon I was sweating profusely, so we retreated to the shade of an irrigation cavern, one of the karez tunnels, to cool off. It was large enough for both of us to sit in comfortably. I looked longingly at the gurgling water that flowed in the canyon below us. We would bathe, Thod promised, but not until the sun lay lower in the sky.

Thod continued to speak about the Supreme Truth.

"It is not merely a philosophical concept. Once you overcome the Supreme Lie that keeps you trapped in your web of personal stories the Supreme Truth will become your guiding light and your source of energy and power."

"So, not only is there a Supreme Truth, there is a Supreme Lie?"

Thod furrowed his brow. "The Supreme Lie is found in the declaration: '*I am.*' Whenever you say '*I am . . .*' and finish the sentence, you're telling a lie, because you are much more than whatever limitation you just created for yourself. When you tell yourself stories long enough you begin to believe them. You forget that they are only stories—and maybe not even your own stories. We try so hard to fit into this world. And in doing that, we can become completely identified with other people's stories." Thod's face brightened. "But you can put the power of this Supreme Lie to your use. All you have to do is give it a different name: *faith*."

"Whatever in the world are you talking about?" We had just gone completely around in another one of his circles of logic.

"Faith, for a shaman, is very different than for an ordinary person. I call it 'Intentional Faith.' Let me explain. When I asked you to tell me who you are, how many times did you give me somebody else's answer? And how much of your self-image is controlled and manipulated by marketers, advertisers, politicians, and the moguls of business?"

It was true. I couldn't think of a single image that I held of myself that was not influenced in some way by a parent, teacher, friend, television show, or fashion trend—or my culture in general. Only my experiences alone in nature could I truly call my own.

"That's why this simple thing becomes so threatening," he said. "It's hard to accept the fact that your world is created almost entirely from other people's dreams. There is only one sure way to become free from being manipulated by the world around you: You have to first learn to be comfortable with the huge emptiness inside of you. Then, if you can learn to be at peace with that emptiness and accept the Supreme Truth, you can learn to shift in and out of that emptiness at will. That's when life becomes a delight. Only when you embrace your nothingness can you fully experience the fact that you are one with everything. Before that experience, talking about 'oneness with life' is only a sentimental sense of comfort that comes from agreeing with everyone else."

Emptiness was still a big question mark for me. I had seen it momentarily the night before and felt the relief of it, but to be able to go there at will . . . that was quite another thing. And when Thod spoke of my nothingness, I could feel the old resistance rising up inside me.

Thod wasn't waiting for me to agree or disagree with his line of reasoning. "The best part of all this," he continued, "is that once you realize that you alone are responsible for choosing how you react to the world, you don't need to feel like a victim of anything or anyone. If you want to live your life with joy and delight instead of suffering and anger, you can make the choice to do so. Whatever suffering and anger you have felt are in the past. They are no longer relevant. You can create any world, in any moment. And change it at any moment. We are creating our own worlds all the time, whether we are aware of it or not. Now, in every moment, you can create it the way you choose."

"I agree in principle," I said. "It sounds good. But I wouldn't know where to start."

"The first step is to accept that nothing is true by itself." He stared at me until I nodded that I understood. "The main reason we keep being angry is that we don't know what else to do. We don't know that we have the power to create something new to take its place.

"The second step is to have complete faith in whatever you choose to believe in. That is what I mean by Intentional Faith. The final step is to use your knowledge—knowledge about the scientific laws of creation. With faith and knowledge you can create almost anything you can imagine." He smiled and added a warning. "Gil-Hamesch is fond of reminding us that no matter which food you choose from the banquet table of life, it's going to be poison for you. So pick a fruit that delights your taste buds."

"Isn't that a bit cynical, or even hopeless?"

"Whatever dream you choose, it's still a dream. An illusion, a lie, a disappointment-in-waiting. So choose a dream that entertains you and fills you with happiness. Before you wake up from the spell of life, people and events in the world hook your attention in every moment. But as you begin to wake up to reality, you discover that you can become the one to cast the spells. You can find the power to overcome the illusions of the world, and even to control the world of illusion like an artist, or a movie director.

"You already know for a fact that every story in this world is not true, don't you? Of course—there is no other possibility. Therefore, you can choose to believe in any one of an infinite set of possible stories. The power that manifests from this kind of faith will astound you."

I had to stop him. "One minute you talk about the emptiness and the meaninglessness of it all, and the next you're talking about faith in a universe of infinite possibilities. Which is it?"

He slapped his knee with a laugh. "You're right! That's what this all boils down to. In fact, you'll find that your whole life will alternate between these two extremes: the whole universe and total emptiness. In other words, between *knowledge* and *truth*. The deeper you embrace the Supreme Truth, the greater will be your power to consciously invest in your dreams, in your knowledge. Believing firmly in nothing allows you to believe more firmly in whatever you intend. That is Intentional Faith."

Somehow, what he said began to make some sense. But I couldn't fully grasp what he meant. I didn't understand how I could see this world as being everything and nothing at the same time. But I wasn't going to let it go at that. "How do you think this entire universe could arise out of nothing?" I asked.

Thod shook his head. "You are thinking too much. Just use these principles to guide you to have your own experience of what I'm trying to share with you. Even the concepts of a universe and of nothingness—they're both only concepts in your mind. When you are centered at that zero point in your mind, the universe appears empty. When you return to interpreting the world you see, then the universe multiplies itself out to infinity."

As my mind swam among this sea of new concepts, I began to appreciate just how much I actually *enjoyed* these philosophical debates with my teacher-tormenter. I hadn't really thought about the nature of the mind or the universe—at least not this way—since my days in college. I wondered what Thod thought about the idea of God. "Do you believe there is a greater intelligence that guides creation?"

"In my opinion, Nature is entirely self-sufficient. It is the result of undirected processes. And it certainly doesn't need you or me, or anyone else to project our human ideas of intelligence onto it."

"Then if it's all just random . . . "

"It is not just random. I didn't say that," he interrupted impatiently.

There he went again. It seemed like every time I would try to discuss anything using the familiar ideas of spirituality, he would cut me off. It finally dawned on me that maybe he was doing this on purpose to throw me off guard. It was just another way of forcing me to be free of other people's reference points.

"There is an order to things that goes beyond our ability to understand," he said. "When you gaze at the world with unclouded eyes you can only be filled with the deepest awe and respect for the beauty, the power, and the order of creation."

If that was his answer to my question about the existence of an intelligence behind creation it was an indirect one. His answers continued to throw me back on my own ability to perceive what was true. "Do the Kashi have a creation myth?" I asked, hoping to keep the topic alive.

"We do not say the world was once created. We say it is still in the process of being created right now. That is the subject of the *Book of Creation*—how to create something out of nothing."

"So you're saying your ancient creation myth isn't about the actual beginning of the world? It's an allegory about the ever-present process of creation itself?" I had never heard of such a thing.

"You must be aware of the Tibetan *Book of the Dead* and the Christian *Book of Revelation*, and the Egyptian *Book of the Dead*," he said.

"Of course."

"If you read between the lines, they are not just about death and the afterworld, or about some events from long ago. They point to knowledge about the living realms of human experience. They're about the present. They're a description of the levels of the human mind. Hell and heaven, demons and angels, and so on. These things exist here and now in the human mind. In the same way, you could call our *Book of Creation* the '*Book of Birth*.' It is our way of describing the natural processes of organic life, as well as the unique world of human experience.

"According to the *Book of Creation*, the moment that consciousness or any other form of energy is born in the universe, creation unfolds in a certain predictable pattern. That first moment is compared to the serpent of awareness biting its tail and awakening from a dream. When the serpent breaks the circle and waves its tail, time begins and a wave of energy sweeps outward, and the whole world is created.

"The *Book of Creation* is a description of the waves of energy. In Western science we say that light sometimes behaves like a particle and sometimes like a wave. The Kashi say that sometimes energy is like a melody and sometimes it is like a rhythm. So you see, they're not that different.

"The melody and rhythm of the first wave of light is called the *Song of Eternity*. It is the universal language of all living things. It calls to each of us to find our unique voice, so we can join in its timeless song." He smiled at nothing at all, saying, "Some of the greatest masters of the *Song of Eternity* still live right here in Central Asia. They are the mysterious nomads who are called the Desert Wanderers."

We were still sitting in the karez, waiting for the heat of the day to abate before we set out again. At this point I had no awareness of whether my body was hot or cool, or even if I was thirsty, I was so involved in the imagery that Thod was setting before me. And now I learned that there are mysterious beings called Desert Wanderers. I didn't want Thod to go on to another subject until he told me more about them.

"I thought they would interest you," he said. "On long caravan journeys through the desert the Desert Wanderers open their perception of sound so deeply that they can hear their own hearts beating. Then they listen even deeper, until they hear the blood flowing throughout their bodies. They say that when you learn to hear your own blood flow you can hear a special kind of inner rhythm. They meditate on that rhythm for days at a time, deepening their silence until they can hear the even more subtle sound of the first wave of creation. Through this practice alone, it is said, the Desert Wanderers have developed highly advanced psychic powers.

"There are other Desert Wanderers who do not hear sounds. On their months-long journeys across the desert they practice gazing at the reflection of light on the desert in a certain way, with their eyes almost closed. Their intention is to see the reflections of the first wave of light. They say it is like a soft white glow that still permeates everything. Desert Wanderers can see and hear in ways that ordinary people do not. That is why when they speak—which is rare—everyone listens."

"And what do *you* think about all this?" I asked.

"Personally, I think what they hear is the subtle vibrations of the nervous system," he said, true to his nature as a physician.

I reflected on my own small experience of the Supreme Truth, and remembered those poetic words about the moonlight that had spontaneously come to me last night by the fire. It didn't seem to originate from any poems I had heard before, but from the desert night sky itself. Thod knew what I was referring to.

"That was another way to hear the *Song of Eternity*," he said. "Our first epic storytellers said that they received the ancient myths from speaking directly with the light from the stars on the darkest desert nights." He looked away for a moment, as if thinking about what to say next. "In the silence of the desert we hear the songs of our own biology. And that song calls for us to awaken to our highest potential."

I asked Thod if he had ever met a Desert Wanderer.

"Yes, they are still around. The first time I met one I was very young. A stranger came to our village to buy supplies. He looked odd and fierce and silent. I didn't know if he was evil or good. Most of the people feared him. But Gil-Hamesch told me he was gentle, and not to worry. He said I could learn an enormous amount from him just by watching him.

"I worked as his helper for three and a half days. I watered his camels and brought him food. He fascinated me so much that for many years after, I tried to imitate him. He hardly spoke, but he radiated a powerful presence that everyone felt. Now I understand that he looked this way because he spent long periods of time in the desert immersed in constant awareness of the Supreme Truth—and because he had mastered the Shield of Power."

The Shield of Power again. Thod didn't elaborate. By now I was confident that he had his reasons for everything he said to me. I imagined that I would learn about the Shield of Power in good time—Thod's time.

16

The Science of the Shaman

HIGH CLOUDS NOW COVERED THE SUN, SO WE VENTURED DOWN TO THE creek at the bottom of the red rock canyon. I looked back at my footsteps in the sand and wondered if they would remain there for a thousand years. Thod took out his dombro and looked at the creek for the one exact spot where he wanted to play it. He did this by putting his ear close to the stream where the water ran rapidly over a group of three boulders. Thod then hummed different tones until he found one note that created a slight echo from the water. Then he tuned the two strings of his dombro to the same pitch as the echo.

He asked me to close my eyes and listen carefully. He plucked one of the strings at full volume and I listened for the sound to fade. To my astonishment, it did not. It reverberated off the canyon walls and returned to us from every direction. Thod sat motionless, his attention focused on the sound. For a long time the tone sustained almost the same volume.

"How did you do that?" The sudden interjection of my voice caused the sound to diminish significantly. However, I still continued to hear faint echoes of the sound long after.

Thod told me to look closely at the dombro. "It is the principle of resonance," he said. "The sound of the water acts like an amplifier. Sound fascinated our ancestors. They mastered the basic scientific principles of music untold ages ago. They learned these principles in canyons just like this one. Watch carefully."

He plucked the string at the quarter point, and released it. It sprang back and forth, forming the perfect sine waves that characterize all stringed instruments. Thod scratched a picture of the string in the sand with a stick: two wave lines over each other, like an elongated figure eight.

"Now look at your gold figure," he instructed. I pulled the caduceus from my pack and saw his point right away. The double serpents looked something like the wave pattern that a string makes as it vibrates to produce sound.

"Next time you see the Western medical caduceus symbol that doctors use, remember that the ancient Greeks were not the only ones to understand the principles of sound waves. Once you understand sound vibrations, you can understand almost any phenomena in life, because it is through sympathetic vibration that we influence the world and attract people and events into our life.

"In terms of the two fundamental principles of life—knowledge and truth—you could say that truth is like pure energy, and that knowledge is the information conveyed by that energy. The way our minds evolve is by increasing the amplitude, the loudness of the signal, and increasing the complexity and frequency, the tone of our own energy, so that we can process information in ever faster and more complex ways."

"This seems like a pretty sophisticated philosophy for such an ancient people," I commented.

"This knowledge can all be derived by a master musician-healer with just the dombro, the river, and the canyon walls. What still amazes me is the knowledge that our ancestors developed that went far beyond these fundamentals.

"Our healers learned from the Desert Wanderers long ago that there is a primary sound that vibrates inside every person. The healers discovered that they could characterize people by the way their individual tones differ from the norm. If a person has a certain illness, the pure universal sound in his body is distorted in a certain way that the healer is trained to perceive. Kashi healers have learned to 'hear' the specific distortion for each different illness. The original purpose of music and dance wasn't entertainment, but healing. The healer uses his will power to affect a person's body through resonance and harmonics. The goal is to raise a person's level of consciousness. Then the patient's own higher consciousness reprograms his or her body so that healing can occur. That is why every healer must have healed himself first. There is a saying we have: If you have offered yourself redemption from your sorrows, then your music will bring redemption to your listeners."

"Physician, heal thyself," I said, recalling the New Testament passage.

"The concept even applies to other areas. In the old days of our people, the healer's work involved understanding all the vibrations of Nature. The healers used music to communicate with animals and plants. There are some who still do, but it is fast becoming a lost art. You may have heard of the *baxshis*, the traditional healers of rural Central Asia. They recite ancient poetry, like the *Song of Eternity*, and they play music on a stringed instrument or drum. And sometimes they enter into a trance with a patient."

"I want to understand more about the use of sound in healing," I said. There had been so many times in this journey of mine when sound had touched me strongly, in both my physical body and my perceptions.

"Different sounds evoke different emotional responses," Thod said. "Again, it's based on our primitive survival instincts. For example, the sound of fire creates fear. Earth sounds make us want to move. Water sounds stir the imagination and wind sounds inspire the spirit. These responses are programmed instinctively in our bodies.

"For the baxshis, light can be used in the same way as sound. Healing is done at dusk because of the peculiar distortion of the light at that time. It allows the baxshi to connect with the light energy that the brain has absorbed through the eyes. They can see, or feel, how the person's illness is interfering with their internal processing of that light. Once the healer recognizes the problem, he attempts to change the person's internal sound or light vibration by resonance through his or her own body. He re-infects the patient with health, by helping the patient break the routines in which their illness lies trapped."

I could see that from this point of view healing was a matter of working with the vibrating waves of energy. "You said that the *Book of Creation* describes the waves of energy, and that those waves can be light or sound. Then did the early shamans intend it to be a sort of healing handbook?"

"All I can say for sure about the author or authors of the books of the *Song of Eternity* is that they were master perceivers. Through the power of their keen perception they discovered a few key principles of life that are as useful today as they were thousands of years ago. And who knows? In the future, doctors may rediscover and study these principles once again."

"Which principles specifically?" I asked.

Thod asked me to look again at the caduceus. Then he pointed to his diagram of the vibrating dombro string traced in the sand. It looked like two figure eights placed end to end, as shown in the following figure:

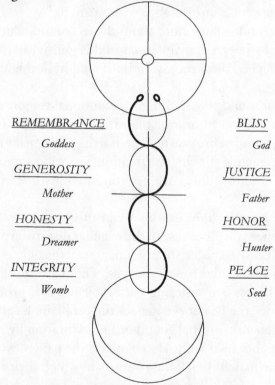

Simplified diagram of the Kashi "Form of Life"
showing the Eight Jewels of Redemption (in larger type)
and the Eight Fruits on the Tree of Life (in smaller type)

"Each wave reaches a maximum point here." He pointed to the crest of the waves, of which there were a total of four on the left and four on the right. "When the string is at its crest, the ear delights in pleasure. Each crest also has a complimentary opposite wave. These eight crests are called the Fruits on the Tree of Life. The four pairs of crests are called, from top to bottom: Goddess and God, Mother and Father, Dreamer and Hunter, Womb and Seed."

He pointed to where the waves crossed each other. "These are called the nodes, or neutral points. When a string is at its neutral point, it is momentarily at rest. There is always a moment when there is no tension, only peace. There are a total of five neutral nodes, including the two end points where the string is attached." Now he drew a horizontal line to separate the top figure eight from the bottom one. "This is called the Plane of Reflection, because what is above is reflected below."

Thod traced his stick along the outline of the waves. "When light and sound enter the eyes and ears, the energy follows this path, from top to bottom. As we respond to the light and sound based on our personal store of experiences, we fill these places with our reactions. We call these depositories of reactions the 'lenses of our perception.' They are the glasses through which we interpret the world. These repositories are filled with our inner stories. If you change your beliefs, your reaction to the incoming pure energy changes. If you embrace the Supreme Truth, the eight clouded lenses gradually become clearer and turn into the Eight Precious Jewels."

Thod began at the bottom this time and worked his way up. Pointing to the crests again, he called out the names of the Eight Precious Jewels: Integrity and Peace, Honesty and Honor, Generosity and Justice, Remembrance and Bliss.

"Everything we know is based on the information we gather from the world through this process. That is where our so-called 'knowledge' lies."

"You're referring to all knowledge, even scientific knowledge?" I asked.

"No. I am talking about your unique set of beliefs about yourself and about your world. We each contain inside of us our own individual *Book of Creation*, our own explanation and justification for existence. It is through accepting this knowledge that we forget who and what we really are, and we fall into a kind of sleep. It is through seeking truth through knowledge that we finally find the path to awaken, and.it is through the renunciation of knowledge that we awaken to the direct experience of ourselves. Knowledge and Truth are gripped in a titanic struggle for our awareness.

"You will discover some day that the *Song of Eternity*, and especially the *Book of Creation*, lays out a universal language that connects science, religion, dance, philosophy, medicine and music. It is the boiled-down essence of the song that plays in our bodies every moment we are alive."

"And the other books?" I asked, very much aware that there were more.

Thod picked up the stick and drew a second set of double figure eights next to the first. "This is where it really gets interesting, because when two people interact they create another whole set of energy relationships. The third book of the *Song of Eternity* is the explanation of those interactions. We call it the *Book of Correlations*. It is a manual for dancers and martial artists. But it is also much more, because to master the art of movement you must master the art of relationship.

"In the *Book of Correlations*, instead of eight crests, sixteen are described—eight for you and eight for your partner. Sound vibrating by itself reaches out to infinity. But when two sounds interact with each other, they create awareness of each other. It is the same with us. It takes another person for us to become aware of ourselves. And that perception of the other person, of course, is made up of information—knowledge again. So everything we know about others, and ourselves, can be studied as the art of observing interfering wave patterns."

It was an overwhelming concept for me to absorb. I knew that Thod was giving me only the barest outline of an entirely different world view. I asked him about the final book in the *Song of Eternity*.

"The fourth teaching, the *Book of Immortality*, describes all sixty-four possible aspects of energy, from pure energy to pure stillness. The book also describes the method for releasing the spirit from its attachment to the body so that one can consciously realize one's true immortal nature. We call this the Art of Immortality. The one who has mastered the Art of Immortality is said to be able to merge with the creative force of the universe at will and manifest any possible creation. The *Book of Immortality* might have been the original inspiration for the 64 hexagrams of the ancient fortune-telling system, the *I Ching* of Chinese Taoism.

"The ancient shamans also discovered that our minds contain a map of the genetic code," Thod continued. "Of course, they didn't call it that—but they discovered it nonetheless."

"I can't conceive of how that could be," I said.

"You need to understand that there is a two-way passage built into our nervous system that allows communication between our mind and the genes that regulate our cells. Someday, after you have mastered the first three books, you will be ready for the final awakening." I expected to see a skeptical look on his face, but I didn't, for which I was grateful.

"Have you mastered all of those teachings?" I asked.

"No, but that is my intent. The first two initiations are given easily. The next two take many years of discipline. It is a matter of deepening your understanding first."

"And what does that involve?"

"You have to ask the water," he said, pointing to a spot where the water tumbled over some rocks. "Put your ear very close to the surface of the stream."

I knelt at the edge of the water and cocked my ear over the surface, listening for subtle sounds.

"Deeper—you have to go much deeper," Thod said. He came up behind me and gave me a sharp push that sent me head first into the water. When I came sputtering up to the surface, he was laughing loudly.

"You have more questions than anyone I've ever known!" he roared.

17

Choosing Reality

AS THE FIRST RAYS OF DAWN APPEARED, WE LOADED THE LAND ROVER and headed across the sun-stricken wilderness in an arrow-straight line towards Turfan, an oasis on the main caravan route of the ancient Silk Road. In the distance, snowy peaks floated dreamily in a vivid blue sky above dark and rocky foothills. The slap of the canvas flap on the back of the Land Rover accentuated the utter silence. An endless sea of platinum sand surrounded us, punctuated here and there by islands of black and white gravel.

Gradually the silver desert floor gave way to fine ochre clay and patches of tenacious shrubs. Streams appeared and disappeared abruptly, and the road became an obstacle course of potholes. Occasionally the remains of crumbling adobe buildings rose lifelessly from the sand, a ghostly reminder of the presence of ancient history. Here lay the pulverized outposts of vanished empires that once dominated Central Asia. Whole civilizations we know almost nothing about have sprung up here and flourished for centuries, only to be conquered by neighboring kingdoms and vanish forever.

Then, abruptly, a skyline thrust itself up above the horizon line: the faded yellow high-rise apartments of the city of Turfan. I felt nervous to be tossed back into the 20th century so suddenly, even if we remained at the remotest edge of the civilized world. We drove into the middle of town and found a small Muslim restaurant on the central square. After the silence of the desert, I jumped at every noise. I cringed at the incessant pop music that blared from the cars and storefronts. The steady clatter from an unseen factory and the blaring of car and bicycle horns set me on edge. Every neon sign and brightly painted storefront glared harshly in my eyes. My senses had been laid open by the silence and emptiness of the desert. And not only my senses, but my sensibilities.

Everything in Turfan, from the paint peeling off the aging hotels to the cramped Chinese collective apartment buildings, looked disheartening and forlorn in a surreal way. I took some comfort in the small piles of windblown sand in the gutters. They reminded me that the desert lay patiently waiting its turn to swallow this spiritless town.

My outer appearance no longer attracted attention because I was dressed in native clothes and wore a white Chinese hat to keep the sun off my face. Inside, I felt raw. I wondered how I would ever readjust to a real city like San Francisco or Los Angeles, or how I could keep from being irritated by the shallowness of everyday interactions—or even have a normal conversation with the people in my old life without reacting to their pain.

Gil-Hamesch noticed my distress and put his arm around me. "Your shield is down," he said quietly.

"He sees the despair of the whole world in your eyes," Thod commented. "You will have to put up a new shield to protect your energy."

I ate my bowl of noodle soup in silence, while my three companions were occupied in conversation. They appeared to be making plans for the trip to their village.

Gil-Hamesch and the Cook left to pick up supplies. Thod let me stew in my dark mood for a while, then brought his hand down hard on the tabletop, rattling the dishware. I looked up to find him glaring at me. "Do you plan to stay in your cave, do you enjoy it in there?" he demanded. "Look what you have forgotten already!"

"I haven't forgotten a thing," I said. "If anything, I know too much."

"Hah!" he barked. "You wouldn't be acting like this if you could learn to see the world through a clear window."

"Easier said than done," I said, hearing the petulance in my voice.

"The one who strives hard to clear the windows of perception from judgments will be rewarded with understanding, and one's path becomes clear." It was a quote from the *Book of Truth*, and I nodded that I did indeed remember it. "Then, how do you think you can reenter your normal life when your windows are still clouded?" he asked.

"That's what's bothering me," I said. "I don't think I'm ready to go back into my old life. Other people haven't changed, but I have, so how do I deal with that?"

He smiled. "Now, *that* is the right question to ask. And you are in the right place to find the answer. It is all a matter of reversing lifelong habits. When you interact with people in your daily life, you are always talking to yourself about how you feel about yourself. Your inner voice says, 'what does this mean to me?' But I can promise you, if you stay grounded in the Supreme Truth there is no more need for self-pity or self-judgment. What other people do or say will not be important to you."

I watched as an old man in a dark blue Maoist uniform yelled at a young boy across the street over and over again. It made me angry and I wanted to tell him to stop.

"Whatever anger you are feeling is not coming from them. It is inside you. You will not resonate with another person's feelings if you do not identify yourself in their suffering. You are still looking for revenge for some past injustice."

I was willing to think about that.

"Since you have surrendered your Badge of Honor," Thod said, "the natural consequence is that the eyes of the heart suddenly open. To live life with your heart open, you have no choice but to learn how to see people dispassionately."

"But not without feeling," I insisted.

"Dispassionately." He glared at me for emphasis. "Otherwise you will be torn apart by seeing the level of pain in the world. Look around you right now. What do you see?"

Following Thod's directions, I directed my eyes to observe each person who walked by the café, and tried to remain detached from judging them. It seemed as if I could now see straight into the heart of each person I saw—and I didn't see much happiness or love.

I watched a merchant selling cheap drugstore items from a wheeled booth on the sidewalk across the street. When I looked

163

closely at his face and body language I felt neediness, petty greed, and dishonesty. A very attractive Chinese woman stopped by his stand to purchase lipstick. Gazing at her with what I hoped was objective clarity, I saw a person who lived a life governed by sexual manipulation and vanity. Their conversation appeared to alternate between blatant flirtation and angry argument over prices. They seemed to be stuck as they kept repeating their demands over and over. I knew I was seeing into the realities of their lives, and for once I didn't make excuses for them in my mind, or romanticize their stories, or assume that I was in some way superior.

As I watched people go about their daily business I felt the pain and loneliness in their lives with uncomfortable clarity. A busy city can be far lonelier, and the people more isolated, than the desert. This was the real desert. How could I shield myself from the things of the world that were painful, or even from the pleasant things that now felt meaningless and numbing to the spirit? Why did I once feel so content in my modern world? I knew the answer: I never truly *was* content. Otherwise, why would I have come here in the first place?

The name of this desert passed repeatedly through my mind: Taklimaken—*whoever enters never returns*. It seemed to mirror my own fate, to be trapped forever in the lonely desert of modern life. Awake and alone. I had faced the Supreme Truth: that all my life as I knew it before had been an illusion, that it was only the reality that I had chosen to believe in. How could I ever again cover it over with the false veneer of rationalization?

How many other people, through some circumstance, are forced to face the realization that life has no meaning other than the one we give it? And how do they react? By becoming alcoholic or obsessed with a relationship? By embracing a religion that requires unquestioning faith? By becoming cynical, selfish, or obsessed with making money? There are so many ways of turning away from looking within.

I remembered a famous Hollywood actor who spoke on the radio show "Fresh Air" about his personal struggle with feeling alone in the world. He said that one day he came to the conclusion that everyone outside of the entertainment world was also an actor in a movie but in movies of their own making—and with badly written scripts. The realization that there existed no escape, no independent reality to guide him, scared him so deeply that he had paralyzing bouts of depression. But this knowledge also made him a powerful actor. Maybe the "dark side" of the Supreme Truth strikes the most creative and sensitive and curious people especially hard.

"This world is a lonely place," I said aloud.

"You're right," Thod said. "But this grim view of life will fade. The *Book of Creation* compares your present experience to awakening in a deep cave surrounded by ghosts who have been trapped for eternity. You are seeing too much before you have the tools to understand."

Gil-Hamesch and the Cook rejoined us and we ordered tea and continued the conversation, with Thod translating most of Gil-Hamesch's words.

"Everything in this world is born out of nothing," Gil-Hamesch said to me while Thod spoke his words in English. "If you stay rooted in this awareness, you can create anything you want. Enlightenment doesn't mean running away from life. Enlightenment seems like the ultimate goal of life, just as freedom is the deepest wish of a prisoner. But enlightenment and freedom are just the beginning. If you want a beautiful life, you must create that vision, have faith in your creation, and follow the natural patterns of life. It will come to you. Once your saboteur is gone, your new creation will be backed by all the power of the universe." Gil-Hamesch was pleased with Thod's translation, and I was well aware that the venerable master understood far more English than he was comfortable speaking.

He was smiling at me, as if to encourage my deeper understanding. "I do want to create a beautiful life," I said to him. "It's difficult to believe that by simply changing my beliefs my entire reality will change."

"Your reality," Gil-Hamesch said in his own words, "is always, and has always been, only what you perceive it to be."

Thod continued as translator: "Watch carefully the ways you re-engage your life-dream. Play with your creative power the way a musician experiments with a new instrument. You used to spend a lot of your energy making yourself miserable. Think what you can do now! You can choose any path, so why not choose a path with heart?

If you didn't like your destiny before, intend a new one!" Gil-Hamesch's eyes were laughing.

"But," I countered, "doesn't each of us come into this life with a particular destiny to work out? Aren't we limited to some degree by that destiny?" It was the same question I had posed to Thod. I still wasn't convinced of the answer.

"Once you fully embrace the Supreme Truth you no longer have a personal destiny to fulfill," Gil-Hamesch said, by way of Thod. "You have effectively cancelled your personal destiny. The only real and true destiny of every human is to awaken from the illusion of what he is not, or she is not, and to realize the truth of one's existence. You have a unique voice, a song that is yours alone. You have rediscovered yours. Your old habits of self-pity and self-judgment are no longer useful to you. That is why you feel so empty. When you let go of the old dreams of your life and overcome the fear of loneliness, you will discover another land, a land filled with wonder and miracles. Beyond the desert is the Valley of Miracles."

I assumed he meant that the Valley of Miracles was a figurative place, a spiritual ideal. Gil-Hamesch read my thoughts and said, "No, no, it is also real—a very special and beautiful valley."

"It is a beautiful place," echoed Thod, "like an unspoiled paradise, only four days' ride by horse north of our village." He sighed. "I dream all the time about riding my horse through those meadows and pine forests, just like in my youth." He caught himself in a moment of sentimentality. "But does it matter where it is? With a clouded mind you could be in paradise and suffer. With a clear spirit you can walk in the Valley of Miracles wherever you go."

Thod directed me to keep looking at the people in the market, making no judgment, and to tell him what I saw.

I looked again at the people on the street, and a realization came to me. Everyone I saw was no different from me. They too had lost their True Voice. They too had forgotten their childlike spirit and traded it for some false promise of happiness. It wasn't anyone's fault. It was just the way of this world. I felt overcome with a deep desire to help them. I knew I couldn't help all of them, but I felt moved to do something. This was a revelation to me. This was a first recognition—and acceptance—that I could freely choose a life of service.

Serving others was the way that I could choose to serve the inner fire that lights each of our lives. This had nothing to do with my old, flawed Badge of Honor, because I no longer cared about the outcome. I could serve just because it made me happy. Whether it ultimately made a difference . . . well, it didn't really matter. "Are you following your old pattern of feeling responsible for the world?" Thod asked.

"No, I don't think so. I feel only compassion for the world now." I meant it with every fiber of my being. "If I can choose to feel anything I want, if I can create any belief I want, I choose compassion."

Gil-Hamesch knitted the deep creases in his brow and looked up into my eyes with a silent smile. I had the feeling he had made a similar choice many, many years ago. I realized I still knew so little about this man. But I was sure of one thing: He did not judge me. He only cared deeply for me. He cared deeply for everyone. Though Gil-Hamesch lives in a part of the world that is often filled with oppression, corruption and violence, his smiling optimism arises out of a deep compassion for all and a belief in each person's potential to make better choices.

"How do you choose to see the world?" I asked Thod.

"When I look at the world I see a place that needs healing," he said. "Whether I was learning our traditional healing techniques or studying in medical school, I have always chosen to be a healer."

I told Thod I wanted to learn more about his native healing practices. "Do you have a hard time reconciling your shamanic training with modern medicine?"

"There is no ultimate truth, as you now know, and this applies to medicine as well. There are only different points of view."

We left the Muslim restaurant and strolled to a small electrical shop a few blocks away. Thod needed to buy some parts for an irrigation pump in his village. Here was something I could help him with, as an engineer. I already felt I could never repay the debt for the personal help and attention I received from Gil-Hamesch, the Cook and Thod. At the very least, I could make sure that the village would have a working irrigation pump. Such a humble thing, but it carried so much meaning for me.

18

The Form of Life

TURFAN BECAME MY BRIDGE BACK INTO THE WORLD FROM THE SENSORY deprivation of the desert. Thod made sure that I took full advantage of the learning opportunities here. Later that day, while Gil-Hamesch and the Cook were about their own business, he took me to the covered market again where we could watch people without being observed ourselves. We found a small table at a tea stand that had a good view of the comings and goings in the market.

"Do you see all of these people?" Thod asked with a motion of his hand.

"Of course."

"And you think yourself rather perceptive now—but I tell you that you could sit here for the rest of the day, and for days on end, and not really see them."

"I'm sure you're right," I said. "And I'm sure you're going to tell me why that is."

He smiled briefly. I think Thod enjoyed our mental play as much as I had finally come to enjoy it. "It has to do with being able to see *into* a person, into the causes of their illness or suffering. Everyone vibrates with energy, just like the string on the dombro. You are energy. Energy and matter. Your unique signature is conveyed through the waves of your inner current. It fills and surrounds you in a cocoon."

"So are you saying we have a kind of force field around us?"

"You could say that if you want to, but it's not really like that."

"Then *what*?"

"It looks like a force field to some people, and to others it looks like an egg surrounding the body. The Kashi call it the Form of Life."

"And you can see this energy?"

"Absolutely."

I had to know how he did it. "And it doesn't interfere with seeing things around you clearly . . . or does it come and go? Can you see it when you close your eyes?"

"It's not like that. You don't see it with your eyes."

"So it's dreamlike—a mental image?"

"No again," said Thod. "You see it with your energy being. You resonate with another person, and then you perceive it with a different kind of perception. That's why mastering the Supreme Truth is so important. You have to learn to be completely detached when you need to be. Otherwise you will resonate with everyone—including those who are ill. This could make you sick too. You have to clean yourself through the practices I taught you if you want to learn the art of healing."

I was fascinated. "So you can see this egg shape, or whatever. Then what do you see? Colors or dark spots . . . ?"

"Sometimes. The Form of Life is always in motion, vibrating like the dombro string, in waves. The old masters were such great perceivers, they learned to see everything—the nodes, the neutral points, everything about these waves. So when I was training, I learned to see the waves too, all eight crests. But it's not with the eyes, exactly, it is a special form of perception. And each of the eight crests in the waves has two aspects. That's why we say we have the eight Fruits of the Tree of Life, which can be transformed into the eight Jewels. We are always in the process of making our light darker—or cleaning it up and making it brighter."

I had a hard time making sense of this at the time. But not for lack of trying. "Do these waves flow through the body?" Even a dumb question might help. Today he seemed to be more patient with me than usual, so I didn't mind pressing him further. At least there wasn't a stream nearby for him to push me into.

"Yes," he replied to my question about the waves. "There is correspondence in the body. When you are able to perceive the waves in another person you can feel them as well as see them. There are four sets of waves, starting with the energy in the loins, which has to do with reproduction. The second set can be seen or felt around the solar plexus, which shows the drive for food and shelter, in its simplest definition.

"Do you remember when we sat at the river and spoke of these things—about the division of the waves? I told you that there was a horizontal line separating the two lower sets of waves from the two higher ones—the 'plane of reflection' at the level of the heart. That is the point at which we open the possibilities of loving beyond the self. Above that, at the breast, is the third wave set, whose energies are most often expressed in the care for our offspring. The fourth is at the forehead, revealing the energies of self-awareness. Very few people have a completely balanced wave pattern, and so their Form of Life will bulge in places, or expand or be shrunken, depending on the state of the person.

"Shamans have the sight to see these shapes in detail. They say that people usually fall into categories such as the mushroom, the cup, the lotus, the eye, the bell, or the basin, according to the predominant distortion and coloration of their Form of Life."

Instead of explaining further, Thod sketched these objects on an old cigarette wrapper that lay on the table next to us. I could see that each of these curved shapes represented a portion of the figure-eight wave shapes—cupping upwards or downwards, and representing an odd sort of shorthand for certain types of people.

I had another question. "If I could see all of this, then I could truly know where they felt pain or had distortions in their physical or mental states?

"The Kashi have developed a way to do this. We call this 'seeing into the egg-form.'"

"And you think this is something I can learn?"

"If you cannot, then you have a fool for a teacher!" he laughed. "It is not difficult. To begin with, you will need to shift your perception until you can see life from the point of view of the egg."

"Of the egg?" It was my turn to laugh.

"The art of seeing it is to be taken as literally as possible. All living things begin their life as an egg or a seed. It is only due to the driving force of the sun's energy that we are compelled to awaken from our egg state and venture out of our mothers' wombs for the purpose of finding a partner with whom to pass on our life force and genes."

I was amused by Thod's reduction of the life force into a primitive drive to reproduce ourselves. He was no romantic when it came to explaining the processes of nature, and I told him so.

"Look," he said, "I tend to talk about these things in medical terms, or in the language of the shaman, because that is how I think about them. But that doesn't make them any less miraculous."

"It isn't always clear, I'm sorry."

"I know," he sympathized. "Maybe there is a simpler way of framing this discussion." Thod started again. "The Kashi say that people usually fall into one of nine personality types. Of course each of us carries all of the Fruits and the Jewels of the Tree of Life within us. But as we grow up from our youth, we develop a tendency towards one of the Fruits more than others—and that becomes our dominant personality trait.

"The energy of the sun flows into our being and we transform it into our life spirit through the vehicle of the Form of Life. Then that energy rises within us from the base of the spine. Some people's energy tends to stay there, focused in the first two waves, the Fruits called Womb and Seed—and that guides their personal destinies. These are the first two personality types. We call a person whose energy is focused in the womb a Seducer, and one whose energy is con-centrated in the seed a Warrior. These are the primal male and female energies at the most basic level."

"How can you put people into boxes like that?" I objected.

"They are not boxes," Thod said emphatically. "They are survival mechanisms for the human organism. The Kashi healer sees that people's energy is focused in one part of their being whether they know it or not. The task of the Warrior personality is to learn to channel one's energy into peaceful action. The task of the Seducer is to find integrity with one's sexual energy."

"How are you defining integrity?"

"Everyone knows what integrity means," he said.

"I don't think so. I am not sure I always know!"

"But you do. There is always a moment when you cross the Line of Integrity," he said. "The moment may go by almost unnoticed or it may be deeply contemplated—and rationalized. That line exists in the heart. When you give up something for yourself, out of love, you cross above the Line of Integrity. And when you lie to yourself you cross it in the other direction. For example, many people struggle over the choice to marry or to have a family. If that choice is made for the wrong reason, like duty, or money, for example, then it hurts a person inside, and it clouds their future. But when a choice is made from true love, whatever the choice, it is likely to eventually bring good fortune."

"Okay, I get that."

"And it's not just about love of somebody else. You have to make choices about love for yourself. You have to respect who and what you are. And that includes recognizing your personality type and working with it."

A lot of questions came up in my mind, beginning with what type he thought I was.

He waved away my question before I could ask it. "The third personality type is called the Dreamer, and the fourth is the Hunter. The job of the Hunter is to learn to overcome a natural tendency towards craftiness and transform it into Honor. And the job of the Dreamer is to overcome a tendency towards obscuring things—to transform his or her way of life to one of unfettered truth." While he was talking I pulled my notebook out of my daypack and found a sketch I had made of the Kashi Form of Life. With that as a reference I began to see how Thod's personality types fell into place.

"The next is the Provider," he said. "This person's energy is focused in the Fruit we call Generosity. He or she could be a parent or a teacher or many other roles. And the sixth type is the Judge. You know you have a Judge when people say about him or her that they seem 'born to lead.' These people become the judges, doctors, politicians and so on."

"Like mother and father figures."

"Yes, as a society we need all manifestations of the Tree of Life among us to keep our society balanced energetically."

He continued with the list. "The Priest is the seventh type, and corresponds to Goddess and Remembrance. The role of priests is to hold the spiritual energy for us to access and to help us remember our highest nature. And the eighth, corresponding with God/Bliss, is the Desert Wanderer, the ones who are free from illusions and have no attachments in the world."

"That sounds rather lonely," I said.

"Not for them. They learn to blend in so that the average person does not detect them. But when they act, they act with a great deal of power, and are always in the right place at the right time. There are very few true Desert Wanderers. You will be lucky if you ever meet one."

"I'd like to."

"Be careful what you ask for!"

"And the ninth—you said there was a ninth type."

"We call such a person a Being of Compassion. This is a person whose energy is focused in the heart—there in the middle of the Tree of Life. In our village we have a man who bakes bread and pastries. Everyone goes to see him, but not only because they want his bread. They want to see his beautiful smile as he asks them about their lives. I do the same, and I miss being around his kindness, concern and compassion when I travel—even though he is a simple man and we rarely talk about anything important."

"The Cook . . . that fits how I feel about him. I love being around him."

"Yes, that's exactly why."

"What about Gil-Hamesch?" I asked. "Or is he above these personality types?"

"Oh, no. He is the master Priest. His role is to radiate his spiritual wisdom to all of us, on all levels. He has accepted that role and plays it well. He is a master of the highest kind."

"And the Desert Wanderers, are they higher—or alongside Gil-Hamesch?"

"The Desert Wanderers barely live in this world. Their task is not to be seen or to directly lead us. Therefore, we leave them alone to whatever it is they do."

"Then what about you, Thod—can I ask which one you are?"

"You can ask me anything you like. My personality type is the Judge. That is why I was predisposed to become a doctor. And why I have done so well with the healing arts. I know it's my role to help the village and I do it with pleasure."

"So, what is my personality type?"

"You must have figured that out by now!" he laughed.

"I haven't. Tell me."

"I want you to think about this while we go on with our lesson." He took a drink of his tea, pointedly ignoring my frustration.

"We were speaking about the art of seeing into the egg-form," he said. "The Kashi believe that our present lives are only the 'exploded' phase of the egg's life. Everything we know in this world is therefore just a temporary representation in the minds of the exploded eggs."

My mind wanted to wander off to the personality types, but I dragged it back to try to imagine such things as exploded eggs. Usually, when Thod introduced a strange concept I eventually got it, so I just listened and trusted that I would.

"For this exercise I want you to use a combination of perception, imagination and intuition, to literally see humans as exploded eggs on a quest driven forward by a compelling force, knowing that their time has been limited by the impending reality of death. Everything in this life comes down to a search for energy. Now . . ." he nodded in the direction of the market crowds, "Look, and tell me what you see. Clear your vision of judgments and see dispassionately."

I closed my eyes partway and quieted my mind, imagining each person I saw as an egg. "I don't know if I can do this," I said after a false start. Thod said nothing, so I tried again, this time not trying to make sense of it, simply using my imagination. After looking at people this way for maybe an hour, I began to be able to create a shift in my normal perception.

"Now, look for the subtle egg-shapes around their bodies."

Soon I wasn't seeing people as people at all, but egg-shaped forms that bounced and bobbed down the street in search of energy —which in this marketplace meant food and money. I could also faintly perceive a glowing luminescent sphere that seemed to emerge from the egg form around the heads of some people.

In this altered state of seeing, people did not seem so different from any other living creatures, and my judgments about them began to dissolve into sympathy. I even felt a sort of affection for everyone I saw. "I don't think what I'm seeing about people is only my imagination," I said.

"You have started to open your eyes," he reassured me. "When you read the language of a person's body you will know much more than their words will say. The body does not lie."

So how, I questioned him, did this translate into the knowledge of healing.

"The goal for the healer is to see the human egg so clearly that you can gradually begin to see the Form of Life guiding the activity of each person," he said. "The old Kashi healing masters perfected their knowledge of the Form of Life. They catalogued and described every detail. By seeing the Form of Life at work a healer can directly perceive the source of illness, as well as predict behavior."

"The world needs more healers!" I said.

"I agree . . . if they are correctly trained and initiated. Seeing the Form of Life takes a great deal of practice and concentration. You have made a first step today by realizing that you can shift your perception and begin to see into the energy forms."

"What would it take for me to be able to see the Form of Life at will and have a healer's insight?"

Thod looked dubious. "To awaken your ability to see the Form of Life directly? That would take unbending effort. It would also take time. Right now I am pushing you to understand as much as possible about it in preparation for your initiation into the *Book of Creation*."

19

The Jewels of Redemption

A WAITER BROUGHT US ANOTHER POT OF BLACK TEA AND A PLATE OF hardboiled eggs. Thod caught my eye. "We live in a world of symbols," he smiled, biting into one of the dusky-colored eggs. "If you are growing tired, we can stop for a while."

"I didn't come halfway around the world to take it easy," I replied and poured another round of tea into our cups.

"All right, then. Out there, in front of your eyes is everything you need to know about love."

"If you say so." I looked at the noisy bustle of people and goods in the covered market, the Chinese faces and the Uighers, and faces whose origins I couldn't identify. In the midst of it all, love wasn't the first word that came to mind.

"Every one of them is in the process of awakening. They are somewhere on the upward serpent spiral that leads to Remembrance and Bliss. Think now about the eight bends in the serpents' bodies as they embrace the central fire, like the wave pattern of the vibrating string. And remember that the natural functions of our life, the Eight Fruits of the Tree of Life, can be transformed into higher functions, which are the Jewels."

I nodded, trying my best.

"See the merchant over there," he said, "the one sitting on the folding chair behind the cart with all the perfumes and cosmetics."

This was the merchant who had been arguing with the woman before.

"Now recall that the Eight Precious Jewels exist in pairs, moving upwards from the joining place at the root. Integrity is the first, and Peacefulness, Honesty and Honor, Justice and Generosity, Remembrance and Bliss. We will concern ourselves with the first four Jewels of the Kashi path, beginning with sexual integrity." He gave me one of his looks, and I immediately assumed he was referring to a character defect of my own. I braced myself for some awful truth.

"If you remember nothing more, remember this: Sexual energy is naturally clean and clear. But if we have filled the lens of the first Fruit with fear, self-rejection or shame, the energy is obscured. It has a hard time rising to the heart and beyond."

I asked what this had to do with the merchant, who didn't appear to be a clean and clear kind of fellow, to my untrained eye.

"I am speaking first of the principles involved," Thod explained. "Then we will see how they apply. Energy by its very nature leads first to power, then to action, and then, potentially, to violence or dissipation. This applies to sexual energy too. Therefore, the first step, the foundation, really, on the path of transformation is sexual integrity—faithfulness, and innocence that is lost and regained. The next step after cleansing one's sexual integrity is the transformation of this energy into the second Jewel, the one that is called Kindness, or Peace. This step is the mastering of the art of non-violence—to others, to oneself, to life."

"That is the work of a lifetime," I said.

"For some it is a lifelong challenge. I choose to say *actively making peace*, instead of the more negative term non-violence. This is a special kind of peace, not a passive or restful state. It is like the great power latent in a slowly moving stream. It links the individual stream of energy to the cosmic flow all around. Where the average person may seek to modulate their excess energy through alcohol, athletics, excessive work, or sex, one who has awakened the second Jewel radiates a palpable feeling of peace and compassion. This power of love for our fellow humans can overcome violence and fear. It is an active principle. When one creates an outgoing energy of peacemaking, it influences those around us to be at peace."

He stopped, as if he expected me to ask about all of this, but I had no desire to speak, being completely engrossed in the concept he was proposing. I felt it more with my body than my mind.

"Look at that man again. I want you to observe how his motivation alternates between planning for the hunt, hunting, and enjoying the captured prey."

"So you would say that his personality type was the Hunter."

"Yes, and his task will be to claim the Jewel of Honor."

The woman had returned to see the merchant again. I noticed that she was wearing a great deal of makeup and that her body language was almost exaggerated in its femininity. Their conversation became strained right away. Thod was clearly enjoying the interaction. "And she is the Dreamer. Try seeing them only as two personality types searching for connection—the Hunter and the Dreamer, each needing to find their own integrity through honor and truth."

The man and woman resumed their arguing, or was it haggling? I couldn't tell. Maybe it was a cultural thing, and they were both enjoying the game. "Even though you cannot understand his words, you can see from his body language that he is lying to her," Thod said. "He is selling counterfeit French perfumes and charging high prices, and she knows it. Fortunately for us, they are demonstrating a point from the *Book of Creation*."

"That lying is wrong?"

Thod stared at me. "You are forgetting again. Judgments about right or wrong only cloud your perception. Now that you are initiated into the *Book of Truth* you need to abandon your prior concepts about 'right' and 'wrong.' You have to learn to accept people exactly the way they are. What is efficient and meaningful to the life of the egg? That's the question that truly matters." I felt a sudden urge to whine and complain, but I stopped myself. Thod continued. "One of the egg's objectives as it hunts is to gather more information to hunt better. When people lie and act with deceit, their deviousness sabotages their own ability to learn. Others can feel their dishonesty and become suspicious. Then the liar can't even trust himself. So in the end an egg hurts itself by lying. On the other hand, if you make the conscious choice to be as honest as you can, people will feel it and put more trust in you. Then you will do better in the world. It is a simple biological law. It is the same with each of the Eight Jewels on the Tree of Life.

"So you see, you don't need anyone lecturing you about moral laws. You don't need a religion to be your moral guide. You choose honesty because it is a better way to live. You will become a better gatherer of information—a better hunter. Your egg self will function with more efficiency and with greater success."

"I'm starting to feel sorry for the lying merchant," I said.

"Remember—try not to judge people," Thod said. "I can see that that man is deficient in the aspect of the Hunter. Every being is hunting, seeking energy, but this man's lack of integrity is hurting him. If he transformed this aspect of his life through the Jewel of Honor, his life would change. If he went to a Kashi healer for anything—even something seemingly unrelated—the Kashi healer would see this in his Form of Life and instruct him to work on this one thing. But there are other things that can bring a person to change—such as love." He gestured towards the woman.

"It is the same path for that merchant as it is for you to escape your feeling of separateness. You must both begin by acknowledging that your world is a false one. You must have faith in the power of life, take responsibility for what you create, stop hurting people, start telling the truth, and start acting with honor."

I was aware that Thod had started using the word "you," meaning me. I had never mentioned to him that there was a woman back home that I cared about, and I wondered what he saw in my own egg-form in the area of my heart—or in the part below the heart that was supposed to already know about sexual integrity. I felt way too transparent at the moment. I was about to tell him I was fully aware that I was a work-in-progress.

"I predict he will marry that woman some day soon," Thod said. "Only through love can they transform their bickering into genuine affection."

I couldn't believe what I was hearing. "How can you possibly say that, Thod? Look at them! Can you imagine the fights if they ever got married?"

"That is a belief you need to look at," Thod said severely. "Put that one back on your list. It is not the natural law of the human spirit. Let me tell you something. When I look at most people from America and Europe I see a vacuum of love in their bodies. You have made the greatest distortion of the greatest emotion. You have an abundance of wealth but are wanting of the love that is free for every human. So many of you are starving for love so much that you have come to fear it. And in the final irony, your fear of love has turned into a love of fear—even an addiction to fear."

I was trying not to react with irritation or take his harsh comments personally, but it wasn't easy, though I didn't feel like challenging him at the moment.

"It is just as true of many people here in China today," he added. "Now, back to that woman: I see that she is deficient in the aspect of the Dreamer. She is wearing a mask, not being truthful about herself and her emotions. Her seductiveness is crying out 'Me, me, choose me!' But this could be transformed through the Jewel of Honesty. The truth is, she does not need anyone else to validate her beauty. When she realizes this her awareness will rise to a higher level. That is what a Kashi healer would tell her. The possibility exists that these two people will fall in love, despite their masks, and that the Hunter and the Dreamer will transform their Forms of Life with the Jewels of Honor and Honesty. And so now we have the first four Jewels and we have the opportunity to awaken to a higher potential. Which brings us to the heart."

HE PLACED BOTH OF HIS HANDS IN FRONT OF HIS HEART, ONE PALM facing upwards, and one down. "It is at the heart that we shift from caring only about ourselves to caring for the life of another being, for the lives of all beings. The *Book of Creation* calls the heart a Magic Lake, the Lake of Reflection, because it mirrors others to us as ourselves.

"What is it that lifts us up into this higher plane?" Thod asked rhetorically. "It is Love. Love means that you care for somebody else, and perhaps that someone else cares for you. Usually we are only obsessed with our own importance."

"I would agree," I said.

"There are only a few ways to overcome this obsession. The greatest of them is with an act of love. When you have a lover, you care only for that person's happiness, not your own. When you love your children you gladly sacrifice for them. When you truly love yourself, you no longer want to suffer. All of these can awaken us from the dream and bring us up into the sunlight."

He returned his hand to his belly. "Look at the merchant. Right now he is filled with feelings of poverty, neediness and greed." Thod moved his hand to his heart again, and then to his shoulders. "Through surrender to love for a woman he will become a proud provider and defender of his family. He will find his integrity." He straightened his shoulders to demonstrate the energy that moved up from the heart. "If these two people were to come to you for advice about marriage you would see that right away. You would find some action that would strengthen those two characteristics. Then harmony would be restored and they would have the tools to live a happy life."

Thod's words were either very naive or profoundly wise. At this point I had to assume the latter. "This will all become clearer once you study the *Book of Creation*," he said, noting my reaction. "Every person's needs are different, but there are certain fundamentals that are universal. Sexual integrity is the foundation of the house of the spirit. Without sexual integrity the house will eventually collapse. With it, a man or woman can build an empire if they want to. Even that man and that woman.

"In order for us to grow, we need first to go back and embrace more fully who we really are. It begins with sexual integrity and nonviolence and rises to honesty and acting with honor. Then the power of love leads us straight to the Jewels of Justice and Generosity, to Remembrance of our true self, and finally to the experience of Bliss."

"The last four Jewels," I said, finally seeing where he was leading me.

Thod put his finger to his forehead. "It is essential that you understand this: The experience of ecstasy that comes from feeling your unity with life has always been available to you and to every person in the world. It is not owned or controlled by any priest, swami, or mullah. The Eight Jewels represent the inner path that you must ascend, the steps you must finally master along the way.

You might skip some steps and still achieve the higher levels of transcendence, but your happiness will soon fade. Only when you master your full integrity step by step will your bliss stop deserting you.

"Integrity with your sexual energy leads to integrity with the rest of your life," he continued. "And integrity with the rest of your life keeps your sexual energy forever fresh and blissful. I have been to the mountains many times in my life, but I do not tire of their beauty. In fact, they grow more beautiful every time I see them. So it is with everything of true beauty in life. Your lover is always different today than she was yesterday. True love is eternal, yet ever-new." Thod's eyes shimmered now. "The secret is to pay attention, so that it never becomes routine. If your relationship is an eternal romance, then the rest of your life will be one also."

This was a new side of Thod, sentimental, even vulnerable. I had no idea. "But what if you don't have that kind of ideal relationship?" I asked, referring to myself.

He waved away my question. "You don't need a partner to know bliss. You can fill your needs for validation, comfort and love from within. When your own bowl overflows, people will surround you to feed themselves. Sexual energy is a special gift from Nature. It is what you choose to do with it that will determine your character. You can choose to waste it or repress it—to express it or transform it. It can be an expression of beauty as you give your partner the unconditional love she once received from a parent. Or it can be transformed into a shiny current of magnetism that radiates from your whole being."

"So you think there's still hope for the merchant over there?" I joked, seeing that the negotiations were still in full cry.

He lowered his sunglasses for a moment. "You don't yet understand the enormous power of love."

"I'm sure you're right," I said. I decided to ask him something I had wondered about. "Is there a woman in your life, Thod?"

"Oh, yes," he said, somewhat shyly, I thought. "You will meet her soon enough."

That was all he said about her, but I was very curious to know what kind of woman would cause Thod to speak in the way he just did. He stood and stretched his tall frame, then sat down again and changed the subject. "We have a little more time before we meet Gil-Hamesch and the Cook at the car. We will drive to the home of friends for the night. I can feel your concern about where you will lay your head tonight."

"Not at all," I said. "I have absolute trust."

He smiled briefly. "You have more questions, I can feel them. Ask."

"Only one at the moment. I want to know more about how to see the Form of Life."

"First of all, the Form of Life is not only in humans, it exists in everything as a signature of Nature, if you can read it. For example, when you think you see a whirlpool, you do not really see a whirlpool, you see water in motion. But your mind is capable of giving a name to the principle that organizes the water into that shape. That is what you are trying to see, the principle behind the forms of life. If you know what to look for you can see traces of the Form of Life in the spiral marks of a pine cone, the petals of a rose, in oak trees and bee hives. It is a matter of training your eyes to perceive it. It is everywhere.

"To see the Form of Life in people requires deeper concentration and knowledge. It requires the involvement of your heart, most of all. One way the Kashi healers have learned to see it is through dance, in conformity with the rules outlined in the *Book of Correlations*. In these dances, every note of music, every rhythm and every movement of the dancer has a specific intention to facilitate communication between the Form of Life and the dancer."

I asked what he meant by "communication."

"Most of the dances were created to foster harmony between a man and a woman," he said, "or to create camaraderie in warriors, or to otherwise bring a group into harmony. But the purpose of certain special dances was to lead the individual dancers into a kind of trance in which they could communicate directly with the Form of Life."

"Like the dervishes," I said.

"Very much. The Sufi dances of the whirling dervishes possibly came from a distant offshoot of the original Kashi 'liberation dances'."

I'd always been intrigued by the whirling dervishes, wondering what was actually happening when they went into their spinning trances. "But, when *you* see or feel the Form of Life, Thod, I assume you're not in a trance."

"No, my training has been to experience it directly, as a healer looking into my patient's needs."

"And what is that like?"

Thod picked up another hardboiled egg from the table and began tracing spirals from one end of the egg to the other, turning it slowly in his hand. "First I see the spirals in the shell of the egg, and then I see a thin vortex spinning in a tube running from one end of the egg to the other, down the middle. The center of the vortex appears like two twisted snakes, ascending and descending. Where their bodies bulge out, I see colors. By the time I see that far, I am usually filled with the knowledge of what I need to do or to say to the person I am seeing, or I know what action I need to take."

Thod gave me a piercing look. "We can talk about this forever, but that will not change you. You can learn to see the egg form and still not change. You can even do the Sacred Dances and awake to ecstasy and see the Form of Life—and still you will return to your life unchanged. What is needed to transform your life is the will-force."

"*Schug*," I said, remembering his word for it. "You told me how you used it to get away from the KGB agents in Moscow."

He smiled again. "All right, then, it is time to speak of it further. Schug is a type of will power different from any other. It does not originate in the mind but in the body. Once it is awakened, it has the power to permanently transform a person. It is summoned up from the base of the spine. The power of schug is unmatched in the human experience and should be used with caution and discretion.

"It is this special will-force that has the power to permanently transform the Eight Fruits of the Tree of Life into the Eight Jewels. And when these shine in your inner being they are felt by everyone around you.

"And so," he said, "we begin the path that leads us to becoming like the pure, unclouded light. But to do so revokes agreements that have been in place for a lifetime. Few people are ready to give up their addiction to suffering and self-limitation. Merely making a choice with the mind is not enough." Thod lowered his voice. "It sometimes takes a life-or-death choice to permanently change the direction of one's life." He left it at that. Even though we had spent a great deal of time together, I still knew very little about Thod's life, or what choices he had had to make.

By now the marketplace was thinning out. Some of the merchants were closing up their stands and shops, while others lit kerosene lanterns and stayed open. For us, it was time to go.

"ONE LAST QUESTION," I SAID, AS THOD COUNTED OUT SOME YUAN AND laid them on our table.

"You still haven't figured it out?"

"No. I really feel like I have elements of all the personality types inside me—not just one."

"Tell me what you have learned about yourself on this journey of yours—different from what you knew before you came here to be with us."

I took a deep breath and closed my eyes. I was very tired from the long day, but I was able to bring myself into a state of centeredness. My thoughts went back to the time at the cabin. "I am the pure energy of life," I said, keeping my eyes closed.

"And when did you first become aware of that pure energy of life?"

"That day I told you about, when I was six."

"And what did you do with the energy that arose in your being then?" he pressed.

I opened my eyes. "I wanted to become a priest."

"That's because you have a very strong tendency in that direction. But where did that get you?"

"Nowhere," I answered, "except that I wrote about it . . . poetry and stories and things like that."

"So the natural direction of your energy was to express itself with art. That should tell you that you have the personality type of the Dreamer."

"I don't think so!" I objected immediately. "I can't paint or draw, or play music very well, or even write very well. How could I be a

Dreamer? I think I'm more of a Hunter." I wasn't sure why I reacted so strongly.

"You say you came here to take a job in engineering—that your destination is the Technology Office in Urumchi. And yet here you are, spending your time with a shaman, a master and a musician. Do you really believe you are a Hunter?"

"Yes, I do . . . because I think of myself as a practical, hard working person."

"And has this filled your heart with love and happiness for what you do?"

"No." I didn't know what else to say. He was right.

"A lot of us take on roles that do not match our personality type. But if you want to see what a person's True Voice is, watch what they do after they retire from their job, or after their children move away. Then you will know."

"Are you saying the True Voice is the voice of the personality type?"

"Yes. It is the voice of your predominant Fruit—calling out to transcend into a shining Jewel."

I looked down at the table for a long time, letting this sink in. Somehow I felt like I must have known this all my life, but just not in words or concepts. And now I had just discovered, or rediscovered, the core roots of my unhappiness, my restlessness. As I reflected on this, I sensed Thod staring at me with his shaman eyes.

"There is another possibility," he said. "You may be destined to become a Desert Wanderer yourself someday. There will come a point in your life when you will have to choose how far you want to go with this knowledge. For now, you still have a lot of inner work to do."

"What kind of inner work do you want me to do?" I asked, assuming this was the beginning of another one of his lessons.

"The task I am going to give you is to write a book about your personal experiences here in the desert. I want you to write the verses from the *Song of Eternity* using your own best understanding. And I want you to deeply contemplate each verse until it speaks directly to you."

I looked up and saw the steady power emanating from his gaze.

"You have neglected your artistic side, your Dreamer self, for too long. When you can learn to speak with your authentic Dreamer voice, you will find that your life will change. You will find a partner, and you will find a satisfaction in your soul that you have yearned for your entire life. Only then will you be ready to return."

"Are you telling me I have to write a book before I can come back here?" I didn't know where I could possibly find the time to fit such a huge project into my busy life.

"You will find the time, because writing this book is an opportunity for your life to change," he said emphatically.

I accepted this assignment with a mix of dread and excitement. "The best I can do is try, isn't it?"

As we stood to leave, Thod put a reassuring hand on my shoulder. "Gil-Hamesch wishes this."

We met Gil-Hamesch and the Cook at the car and drove several miles outside of Turfan to the private residence of a friend of the Cook's. The owner was a gracious man, a Uigher who had a small vineyard.

After dinner I retired early to write in my journal. I sat on the low bed of my closet-sized guest room with the pages open on my lap. I still couldn't imagine myself writing a book, but far stranger things had already happened to me. I was energized to make much more detailed notes than before. I recounted today's lessons with Thod and filled in some of the gaps from previous days' entries. When I closed the journal for the night I took out my golden caduceus and looked at it for a very long time, quietly exploring the depths of its symbolism—the twin serpents, the eight curves, the Fruits and the Jewels . . . the Form of Life.

It was beginning to tell me its secrets.

PART FOUR

The Nature of Power

20

The Desert Wanderer

WE DROVE AWAY FROM TURFAN EARLY THE NEXT MORNING, LEAVING A cloud of billowing dust in our wake. I watched the fine powdery cloud reach slowly up into the glow of the predawn sky. The long desert floor stretched out ahead of us. It was such a liberating feeling to be out in the wild country again. Once again we were immersed in vast expanses of barren valleys and dry river gorges. We drove for most of the day, sometimes on tracks and sometimes not. Several times the wheels sank into soft sand and only our high speed pushed us through. I had assumed, wrongly, that Gil-Hamesch, Thod and the Cook lived much closer to Turfan than this.

During the last part of our journey the scenery shifted gradually from a windswept, gravel-covered moonscape to numerous small creeks with stands of willows and birches, and occasional wetland marshes. As we drove up into the hills, rivers appeared looking like tangled threads, turning back on themselves, splitting apart around rock formations then coming together again. We seemed to be approaching an oasis of some sort. We entered a small valley which showed signs of having been irrigated and planted, and drove up to an adobe livestock barn with a thatched roof that sat among a grove of trees at the foot of a shrubby hill. I didn't see a village, just scattered farms.

I looked a question at Thod. This couldn't be our destination.

"Do you ride?" he said offhandedly and got out of the car. He swung open the double doors of the barn and I saw what he was referring to. Horses. Small, tough looking Mongol horses.

We spent the next hour transferring our supplies from the Land Rover to the backs of four of the horses, while three others waited to carry their human cargo. Thod chose a mount for me that looked well fed and groomed. He saddled him with a red wool blanket and handed me the rope bridle. I was comfortable around horses, but I had my doubts about the lack of padding for my backside.

Our little caravan set out slowly along a narrow path through a steep canyon. We followed a small rapidly flowing river with tall stands of birches, then turned up a narrow tributary, with soaring red canyon walls enveloping us. We emerged from the rocky canyon into a surreal landscape. On one side loomed a mountain of perfectly smooth red sand. On the other side, wind-carved beds of pink granite tilted at an angle as they jutted from vertical cliffs of ocher sandstone. The first sign that we were nearing habitation was the presence of low clay domes along the trail, their tattered prayer flags flapping in the wind.

Gobi Desert domed structures

As we rounded the corner of the last cliff, a howl of warm air blew through the canyon and our horses snorted and whinnied as they smelled the approaching oasis. Then the entire village suddenly appeared, one moment invisible, the next in full life and energy. A dozen children ran to greet Gil-Hamesch who threw them a handful of candy from his horse. In no time a greater crowd had gathered, and Thod introduced me all around. Children in handwoven clothes and old men with toothless grins greeted me with formal bows and less formal cheers. When Thod told them that I was a student of the Gardener the cheers turned to impressed looks of respect. I almost wished he hadn't said it.

A smiling man took our horses and supplies and I picked up my duffelbag and backpack. "Where will I be staying?" I asked Thod as we started walking.

"Over there." I looked up at a large, ancient building that dominated the village and appeared to have been built into the side of a cliff. "The Monastery of the Sacred Tree," he said matter-of-factly.

A small voice in my head dared to whisper, "*oh . . . of course.*" As if this moment had never been in doubt.

⌒

WE WALKED IN THE DIRECTION OF THE MONASTERY, THROUGH NARROW medieval streets lined by neatly swept clay homes with silver bleached timber roofs and brightly colored windows and doors. Every garden plot had a space for flowers and vegetables. There were trees everywhere. Pleasant faces greeted us as we passed. This was a gentle place, a good place. I could be happy here, I thought.

The original craftsmen, whoever they were, had used great skill in the creation of the monastery. From a distance it was nearly invisible to the eye, because it blended so artfully into the formation of the hill behind it. As we came closer I could see five separate levels of terraced patios with wrought iron railings and many old wooden doors leading inside. "No one lives here any more, at least not permanently," Thod explained as we entered through a heavy iron gate. "Occasionally there are travelers, and there are always a few goats." I couldn't see anyone, except for one long-haired goat who met us in the first courtyard.

The atmosphere inside was cool and silent. Some of the walls had beautiful but faded frescoes of Buddha painted on them. The remains of a portion of the structure were so old that only a few walls still stood. "Nobody knows how old this is," Thod said. "So much of the monastery is built upon still older ruins that long predate Buddhism."

"It didn't start out as a monastery then?" I was intensely curious.

"It was always a place of spiritual teaching, but who built it and for what particular devotion, that I don't know. Over time it has been used as a monastery, though what you see today is not a monastery in the usual sense. There are no monks or nuns here. Gil-Hamesch oversees the spiritual energies and the deeper meaning of this place. You will learn more, don't be impatient."

I didn't ask further. We came to a more recent looking building with multicolored murals of ancient scenes vividly painted on the doors and patio. I noticed an ornately carved fountain, but at the time there was no water in it. The paintings and tile work consisted primarily of colorful, complex patterns of flowers, birds and geometric shapes. There were other patios too. Some of them had been entirely tiled with orange, white, and blue geometric figures. Still, there were no people to be seen. I wondered about the countless people who had spent time here over the centuries,

Further on, we entered an ancient cave that had been dug into the rock cliff. Thod opened a low plank door and we stepped over a stone threshold into a room, a cell, really. He lit a candle as we entered and I could see a fireplace, a simple bed, a pitcher of water, and on one wall an altar. "You are not the first to stay here," he said with obvious understatement. The walls were stained and smudged from ages of use and soot. In the close, damp air of the cell I could smell the residue of incense. It was the fragrance of antiquity.

Thod left me there to sleep for the night. I walked the perimeter of the room, touching the plaster walls, taking in the atmosphere before sitting down on the floor to collect my thoughts. I couldn't help wondering who had been here before me, what meditations were imprinted in the memory of these walls. Wanting to calm my mind, I started thinking about the Jesuit priest who had come here seven hundred years ago and discovered the *Song of Eternity*. What had Dorothy called it? an instruction manual for the human soul. I was finding that out for myself, in my own stumbling way. I thought about the Order of the Sacred Tree, the group of people that the priest drew around him, who loved humanity and lived by the principles of the ageless *Song*. And then, centuries later, the Gardener, who breathed new life into the work of the Order. I never forgot what Dorothy told me about those people and their deep commitment to service. In what way the Order might still be connected to the monastery I didn't yet know. Thod had been a little mysterious about what went on here. I couldn't help wondering why the monastery was kept up as well as it was, and what purpose the new buildings served if there were no permanent residents. Who were the *non*-permanent residents, then? And why were they here? Why was *I* here? I still had no satisfactory answer to that question.

Ancient Gobi Desert monastery near Turfan.

After a while I couldn't think about it any more. Fatigue drew me to my bed, but I resisted falling asleep, fearing that I would have unsettling dreams in such a place. But there were no dreams at all, as it turned out. I slept more soundly than I had in ages.

When I woke, it was difficult at first to orient myself to where I was, or even *who* I was. I had no awareness of time or place. I could have been Rip van Winkle. It was only when I heard Thod's voice outside my door that I snapped back to the here and now. He opened the door as he spoke. He was shaking with excitement. "A Desert Wanderer showed up here last night! It has to be an omen, that you both arrived at the same time. And now he wants to see you!" I had never seen Thod like this.

I was still wrapped in the deep stillness that I had awakened to, so it took me a moment to realize what he was saying. And then nerves and apprehension kicked in. What would a Desert Wanderer want with me? Thod waited as I dressed and spread up my bed and grabbed my daypack. "Hurry," he urged. "He's waiting for you downstairs."

We headed down a narrow adobe stairway to a wide patio that looked out over the village. At the edge of the balcony, with his back to us, stood a man with long, wild black hair, wearing a wool coat that reached down to his worn leather riding boots. Ragged and disheveled as he appeared, there was no doubt this man had power. It emanated from him like an electrical charge. As he turned his dark, weathered face to us I saw his eyes. They looked directly at me with a steady intensity. He gave a slight nod and Thod whispered to me, "Go with him."

The man turned abruptly and walked down the stairs that led towards a grove of willows. With a last glance back at Thod I followed him down the stairs to a winding path in the sand that was punctuated with jagged stones. We walked in silence for some distance, then stopped at a large boulder and climbed a steep, sandy hill, which he effortlessly mounted while I slipped and slid with every step.

At last we reached a small cave cut into the foot of a high, red granite cliff. The old plank door over the cave entrance had been left unlocked, but he had to push hard to open it. Once my eyes adjusted to the dark I noticed a wooden box in one corner. The Desert Wanderer blew aside a thick layer of dust and opened the box. Inside the case a cluster of old artifacts lay in a jumble. I saw an old knife with a bone handle, a braided leather horse bridle, several coins, a broken clay pot, and a curious carved spiral staff. In a corner of the box lay a frayed pair of white leather sandals with thin straps.

As my eyes further adjusted to the light I could see a wooden altar attached to the wall. To my surprise, it held a small silver crucifix and three gold statues of the caduceus identical to mine. All at once I knew that this was the room where the Gardener had stayed more than a hundred years before. And I knew what I had to do. I reached into my pack and placed my amulet next to the other three. Still, there were no words or gestures from the cloaked man in the room with me, only the crackling energy of his presence. This was an important moment, that much I understood—some kind of completion that I was a part of, that I had been led to. This was what Dorothy could see for me.

I leaned back against the cave wall and closed my eyes, silently offering a prayer to my dear old friend and mentor. I thanked her for inspiring me to come here, and I promised her two things—that I would someday find Father Franck, and that whatever knowledge I might gain I would share with the world. I knew without a doubt that I would make good on my promises.

I opened my eyes and saw the Desert Wanderer removing the curved staff from the box. He blew off the dust, then with his right hand he turned the stick gracefully in several broad arcs before offering it to me.

It felt smooth and comfortable in my hand. Emulating his motion, I made slow spirals in the air with it.

He sat down in a corner so dark I could barely see him. I knew I was expected to sit down too, which I did, facing him several feet away with the stick at my side. Something was about to happen. I closed my eyes and tried to move into a receptive state. He began to hum a quiet monotone chant that thrust me immediately into a startlingly vivid dream.

I wasn't in the cave, I was walking across a barren, windy reach of the Gobi Desert, with the Desert Wanderer following a few paces behind. I looked down and saw that I was wearing a white robe. The sandals on my feet matched the ones I had seen in the box. We carried on a long conversation, he and I, using only our minds.

We reached a fire pit where three men in white hooded robes sat quietly waiting for us. I sat down beside them, while the Desert Wanderer stood a little behind me. The dry wind whipped roughly around us as one of the men began chanting and drawing in the sand with a stick. The scene was familiar. He was chanting verses of the *Song of Eternity*. I already knew everyone here, but I couldn't remember from where. And I couldn't quite see what it was that they were drawing in the sand.

Then, each of the three men stood up, turned, and walked away in a different direction. I remained seated while a single thought expressed itself in my head, again and again: *I must keep repeating the verses so that I can remember them forever. I must share them with others so that the verses will never be forgotten.* At last I stood and walked away from the fire, straight out into the desert—in the fourth direction. The dream was as vivid as any experience in the real world, so I was startled to find myself suddenly back in the darkness of the cave. My guide motioned for us to leave. He stood up, as fierce and mysterious and silent as ever. I picked up my staff and followed him from the cave, still immersed in the dream.

We returned to the monastery and the Desert Wanderer left me at the gate. Not a word had been exchanged between us. I had no idea how much time had passed, but the sun was high in the sky now.

I opened the gate and found Gil-Hamesch seated in a large chair on the patio. He grinned and waved me over to his side. In the next moment Thod appeared, dressed in burgundy pants and shirt, his black hair shining in the sun. The Cook was with him, carrying a long musical instrument that looked like a cross between an oboe and a trumpet. He raised the horn above his head and sounded three long notes. By now, I was in a state of simply watching things unfold around me. "We are summoning the elders of the village," Thod said, putting a brotherly hand on my shoulder. "They are coming to celebrate your initiation into the *Book of Creation*." I looked at him questioningly. "Such an event always calls for celebration," he explained, "especially since you have come from so far away. It is not a time to be somber."

"I'm not somber," I said, "just a little overwhelmed by everything." It was then that I noticed the Desert Wanderer standing silently near the stairs, watching us. "Where will he go from here?" I asked. Thod looked up at him and then back at me. "That depends on you," he said, to my alarm. I had no idea what was going on. And then suddenly, I did. "Please tell him for me to go to the province of Amdo in Tibet, and tell him I have seen the first sign for a new alliance," I said. I remembered the old Tibetan master's words about the terma. Thod walked over to the man and whispered in his ear. He abruptly turned and left without even a look back.

Thod returned and looked at the stick in my hand. "I see you have found your immortality staff."

"It feels good in my hand. What is it?" He motioned for me to walk with him back towards my room.

"The Kashis use curved branches to mimic the spinning of the Form of Life," he said. "By concentrating on the spinning they believe they create energetic life forms called 'spirit seeds' that have enough power to continue on after a person has died. Many of these seeds will ripen and bring about spontaneous awakenings to the Supreme Truth. It is like the sound from a plucked string—it continues long after the instrument is still." He explained that by repeating the motion and reinforcing the intent, the Kashi believe they might create enough energy so that after they die, they will re-awaken in a future life to their memories in this life. "The Desert Wanderer gave it to you for a reason."

"I assumed he did," I said, still trying to clear my mind, and not sure what I thought about my impending public initiation in front of the village elders. I tried to discuss the dream I had when I was with the Desert Wanderer, but Thod refused to talk about it. He said that if I didn't understand it now, I would some day. And then he left me alone in my cave room again.

I didn't feel ready for anything more today. All I wanted to do was reflect on the puzzlingly real dream and what it could mean. After what seemed like a long time, but was probably only an hour, I heard temple bells ring out from somewhere in the village. A young man with dark wavy hair, a large nose and dark eyes came to my door and very politely asked me to follow him.

He led me through a part of the monastery I hadn't seen yet, and into a large chamber with a domed ceiling. I entered alone and seated myself on one of several cushions on the floor. A few large candles dimly illuminated the room. I looked up and saw a single skylight with a figure eight painted on it. Barely visible on the walls were old frescoes portraying what appeared to be Kashi patriarchs and matriarchs of the past. No one else was here at first, then Thod entered and sat at my right side. "Be silent," he whispered, "and immerse yourself in the Supreme Truth as deeply as you can."

I felt uncomfortable with all this attention. I didn't feel that I had earned the right to be initiated. I finally put these thoughts aside and focused on being silent within myself.

A loud gong sounded from the courtyard and Gil-Hamesch entered the room. He seated himself in front of me, radiating the most comforting lovingness. After a while he cleared his throat and began reciting the *Book of Creation* to me, two stanzas at a time, pausing as Thod translated. His voice rose and fell in a loud rhythmic chant. I could feel his eyes sweeping over my body as he recited the verses. "Here begins the verse that is called *The First World*," Thod said after the customary Invocation—and once more I was transported into the powerful energies of the *Song of Eternity*:

The Ocean of the Cosmos slept for eternity, unseen and unknown.

In it floated a great sphere containing the potential of all things.

The Serpent, which lay sleeping, encircling the great sphere,

bit its own tail and began to awaken.

The verses described the unfolding of life from the undifferentiated cosmos to the manifestation of Form in the Tree of Life, with its great Fruits that would become the Jewels of Redemption. The words vibrated in every atom of my body and into my soul. They spoke of male and female and the spiraling dance of life and the great compassion of the primordial Serpents, from which all life arose. The recitation closed with these words:

Herein lies the Road to the Valley of Miracles.

May all living beings find joy!

After the recitation, Gil-Hamesch signaled me to follow him out to the large tiled courtyard. He walked slowly and with measured steps. I couldn't imagine how old he could be. I guessed somewhere between seventy and ninety. Several dozen people were seated around the plaza waiting for us, equal numbers of men and women—the village dignitaries. I sat down on a brown wool blanket with Gil-Hamesch and Thod. The Cook was seated on a wooden chair in one corner. He picked up a dombro and placed it across his lap and began to play. Then he stopped and proceeded to sing a song, eerie in its beauty and different from the ones I had heard in the desert cabin. I leaned to ask Thod about the strange tonal quality, and he said that this was Central Asian throat singing, where the singer produces two or even three harmonic notes simultaneously. It was mesmerizing.

Two men dressed in orange and two women in light yellow dresses stepped out through an open doorway and moved gracefully to the center of the patio. In unison they raised their hands to heart level, palms facing upwards, as if they were making an offering. They stood motionless with eyes closed, awaiting some signal to begin.

"Watch closely," Gil-Hamesch told me, just as a truly astonishing music and dance performance began.

First, a deep resonant sound came from behind us. Looking around, I saw that musicians had stationed themselves all around the patio, not in a single group, creating the effect of sound rising from every direction. The dancers moved in seamless coordination with the melodies. The Kashi music was a thing unto itself, yet it was faintly familiar to my Western ear—like a combination of mournful Celtic pipes, contemplative Middle Eastern drones, pulsing African rhythms, and devotional Tibetan chanting.

The soul-wrenching pleas of an oboe-sized horn overlaid the deep rumbling of a long trumpet, accompanied by more throat singing. The repetitive melodies were produced from a bowed instrument, like a cello, and a plucked long-necked instrument with drone strings. Now and then, high pitched wails pierced the air from a small bone flute.

It took no imagination to be transported into the timeless landscape of caravans and camels crossing the steppe lands. In that music I felt the suffering of the nomads of Central Asia, but also their nobility to rise above all challenges. And I intimately felt their deep love of life. Without a word, or even suggestion of religion, they managed to create a profoundly moving and spiritual experience using only the sound from strings, flutes and voices.

Like the musicians, the dancers seemed to be focusing their attention inwardly, as if performing a precisely choreographed meditation. The whole performance affected me in some way that I cannot adequately explain. I felt it directly, in different parts of my body. I wasn't moving my body to the harmonics, the harmonics were moving me.

Between numbers I asked Gil-Hamesch to explain their meaning. Thod translated. "In the dancing," he said, "you are seeing the balanced energy of male and female. The Kashi believe that for a man to be fully awake he must contain within himself certain qualities of the female. For a woman to be complete she must do the same with traditionally male qualities. The ideal is to express the highest degree of one's body-form, while balancing it with the qualities of the opposite form. And so we teach dance and martial arts and music to everyone, and we give equal honor to men and women. In this way we create a culture of balance and harmony, with the greatest potential for wisdom. Your golden amulet showed that to you. Did you recognize the symbols?"

"The two serpents . . . "

Gil-Hamesch nodded, and Thod continued: "In the simplest terms the serpents represent the equal male and female energies of the created world—the dynamic tension that drives the cycles of time and growth. And here we are, the human versions of those twin forces. And so we dance . . . and we sing." Thod grinned at me, and I felt truly welcomed into their ancient culture.

The final piece of music was quiet and contemplative, ending in the barest whisper of sound, like the gentle exhalation of a breath. When it was over, I expected everyone to slip into meditation. Instead, an enthusiastic roar went up around us and everyone stood up. Several of the elders came over and embraced me, smiling and laughing. I smiled and laughed with them.

I caught Gil-Hamesch's eye and whispered *thank you*. Sometimes the most ordinary words are the only ones that will do.

21

Soham

AND THEN THE REAL CELEBRATIONS BEGAN. IT QUICKLY BECAME A NOISY, happy scene as the entire population of the village converged on the terrace carrying platters of food for a feast. There was such clear good will around me. Thod did his best to introduce me to everyone. We sat on the ground at low tables, eating carrot lentil soup from unfired clay bowls and enjoying the yellow Xinjiang grapes mixed with hummi-melon, yogurt, rice, and raisins. I was an object of great curiosity, especially with the children, who laughed delightedly at my efforts to communicate with them. At some point two of the grandmothers gathered the youngest children into a group and escorted them from the terrace and down the outside steps.

When we had finished eating, a spontaneous band of four men started playing music, which brought others to their feet to dance. This was so different from my first initiation in the desert, when I had gone immediately into the privacy of my room to meditate on the meaning of the teachings. Today, there was no time for reflection. Apparently, it wasn't intended for me to be alone right now. Maybe the music and dance and the sheer life-affirming joy of these people were also part of my initiation.

Thod leaned close to my ear. "I want you to meet someone." He led me over to a place where we looked down into a garden terrace below. There, I saw a circle of children sitting in rapt attention while a beautiful woman dressed in brilliant tribal clothing and heavy silver jewelry was performing a dance in front of them. She moved every part of her body in a slow, harmonious motion, tracing spirals and circles in the space where she danced. I could see that she was speaking in a poetic rhythm as she moved, but I couldn't hear the words because of the noise around me.

"Who is she?" I asked, fascinated.

"Soham," he said. "The special friend I told you about."

This was the woman? I had just assumed that Thod's "special friend" would be a female version of Thod, but that didn't appear to be the case. As we watched, I realized that Soham was telling a story to the village children and illustrating it with the movements of her body. The children swayed and sang in response. "She is the Keeper of the Stories," Thod said. "This is how Kashi children learn, through hearing the stories of their elders. Knowledge must be repeated for it to live. It must become part of one's body as much as the mind."

"What is she telling them?"

"She sings about the Time Before, when all the tribes of Central Asia lived in peace and plenty. The children need to know that there once was such a time . . . before the tribes grew into nations and the nations descended into the Great War, with its plagues and starvation. That was many thousands of years ago."

"It sounds like you're talking about a lost Eden," I said, ". . . prehistory."

Thod gave me one of his looks. "What do you mean by prehistory? In our tradition it *is* history. It has been handed down as carefully as if it were printed on the pages of a book—generation after generation of the Keepers of the Stories, sworn to preserving the meaning of the past."

We stood at the iron railing watching Soham dance her story for the children and listening to their voices respond. I didn't venture any more opinions about what was or wasn't history, let alone mythology. In a way, I was surprised that Thod was being so non-analytical. What he said next surprised me even more.

"The two world wars of the 20th century were only the latest tidal waves to reach across the millennia after the upheavals from the first Great War that took place here in Central Asia. The world is still healing from it. That war resulted in a massive slow migration and relocation of people across the continents of Asia and Europe. Some say that the distant ancestors of today's Jews were among the surviving tribes."

I had a quick image of Zeker, the Jewish CIS agent, and our bizarre conversation on the park bench in Kashgar—and how convinced he was that Hitler had been trying to find the secret temple of the Jews in the Gobi Desert, searching for secret powers. Before this trip, I hadn't known that there were large populations of Jews in Central Asia.

"Do you really believe that the Jews originally came from this part of the world?"

"I have no belief. But there are tales about groups who migrated to the Middle East from a Central Asian homeland. They practiced the faith of their ancestors, which was possibly the first true monotheistic religion in the world." Thod stopped. "Is this of interest to you, or shall we return to the celebrations?"

"It's of great interest to me," I assured him.

"The story is this: After the Great War some of the survivors who migrated to northern Europe believed that the ones who went into the Middle East had secretly carried the Central Asian spiritual books and teachings away with them—had, in effect, stolen the knowledge that could give them the power to win back their lost homeland. That was the knowledge contained in the *Song of Eternity* and, especially, the Shield of Power."

I recalled Thod's earlier mentions of the Shield of Power. So far, he hadn't volunteered to teach me anything about it, and I don't know what I'd have said if he did. I was in no hurry to become a warrior.

"As you may know," he continued, "Hitler was fascinated by the mystical and occult, especially the secret teachings of Central Asia and Tibet. Somehow, he learned about the Shield of Power and how it gives absolute invincibility against any enemy. It became part of his fixation about the Jews. He wanted that power for himself. But he failed to understand that such a thing is under protection and cannot be stolen."

"Under protection how? By Gil-Hamesch?"

"Think about what you already know," Thod said. "Think about the centuries of people coming here to be initiated into the *Song of*

Eternity. And about seekers everywhere who have cleansed themselves for service to humanity, in whatever spiritual tradition. What happens to the energy of such dedication? We know about the Jesuit priest who took his knowledge to Europe, and the Gardener, and how they gathered people around them of like mind and heart. Those and others like them are the ones who work quietly behind the stage of history, while others choose to become well-known teachers of truth. Over time, the combined spiritual power in such people builds upon itself until it becomes a living Shield of Power. Evil intentions can only advance so far before they are turned back. In that way, the greatest knowledge becomes its own protection. It is a matter of intention and the proper uses of the will." He glanced over at me with a quick smile. "That is how Gil-Hamesch or Soham would explain it."

Thod waved to Soham, who was now walking up the steps to our patio level. The children trailed behind her, looking like a flock of colorful young ducklings trying to keep up with their mother. He spoke in English to her. "Soham, this is my friend Larry, from the United States."

"I know," she said, extending a graceful hand to me. "Welcome. I hope that Thod has not been too harsh a teacher. I know he has." She was smiling as she said it.

"Not at all," I protested.

Up close, Soham was a beautiful woman with striking cheekbones, long black hair and large dark eyes that looked deep and thoughtful, yet playful. I recognized her accent as Kazakh. She had the Central Asian features that reminded me of Native Americans.

We sat for a while on the ledge of the patio, sipping tea and watching the colors of the red cliffs change with the movement of sun and clouds. "Your English is very good," I said to her.

"I studied it in school, and once I worked in a bank that catered to foreign customers and oil companies," she said. "But now I spend much of my time with the children. I want them to know the power of their cultural roots. We go out into the hills and I teach them about Nature, and we listen to try to hear the *Song of Eternity*. It is very sweet working with the little ones."

Soham excused herself for a few minutes when two young girls pulled at her skirt wanting to show her something. "Everyone loves her," Thod said when she was gone.

"I can see why. How did she come to live in the village? I can tell by her speech that she wasn't born here."

"No, she came from a region to the west, in what is now Kazakhstan. Her people had the same cultural roots as ours—roots that are slowly disappearing with the advance of the modern age into Asia. Her family was forced to flee to Xinjiang for political reasons. But through all the hardships she always loved books and had a mind that was hungry for learning. She was befriended by a Chinese woman doctor who secretly brought her books and talked to her about Eastern philosophies and Western ideas. When Soham was older she returned to her homeland. Her passion and dedication was to revive the ancient spiritual teachings."

"How was she able to find teachers there who hadn't been silenced?" I asked, having recently been exposed in a very small way to the intimidating atmosphere of the Chinese authorities.

"She told me that she was initiated directly by the mountains, not by any teacher. After that experience she finally realized the true essence of the teachings of her ancestors. When Soham came to our village Gil-Hamesch immediately recognized her depth and asked her to stay and teach. She calls this her home now, but her home is really everywhere. We call such a person a 'knower'—one who understands. She radiates wisdom like the sunlight."

We watched Soham in the distance, encircled by young girls. "When we go out walking in nature together she looks for special places of beauty," Thod said, "like entrances to valleys, or rivers, and there she builds a small shrine of sticks, sheep horns, cloth flags and rocks to focus the natural energy. That is her description of the process. I see in it the power of her intention to affect the energy field around her. We are alike in our love of truth, but different in our ways of expressing it."

"You are a fortunate man," I said.

"She has been trying to show me what she sees when she looks out at the world. She tells me that I am not hopeless." Those were the first self-deprecating words I had ever heard from his lips.

Soham rejoined us. "We have been talking about you," Thod said.

"I know, I could feel it. And now I am going to take your student away for a little while," she said. For an instant I glimpsed the power in her eyes. "Gil-Hamesch wishes me to explain certain things to you about your initiation—about the *Song of Eternity*. Come with me . . ."

22

The Fundamental Harmonic

I FOLLOWED SOHAM THROUGH THE RAMBLING MONASTERY GROUNDS until we came to the carved double doors of a temple hall and entered. Her feet glided softly and without effort, as the embroidered hem of her long dress whispered across the tiled floor. In this large, white walled room high windows opened to the cool air. We seated ourselves on a blue and gold wool carpet, facing each other. A tapestry on the wall above us depicted the two entwined snakes of the caduceus superimposed onto a tree, with a field of stars in the background.

"I know that you must return to your homeland very soon," Soham said, "but there is so much more for you to understand. You have experienced only the beginnings. This will continue for the rest of your life and beyond, believe me."

Her warm voice put me at ease, even as I prepared myself for whatever it was that Gil-Hamesch had instructed her to teach me. I recalled the cryptic words he had said to me that first day in the Kashgar marketplace: *the beginnings*—and my not knowing what he meant. It was becoming clear to me that I was only at the first stages of a long, long journey.

"By now, you have your own idea of the *Song of Eternity*," Soham said, "but I want you to see it in a new way. What if I told you that the *Song of Eternity* is a romantic courting song . . . and as with every courting song, there are two versions: the one you sing, and the one your beloved sings to you. The *Song of Eternity* is a powerful love song directed to the Divine, pleading for the power behind the

Supreme Truth to draw closer and set us free. And it is also a song *from* the Divine, imploring us to return home."

She paused while I absorbed her poetic imagery. "Your cry at birth is your first call to the Divine. That call is always answered, though you do not remember now. Your next call to the Divine is the first expression of your True Voice during your youth. And that call is always answered too, by the appearance of an opportunity that comes only once in your lifetime. But when we are young, we are often too weak or distracted to respond when our destiny appears before us. That is why we have the *Song of Eternity*. It is a new opportunity to regain what we have lost." Soham looked deeply into my eyes and I saw the eyes of the goddess in my dreams—what I know now was the archetypal symbol of life itself. I saw the essence of compassion and strength—impersonal, loving, offering me the gift of insight, challenging me to rise above my small identity as Larry Andrews.

Suddenly, I couldn't draw breath. The sense of loss, the loss of connection with the Divine, was so profound that I wanted to weep for the emptiness inside me. I was still the six-year-old child who had, just once, seen the unity of life; I was still the teenager whose mentor tried to help him remember it; I was still the man whose mind had overridden his heart too many times because his heart couldn't be trusted. At least I could admit to that now. And maybe, just maybe, I was being offered a new chance at life.

Soham smiled again and passed her hand through the air between us, as if to clear it. "Your past wounds have no ultimate reality, they only cloud what is true. In this moment I am speaking to the real you, the one with the True Voice, and I tell you that there is a dormant awareness sleeping in the cells of your body and in your heart. It is called the Dormant Key, and the *Song of Eternity* is meant to awaken it. Do not be sad," she said, laughing at my sober face. "There is every reason to be joyful."

"It's just my feeling that I haven't done what I could have done with my life."

"Oh dear," she said in mock horror, "and now your life is over and you have failed. What a sad way to want to be!"

I saw what she meant immediately. It was my choice . . . it was always my choice.

"You see," she said, "activating the Dormant Key means that you stop debating religion or philosophy with yourself and start a dialogue with the Form of Life inside you. And that dialogue will begin to change you. If you do not activate that key, then the *Song of Eternity* is only meaningless words.

"Look at the entwined serpents, and the tree that is heavy with its fruits." She indicated the tapestry above us. "That is the Form of Life in its simplest representation. You may think of it as the primeval cosmic sound that impels every living being to unfold its highest potential and return to its Divine source in full knowledge. The Form of Life is inside you and has always been inside you, like an ideal plan—but you shape it by your own thoughts and beliefs. Most people's Form of Life is distorted in places. A trained observer can see this clearly. Illness, mental or physical, will deform it, as will attitudes that are uncompassionate or excessively sexual or too coolly intellectual. The ideal Form of Life is rhythmic, smooth, spinning, not fixed in its shape. If you could see a highly evolved person's Form it would appear bright with light, but within it would be the constant interplay of energy that shows itself as spinning filaments of golden light."

"Soham," I interrupted, "I had a vision of such a thing . . . with an Indian sadhu in Benares. It was a swirling golden vortex, with a serpent spiraling inside it. I remember the sadhu called it the sign of life. But really it was the Form of Life, wasn't it?" A light went on in my head: the Tibetan dorje, the Greek caduceus and my amulet— they were all the Form of Life. This was the thread connecting the experiences of my journey through Asia.

"One day you may be able to see deeper into it. The serpent is your life force. It is probably the most ancient of the world's symbols—that, and the Tree of Life. You have come here to understand the origins of these symbols, even if that is not what you thought you were doing," she said with a gentle smile. "Perhaps the oldest depiction is contained in the *Song of Eternity*. It has made its way around the world many times over countless centuries. Whenever you hear a myth about a sacred serpent, or a tree with divine fruits, you are probably hearing the traces of the *Song of Eternity*. So many of the ancient tribes of Asia adopted these symbols.

"In the far past, when our people experienced the first Great War, and the plague decimated our village, there were only a few cures that could help us: our knowledge of the healing herbs, our practice of the sacred dances, and our reciting of the *Song of Eternity*. We will never forget the fires of the invaders or the diseases that they brought. But we have learned to forgive. And we have faith in our ancestors' wisdom. That is why we are able to be a peaceful people deep in our hearts."

"And so, when you danced for the children . . . "

"I was dancing the Form of Life. I was offering them my energy to take into themselves with my words, so that the meaning of the words would become part of their own Form of Life. You see, the first Kashi masters created a powerful intention to ensure that the *Song of Eternity* would be an immortal teaching—that it would pass down to every generation."

I felt that she was inviting me to ask questions, and so I did. "How were you chosen to teach the children? It must be a great honor."

"A great trust," she corrected. "After the Great War a band of men came together to find a way to protect the ancient wisdom. They became the first Desert Wanderers. They traveled the world as storytellers and recited the *Song of Eternity*. In each village they would find an individual, usually a woman in the tribe, who was the keeper of the stories. And they would initiate her into the direct experience of the Supreme Truth, and then teach her the Dance of the Form of Life. She was entrusted to keep the power of the Kashi teaching alive. In this way, through the travels of the Desert Wanderers, the *Song of Eternity* came to be absorbed into the many religions of Asia and Europe."

"And yet it's not a religion in itself . . . "

"I think of it as the great mother of spiritual wisdom, endlessly nurturing her children, all of them, without exception. As for me, I was not exactly 'chosen.' The children came around me and their mothers saw that I was the one to tell the stories and teach the *Song of Eternity* to their sons and daughters. Women sense these things," she winked playfully. "It is an unspoken arrangement that works very well."

She pointed again to the tapestry. "You will find this ancient symbol in the story of the Temptation in the Garden of Eden, in the

Jewish Old Testament," she continued, "but the inner meaning is not generally understood, except in the teachings of the Kaballah." She went on to describe how the ten fruits on the Hebrew Kabalistic Tree of Life are similar to the Kashi Tree of Life, and how she believed that the eight crests of the entwined serpents' bodies corresponded one-for-one with the Buddhist Eightfold Path.

"In India, the *Song of Eternity* resonates in the yogic practice of awakening the chakras by a magical serpent. The Chinese Taoists believe that the world and the Taoist religion were created by two serpents—one male and one female, named Fu Xi and Nu Hua."

Those were the twin serpents in the art book I bought in Kashgar, when I first met Thod. "But, couldn't these universal archetypal symbols naturally occur to people everywhere in the world, rather than coming from a single source?" I asked.

Instead of arguing, Soham agreed with me. "It is true, snake and tree symbols can be found in art everywhere. But I believe that there is a unique symbolic signature that identifies an intentionally placed Dormant Key from our Kashi ancestors: The snakes need to face each other in a male-female pair, and have exactly four bends to their bodies, like a double figure eight. Other typical embellishments might include wings, a sun and moon, a halo of stars, or fruits on the serpents' bodies."

"That was the form on the caduceus I was given."

"Yes. But really, it doesn't matter whether this song was first sung here or somewhere else, or arose spontaneously to many people in different places. Spiritual traditions have been shared for centuries as they passed along the Silk Road—and each tradition has enriched the other. Whether you hear the Divine speak to you through the Bible or the Koran or the *Baghavad Gita* is only of secondary importance. What matters most is to respond by awakening to the Divine Spirit that lies hidden within you. The Supreme Truth is everywhere. Every person can discover the whisperings of the *Song of Eternity* if they stop to look closely at their life."

From somewhere outside the hall where we sat a wind chime tinkled in the breeze, like a reminder for me to just listen and just feel. Even in this serene setting, even with Soham's calm voice, I couldn't completely stop my logical brain from intruding on the delicate presence of Truth.

"You have heard the *Book of Creation* for the first time today," she said quietly. "Do you remember where it was said that when the two serpents rose from the Great Lake they shed their skins, and those skins became the many religions of the world? Every religion has an outer form that is beautiful and unique to its people. But the inner essence of all religions is the same."

"I believe that," I said. "I have since I was very young."

"It isn't necessary to believe any more than that. But now you are at another place in your life where you can be shown what is behind that belief—the power of it. In the *Song of Eternity* is the power to awaken and the power to heal. This power can be transmitted in a strong way through initiation, and in a lesser way by studying, reciting, and singing the verses."

Here I sat, far from the world I was born into, far from the ideas that that world thrived on. I was an initiate, yet I felt like a complete novice. And yet... I *was* changed by what was taking place within and around me. It was a small change and it was a stupifyingly huge change. It would take a while for me to know exactly in what way. But *change* was the operative word, that much I was certain of.

Soham wasn't finished with me. There was more to our session beneath the tapestry in this empty temple room. "Gil-Hamesch has said that some day soon many people will begin an evolutionary shift just from hearing the verses of the *Song of Eternity*." Her voice was the storyteller's. " . . . whether they have been here or not, and whether they receive a direct initiation or not. We believe that our people are like great-grandparents in a modern world that rarely stops to remember its roots. We have a message to share. The message is that wisdom is more important than knowledge—and that true wisdom comes from within. The Divine hides just beneath the surface of everything that you can touch or believe in. And it hides inside each of us, too." She lowered her voice. "If I could be sad, it would be because I believe the message is still ahead of its time for most people."

We sat in silence for a long time. "Why didn't Thod tell me these things?" I asked at last.

"Thod isn't so interested in myths or in history. And he has no use for talk about 'the Divine.' He is fascinated with modern science.

He thinks the *Song of Eternity* should be taken as a mirror of the body's physiology, and that the gods in our epic stories are only biological symbols. I'm not saying he's wrong. He and I debate this all the time. That is how he chooses to paint his world. I prefer poetry over science."

I liked Soham immensely. It made me feel good just to listen to her speak. "Can you tell me about your own philosophy, and how you came to it?" I asked.

"I told you—I don't have a philosophy!" she said and laughed. "I only have a dialogue with the Divine, who already knows everything!"

"Then what about the Divine . . . how would you describe it?"

"In words? That is the most difficult. The Divine is that which everyone knows intimately—and no one talks about. It is the presence of Spirit that sparkles in the light and touches you in the wind." She moved her hands as she spoke, imitating the wind and the dancing light. "It is the eternal awareness that wants to experience life through your eyes. It is the true author of your deeply personal life story.

"The Divine is the universal singer that wants to sing through your True Voice. And in the long run, your True Voice is all that matters—not your body, not your emotions, not your personal history or your accomplishments. Only the unique message that you have to share. Because life is a symphony, an eternal song, made up of each of these unique voices singing their songs to the stars, over and over again, but in ever-new combinations. *The Song of Eternity* is the Fundamental Harmonic that goes on forever, ancient and new at the same time. Hold this in your heart and never let it go."

She looked into my eyes and smiled, with a depth of lovingness that seemed to reach back to the very source of life. "That is the gift that Gil-Hamesch wished me to transmit to you today. It is the rest of the initiation. Now, join with me in meditation for the awakening of all beings."

My eyes were closed and I had moved into the silence of meditation, when the room began to fill with sound, very soft at first, and very beautiful, like the sounds of nature stirring at dawn. Soham was singing a song in a language that I had never heard before. Something ancient, I was sure of that, and it pulsed through my body. When the song was done I didn't want to move from this place.

Soham touched my forehead to impart a blessing. It was time to go.

We returned to the central patio and found only a few people still there. I said goodnight to Thod and Soham and stumbled through the dark until I found my small grotto. I lit a single candle and lay down on the bed with my hands behind my head, just being there, which I now understood was everywhere.

23

The Shield of Power

DAWN INFLAMED THE DISTANT MOUNTAINS LIKE A WIND BLOWING over ash-covered coals. I was seated on the parapet of the terrace outside my cell. Behind me the crescent moon hovered in a field of stars. A woman's song drifted over the monastery fortifications, rising slowly and with feeling, then dropping in exotic scales. I wrapped my hands securely around a hot cup of jasmine tea and tried to imagine how I could return to the frame of mind I would need to meet with the Chinese engineers in Urumchi. In the last weeks my thoughts had been almost completely immersed in contemplation of inward things. My senses were still feeling exposed, almost painful. My perception of colors and sounds, and my emotions themselves, had become so heightened that I continued to worry about being able to fit back into the normal world. But I had to.

Before I had left home I faxed the Urumchi Office of Technology with the approximate time of my arrival, give or take a couple of weeks, and they had replied that they were eagerly awaiting my visit. Now, that window of time was quickly closing and I had no choice but to honor my commitment as soon as possible, even though Urumchi had long since become Plan B. I couldn't afford to ignore the realities and responsibilities of my professional life.

Over a breakfast of stewed grains and grapes, I spoke of my concerns to Thod. He suggested I stay a while longer here and work with Li Po, a Chinese martial artist. "Li Po will introduce you to the Kashi Shield of Power," he said. "It will act as the buffer between the inner stillness of your life in the desert and the chaos of the world you will soon return to."

"I don't know," I said. "Isn't there something less . . ." I searched for the right word "*drastic*?" I couldn't see myself wielding the Shield of Power, when all I needed was a little help reassimilating.

Thod barked a laugh. "Gil-Hamesch gave me permission to offer you the first degrees of training. You won't be able to do any great harm, no matter how hard you try. But you will be more in control of your reactions. Li Po is a master."

"So I won't be invincible in war?" I smiled back at him.

"It depends on how you define war," he said. "I will arrange for your training."

~

AFTER BREAKFAST THOD OPENED THE NOTEBOOK WE USED FOR OUR translation of the *Book of Truth* and the *Book of Creation*. We spent the rest of the morning refining the translation of the text. The difficulty, and the art, was in finding English words that could adequately convey the multiple layers of the original language. Sometimes we just had to trust in the power behind the words to reach directly into the reader's mind and heart.

In the afternoon Thod took me to the Courtyard of the Sacred Dancers, where a middle-aged Chinese man waited for me. He was dressed all in black and appeared gentle, even childlike at first, but I suspected that underneath the unprepossessing exterior hid a jaguar, keenly sizing up everyone and everything. Because his English was awkward, Thod stayed for the first part of our session together, to help with the introductory concepts.

We began by sitting opposite each other on the stone pavement. "There are two kinds of power," Li Po said, looking steadily into my eyes while Thod elaborated on that statement. "One comes from manipulating people and situations," Thod said, "and the other derives from strength of character. At its root, the Shield of Power is the science of character development."

It was something of a letdown to discover that this tremendous energy, which apparently could be unleashed to stunning effect, was all a matter of character development. I had expected something far more focused and pre-emptive—more warrior-like. But I reminded myself that I was only being shown the first steps of an ancient discipline, and that this was my first day.

For the next hour, my two teachers separated the myth from the realities of the Shield of Power. Li Po began. "Thousands of lost lives have gone into the forging of the Shield of Power," he said. "These were the methods used to train the warriors when everything was at stake—even the very survival of the people. These techniques evolved in a time of need, of crisis. And therein lies their power. Your own end may come sooner than you think. There is no time to waste. Trust me on this. The success of your own mission depends on your doing your very best. But much more is at stake. This world is always in a state of virtual balance. It takes only a little bit to tip the scales— one way or another."

That was a somewhat daunting idea, especially about the state of the world, and there being no time to waste.

"Now the shield of power is quite intentionally cloaked in vagueness," Thod said. "Our ancestors did not give it to us to conquer the territory of our neighbors. They gave it to us to conquer our own enemy within us. It is the ultimate weapon for the ultimate adversary—the ego."

Li Po spoke again. "The ego is made out of fear," he said. "This is a great truth." I nodded. Thod and I had had some good discussions about the ego already. "If fear overcomes you," Li Po said, "you have turned away from your True Self."

Thod elaborated: "Even in the gravest crisis you must claim your natural state of grace. If you wrest control from your ego, your chances for success will be greater."

"Far greater," Li Po emphasized, rising from his seated posture. "I will teach you the six Stances of Power." He walked a short distance away and took a position in one quadrant of the broad courtyard.

"First," he said, ". . . the Stance of Humility." His gaze went within, and he began moving his body in a slow, balanced maneuver that looked like a combination of Tai Chi and Soham's Dance of the Form of Life. I could feel the meditative focus of his movements, as if he were creating an invisible force field around himself, in the space where he placed his feet and the space enclosed by the sweep of his arms. Something was definitely happening in the Courtyard of the Sacred Dancers.

"There are stories and lessons associated with this and with all of the other Stances," Thod explained as we watched. Finishing the demonstration, Li Po stood silently for several breaths before rejoining us. My teachers then instructed me in the stories that belonged to the three degrees of the first stance—the Stance of Humility.

The first degree is called the *Humility of the Prisoner*. "In ancient times," Thod said, "the first step in both the warrior's or the shaman's training in the Shield of Power was absolute surrender of his freedom. The object was to break the shell of his ego. Li Po teaches that our ego is not only the source of our false arrogance, but also of our laziness, which is why it must be broken." Li Po smiled and said something for Thod to relay to me, which was that it wasn't necessary for me to go to jail to learn the Stance of Humility. Any situation that requires servitude to another is an opportunity to learn to overcome the ego. This could even include my job, he said—a great relief to hear, since I had no wish to go to jail, and I had already experienced plenty of workplace servitude. "In that way you are forced to overcome your self-pity and anger and develop humility," Thod said.

"But the ego is still strong," Li Po warned. "And so the second degree is called the *Humility of the Priest*. Those who have dedicated their lives to service know the second degree. Out of such dedication comes moral power and lack of ego not available to the average person."

"I have always admired people who served without thought for themselves," I said. I saw Li Po raise his hand at my words. He nodded to Thod to explain.

"Li Po teaches that even the attachment to service can be a subtle form of egotism. Therefore, the third and highest degree of the Stance of Humility is the *Humility of the Peasant*. You recognize the honorable power that lies in the weathered hands of the humblest farmer or blacksmith or weaver of baskets, whose constant focus is on mastering the work at hand. There is little room for ego. Li Po told me that Mao Tse Tung's mastery of this Stance empowered him to take control over all of China. Everywhere he went he would speak of his roots as a farmer. His cunning image of humility seemed so sincere that it won over the masses. An example of the way in which this knowledge can be corrupted."

After that, Thod left us in the courtyard, and my hands-on training began. Li Po gave me a breathing exercise and told me to meditate on the Supreme Truth. The breathing took me easily into a state of mental freedom and openness. Or maybe Li Po was helping me with his dynamic stillness. We then practiced the first of the three forms of the Stance of Humility, and I concentrated on breaking the prison of the ego while my body made the movements that related to that concept. Even in the first few clumsy attempts I could feel a shift in my energies.

As we moved through the three forms I felt them building, one upon the another, not in any way I could describe, but real enough that I knew I wasn't imagining it. At the end of our session he asked if I had questions.

"What else will help me to prevail over my ego?" I asked.

"Go inside," he said. "Find the secret place where you hold revenge." He looked benignly at me and waited for me to think about this. Then he said, "So long as you are fighting one hundred injustices from the past you will be weak . . . an easy target for others. Because the roots of that desire for revenge might be very old, many people don't even remember why they are angry. That is your meditation until we meet tomorrow." He stood, and the lesson was over. We bowed to each other in mutual respect.

⌒

AND SO IT WENT, FOR SEVERAL DAYS, UNTIL LI PO HAD TAUGHT ME ALL of the Stances of Power and all of the meditations and stories that belonged to them: the Stance of Innocence, the Stance of Knowledge, the Stance of Wisdom, the Stance of Love, and the Stance of Discipline. As with the Stance of Humility, each of the others had three degrees—eighteen in all. The goal of practicing these mental exercises and their corresponding body movements was to learn to react to events from choice rather than reflex.

In between my times with the Chinese master I practiced on the terrace outside my cell, where my mistakes wouldn't be very public. I attempted to connect my mind and my will to the meditations that pertained to each of what Li Po called "The Eighteen Primary Maneuvers." I was just a beginner; I could only imagine what the advanced teachings must be like. I knew that I felt more clear within myself, yet I worried that I could still be ambushed by some unexpected challenge and thrown off balance. I hadn't been tested in the real world yet. The closest was one day when I worked with several of the village men to repair the irrigation pump with the parts we had brought from Turfan. But that pleasant, cooperative experience was hardly typical of the world in general. Again I thought to myself, I could be happy here.

I took many of my meals with Thod or Soham or both together. Occasionally I saw Gil-Hamesch and the Cook, but our lives hadn't intersected very much since my initiation into the *Book of Creation*. At breakfast one day Soham asked me what part of the training I found most difficult. I told her that I was trying hard to do as Li Po asked, searching inside myself for the secret place where I held revenge—but I kept coming up against a block. "I don't understand it," I said. "I truly want to empty myself of old bitterness, but I seem unable to do it all the way. Mentally, I can. Emotionally, it's another thing."

Soham smiled sympathetically. "Thod once researched the effects of the plague that decimated Asia many thousand years ago. He believes that the virus may have permanently altered human behavior—that it changed us for the worse, and made us into vengeful creatures."

"Or is that just Thod's opinion of the human race?" I said.

"Not at all. When you consider it, you know that a wounded animal will strike you, but only a human being will plot revenge long after the wound has healed. Revenge is our greatest weakness. If you look around at the problems in the world you might agree that it is one of the greatest evils."

"No question."

"But there is a way out of this unnatural tendency of ours—a slow and steady pressure to overcome the desire for revenge and self-justification. And the last step is forgiveness. I can tell you that the slow way is often the fastest way to achieve a goal. To force a state of forgiveness before you have prepared the way is to build a structure with no foundation."

"You sound just like Li Po," I said.

"You are not the first one to suffer under his gentle hand," she laughed. "He was my own teacher when I first came to the village. Has he spoken to you yet about the bamboo scaffold?"

"That was yesterday's demonstration," I said, recalling Li Po's imagery of how old belief structures finally give way to new ones. What I understood was that every religion, occupation and cultural tradition—every strongly held attitude—is a mental construct that is a belief structure. And because life is in a continual state of change, every belief structure is subject to collapse in a chaotic way before it is replaced by another. He compared belief structures to bamboo scaffolds erected to hold holiday decorations. When the holiday has passed, they no longer serve their purpose.

"I'm sure he told you that the art of power is learning to recognize the right moment when a small push can cause the structure to collapse, making room for something new."

"You're speaking of my emotional block," I said, and she only smiled again.

"Perhaps its time for usefulness has passed, and you have been fearing it for no reason. What would happen if you gave a small push and sent it off with gratitude for what it had to teach you about forgiveness?"

It sounded so simple. Soham was as much a master of logic as Thod, but in her own nurturing way. "I can't possibly argue with that," I conceded.

"In world affairs or large organizations or in one's individual life there are these decisive turning points. When they happen, many other things change as well. For a time it seems like the end of the world . . . chaos. When you are invested in an existing belief structure you fear the turning points. They are deeply frightening. Now, multiply the power of your personal internal crisis times the whole world, and you see how people come to expect disaster, Armageddon. In every part of the world, in every time, there have been stories like this. But you know what? If it could happen, it would have already."

"And why hasn't it happened?"

"Because there is another force at work. And this is where the Supreme Truth comes in. You have to conclude that there is an active, beneficial power guiding all our lives. You can call it God or Chi or Allah or the Tao. There is no ultimate disaster, no end of the world—only the continuing play of the Supreme Truth as it calls us to awaken. Whatever you call that great power, the real purpose of meditating on the *Book of Truth* is to clear your mind so that you can perceive that subtle but active voice of infinity."

Whoever seeks diligently for that presence which has no body, or color, or sound or other description, cannot fail in the quest. The words from the *Book of Truth* came into my thoughts and I repeated them to Soham.

"The power of the Supreme Truth is so subtle that it cannot be seen or heard or touched. So we must work with it in a different way—according to its terms, not ours. Few people have the courage and discipline to set aside their self-importance and unquestioned beliefs long enough to experience this power, let alone develop a relationship with it. And so it is called by many people a 'secret source of power,' although there is nothing secret about it."

"Hence, all those stories about the Shield of Power and its invincibility," I offered.

"Of course!" she said, as if it were a wonderful joke. "You cannot command the power that lies behind the Supreme Truth any more than you can know the future. You can only beckon to it."

Thod arrived at our terrace table in time to hear Soham's last statements. "My timing is excellent," he said as he folded his tall frame into one of the wooden chairs. "Li Po wants me to prepare his student for this morning's exercises. He wishes me to explain the concept of 'beckoning the future,' but I see you have already begun." He broke a piece of flat bread and popped it into his mouth, looking not at me but at Soham, and with the most loving expression.

Thod had laid the groundwork for this concept on our first trek into the desert, when I experienced the painful process of 'culling the past.' We never did get to the second part of it, 'beckoning the future.' I'm sure for good reason.

"The first step in beckoning the future," Soham said, "begins with complete faith in that unknowable Presence which exists every-where without measure."

"There are three steps," Thod said, looking at me now. "The second step is to wait for an indication from that ever-present force. If you act before you see that sign, your actions may lead to failure. Most people grab at power the moment it comes their way."

"In the short term," Soham said, "power does come to those who act solely on instinct and impulse. But true and lasting power comes to the one who waits patiently and acts with integrity at just the right moment."

"That is the essence of the art of changing your luck," Thod continued. "It is the surest method of influencing the future to effect a positive outcome for the long term. I cannot emphasize enough that power comes from patience."

"You mean I'm not the most patient of men?" I said.

"If I have taught you well, you know exactly who you are by now," he said. "I will tell you a great truth, as Li Po would say: A single individual acting in a small way at just the right moment can change the course of history."

"And there is the third step," Soham said. "It is to take action when you see a sign of the Supreme Truth. This sign might manifest in the most subtle way, but you will know it when you see it. So you should be open at all times and in every way. When that moment comes, do not question your need to take action, no matter how unreasonable the direction of that action may seem in that moment. As you practice this you will find that these moments come more often and closer together. And you will be able to sustain longer periods of direct connection with that subtle presence."

"Now you are ready for your final lesson with Master Li Po," Thod said. "He tells me he's pleased with your progress." He paused. ". . . and so am I."

I couldn't reply because of the sudden tightness in my throat.

"And bring your immortality staff with you," he added.

24

The End of the Beginnings

I MET LI PO IN THE COURTYARD OF THE SACRED DANCERS. HE WAS holding a curved wood staff similar to mine. The lesson today was to master the use of it, not as a weapon, but to energize and expand the boundaries of my Form of Life. At least that's what I gathered, since Thod wasn't here to interpret Li Po's limited English. After he coached me through a series of slow, sweeping spiral patterns with my staff he said, "Now, do it with your mind only."

I closed my eyes and concentrated, mentally drawing the lines of the double figure eight around myself. But I couldn't hold onto the pattern. It swayed and bulged and wouldn't obey.

I heard Li Po's discreet laugh. "Again," he said. I tried harder, but the more I tried, the less control I had of the lines. "Do not force," he said softly. "Never force." I tried once more, placing myself in a state of quiet expectation instead. Now I was able to draw the spiral form and see it with my mind's eye, perfectly balanced, pulsing and spinning with a golden light in the center. "The power comes when you hold lightly," Li Po whispered.

This was to be our last time together. Li Po wanted to give me as many ways to understand the Shield of Power as he could. The exercise with the immortality staff wasn't part of the Six Stances of Power, it was meant to help me visualize my own energy field, and to see how responsive it was to my intentions and my inner states—how easily it could be disturbed when the will-force was uneven. We sat down on the stone pavement to meditate together one last time. Again, I heard his thoughts in my mind: *You will not need my guidance when you leave here . . . nor will you need the guidance of Gil-Hamesch. But you will forever need the guidance of the Supreme Truth. Place your faith in the greatest power there is, and act with humility.* When I looked up he was smiling at me. "Do not worry any more . . . about anything!" he said, and a further thought came into my mind: *And don't try to add self-improvement onto your back, like a heavy burden. Instead, resolve to revitalize yourself at the core.* He knew me very well, this master warrior, this powerfully gentle being. I was going to miss our sessions together. When I bowed to him it was with profound respect for his knowledge and heart.

Afterwards, I met with Thod. We took a long walk together, out beyond the monastery and into the rocky hills. Mostly in silence. Even when we talked, our conversation never went deep. "No more lessons," Thod said at one point. "You have enough to think about for now." He was right. I was filled to the brim.

Walking the path near the monastery

"Concerning the book," I said, "I'm getting used to the idea of being a Dreamer. I wish I could feel more confident of my creative side."

"How will you know as long as you keep it a secret from yourself?" he said, and I knew he was right.

Maybe all I needed was to beckon the Dreamer in me and he would come. "It's easier for me to think of you as the Judge," I said.

"That is because I know who I am and I accept it."

"But what about Soham? Who is she?"

"Soham is the consummate Provider. This made a very strong attraction between us, since ours is a complementary pairing."

"And if I should find my complementary 'other,' who would she be?"

"A woman of honor to match your Dreamer's honesty. She would be a Hunter."

While we were speaking of the personality types, I asked him to tell me about Li Po and the Cook.

"You know this already," he said. "Li Po is the Warrior who has transformed his ability to fight into an ability to awaken the higher faculties in people. The Cook is the Being of Compassion."

I stopped asking questions and simply enjoyed my last walkabout with Thod. I could no longer put off going to Urumchi, I knew that. Reluctantly, I asked him to make arrangements to get me there as soon as possible. He said I could leave later today if I wished, but after dinner, because the Cook was preparing a special feast for me.

When we returned to the monastery Thod put a hand on my shoulder. "You have a lot of work to do, my friend. When the time is right for you to return, you will know it."

"I'll probably have another of my vivid dreams and you'll be in it, saying 'Larry, it's time,'" I tried to joke. This was difficult. I wasn't looking forward to leaving tonight.

"I will give you an address to send a message to me when the time comes." As an afterthought Thod said, "I think you'll have to start wearing your wristwatch again."

He left me at the door to my room. I had a couple of hours to pack and get ready before the Cook's feast and my departure. I carefully wrapped my immortality staff in burlap and twine for my eventual flight home, hoping it would qualify as carryon luggage. I didn't want it out of my hands. When I had everything packed and I had changed back into my own clothes again, I went outside on the terrace to sit with my journal and my thoughts. The air was becoming cooler now, I could feel that winter was approaching. I drew long, deep breaths, trying to hold onto the essence of this place—the monastery, the vast desert, the mountains. I was already feeling homesick for it. I still couldn't imagine writing a book that would tell even a fraction of what I had experienced. It didn't seem possible.

So, here I was, at the end of my journey. Wiser than when I began, I hoped. Maybe a little more aware of the ways of the universe. What I chose to do with my knowledge was entirely up to me. I had my indelible memories, my immortality staff, my journal. I had returned the golden amulet to its proper place, and a few minutes ago I had tucked two books of the *Song of Eternity* deep in my carryon bag. I couldn't help thinking that I had traded one symbol of the Divine Sacred Fire for another. The first was for me alone, to carry for a while—the second was for me to share. A fair trade.

I sat watching the glow of afternoon light against the red cliffs. I had come here with questions and some of them were now answered, but many were not. Even though it seemed unlikely, I believed deep down that I would return one day and that more answers would be given to me. I would beckon the future and the future would take care of itself.

Thod and Soham came to escort me to dinner in one of the larger monastery rooms. There were about ten of us around the long, dark wooden table—Gil-Hamesch, the Cook, Li Po, Thod, Soham and myself, and several of the village elders—while three young women from the village served. The Cook had prepared the most amazing feast: fried vegetables of great variety, gingered rice mixed with lentils, lamb kabobs, yogurt, noodles, a spicy lamb and carrot soup, along with plates of honeyed sweets. The Cook told outrageous jokes and everyone laughed. Even Thod.

From time to time, in the midst of the animated dinner table chatter, I felt Gil-Hamesch's attention on me. I wondered if he was having second thoughts about giving me the task of finishing the translations of the first two books on my own and sharing them widely. The Cook kept plying me with food, delighted when I tried something new and discovered that it was delicious.

Inevitably, the time came for goodbyes. We all walked outside and out the front gates of the monastery, where a small group of the village men were waiting with donkeys. They had volunteered to escort me back to the place where we had left the Land Rover. A driver would then take me back to Turfan and I would hire another driver to take me to Urumchi from there.

Out of respect for the Asian tradition, I bowed to the ground to Gil-Hamesch and did not rise until he touched my head. I bowed less formally to Li Po, and when I came to the Cook he held his arms out wide and wrapped me in a tight embrace. I extended my hand to Soham and felt her warm blessing in return. Thod had no choice but to accept a hug from me, his grateful student and sparring partner. I didn't look at his face, but quickly mounted my donkey, picked up the braided rope reins and started off.

We retraced the route past the fluttering prayer flags and shrines, along the hilly, forested trail and down the narrow canyon to the barn. A somber man in a white turban was waiting for me with the Land Rover and we started out in silence on the lonely desert highway.

25

The Stance of Innocence

WE ARRIVED IN TURFAN LATE THE NEXT MORNING. IT LOOKED JUST THE same as before—the rows of yellow high-rise apartments, the dust and congestion, the factories. I was still between realities, not quite ready to reenter this one all by myself. I missed Thod. I missed all of them.

I checked into a modest hotel and napped until noon. When I awoke, I placed a call to the Urumchi Office of Technology to tell them of my impending arrival. After extensive and confusing conversations, I learned that the man who was supposed to meet me had been reassigned to a different post in another part of the country. They did not expect a replacement for at least two months. Supposedly they had faxed this information to my office in the United States, but I had received no word of it. How could I have? I'd been essentially out of contact with the world since Dharamshala. They cheerfully invited me to wait for two months, or to return home and come back again when they needed my services.

I put down the phone. Instead of feeling like someone had just pulled the rug out from under me, I started to laugh. I couldn't stop myself. So, there never was a Plan B, after all! I was never going to meet the Urumchi engineers on this trip, because Plan A was everything! What perfect irony . . . worthy of the most convoluted logic trick Thod ever played on me. I still had a smile on my face when I left my room and walked outside from the hotel lobby. I felt like Nasruddin, the wise fool in the Sufi stories who had nothing but misadventures, yet somehow each one left him a wiser fool than he had been the day before. All I needed was my donkey.

I briefly considered hiring a car and returning to the monastery, but I knew that wasn't right. It was time for me to go home. I'd take a day or two here in Turfan to get my journal notes in order, and maybe even plot out a rough draft for the book. A couple of days of down time sounded good right now. Even in Turfan.

I went for a stroll through the town, reflecting on the incredible effort it had taken me to make it this far. I now wore my jeans and a Western style shirt, which made me a lot more conspicuous than when I wore the clothes Thod had lent to me. I sat in the town park eating from a bag of golden Turfan raisins, thinking about the last time I was here, when Thod tried to teach me to see the Form of Life. For a while I occupied myself watching a group of children chasing after pigeons. I tried practicing seeing them as bouncing, light-filled egg-forms. But something distracted my attention when I became aware of a young Chinese man in a blue Mao hat. As he casually thumbed through magazines at a small stand nearby, I saw him glance back at me. My instinct told me that I was once again under surveillance.

I went directly back to the hotel. By now, the man made no attempt to hide the fact that he was tailing me. He followed me all the way upstairs to my room, then entered the room next to mine. I opened my door, and my heart sank. All my belongings had been rifled. Fortunately, I had carried my money with me in my daypack, along with my camera, plane ticket and passport, and my journal. But my immortality staff had been torn from its burlap wrapping and tossed on the floor. Gifts I had bought were likewise opened and discarded. I did a quick inventory and found that nothing had been taken. I had to conclude that this was the work of the police.

Feeling lucky and paranoid and Nasruddin-like, all at once, I stepped out onto the wooden balcony and watched the setting sun shimmer through the smoky orange haze on the horizon. A dog barked and I looked down to see three uniformed policemen marching towards the front door of the hotel. Two of them carried rifles, and the third held a bundle of papers. I stepped back inside, closed the shutters behind me and started packing my bags, when a loud knock shook my door. My heart pounded as a key turned in the door. A petite woman in a blue and white maid's uniform poked her head in shyly. I motioned for her to come in. Behind her came the three soldiers. The man with the papers waved them at me.

"Come with me!" he barked, without taking the cigarette out of his mouth. He motioned for me to step outside. I picked up my daypack and obeyed. As we walked down the hall, only the thump of military boots could be heard. I thought frantically about what to say and how to act. I thought of Li Po. He would have reminded me that my feelings were real only because I made them real. I relaxed a little and focused on looking for a subtle sign that would give me a clue about what to do.

Down the street from the hotel, we entered a small office with nothing on the walls. The gruff soldier with the papers sat down at an old gray steel desk and motioned for me to sit across from him in a folding chair. The other two officers waited outside the door. I tried not to betray my feelings, not to allow myself to be intimidated. He began interrogating me in detail. Where was I born? What business did I have here? Why weren't my permits in order? I tried to reply with enough candor to appear innocent, but at the same time protect my friends at the monastery. The interrogator did not write any of my answers down, but just stared at me as I answered. He stopped the questioning and went to the door to growl an order to the guards, one of whom returned in a few minutes with a pot of tea. The officer waited for him to leave and then locked the door behind him. He sat down and sipped his tea as he scrutinized me closely. Then he reached into a satchel.

"Where did you get this?" he demanded, pulling out a small blue flag with an Islamic white moon and star. I had purchased it from a merchant at the Sunday Market in Kashgar.

"I got it from an old man," I said. "I don't know his name."

"This is the outlawed flag of East Turkestan!" he declared.

He stopped to watch my reaction. "I'm sorry," I told him. "I don't know anything about local politics. Nor am I particularly interested in getting involved."

"You don't know about the Uigher fight for independence and self-determination?" he demanded.

I looked up at him, and for the first time, noticed that he himself looked like a Uigher. I should have noticed this earlier. It is unusual to see a Uigher man or woman in a Chinese police uniform.

"This flag is outlawed by order of the Chinese government. It belongs to people who want to break away from China and form their own country. In fact, it is even illegal to talk about Eastern Turkestan. That is why you must tell me who has approached you and if you are supporting them."

I told him again that I knew nothing at all about this. The *Stance of Innocence*, I reminded myself.

A sudden gust of wind blew open the shutters. The soldier stood and shut the window. I noticed that his expression had changed. He looked older, and more resigned. "People are not always who they seem at first appearance," he said. "In fact, everything you think you know is not really true," he added, as if to himself.

His words startled me. It sounded like he was quoting a passage directly from the *Song of Eternity*. I intuited that things had shifted somehow, that they would not put me in jail, and that, in some way, I might even help this man instead. This awareness came to me just as Li Po said it would. *Have faith in the natural order of things*, he told me. *Be patient, and act only when you see an indication from the Supreme Truth to do so*. In the past, I would have ignored these brief moments of change that I didn't understand. Now I seized the opportunity.

"Are you sure this Uigher—or Eastern Turkestan movement—is such a bad thing?" It was a risky ploy.

The officer lowered his voice and relaxed his posture considerably. I did the same. He looked at me for a long time, as if sizing up whether he could trust me.

"I want to tell you a story," he said quietly. He glanced up at the closed door and back at me. "It is a true story about my great-grandfather. He lived in a village near Kyrgistan. I heard this story from my father many times."

"I would like to hear it," I told him, as if I had much choice.

"It seems that our village suffered through a drought many, many years ago. The lack of water forced almost everyone to abandon our village. My great-grandfather decided to go to the Kashi village, which was only a few days' ride away. He thought their baxshi shamans might know why our village had been cursed by drought and why the wells had all run dry. He believed the gods must be angry. When he got to the village he met a man who was not a Kashi shaman, but had come from some place far away to the west. He told my great-grandfather that he would help him and our village. However, he told my grandfather that he would first have to work for him. My grandfather agreed to this, and the man handed him a shovel. He told him to dig a long, deep hole in the side of a hill and not stop until he found a buried mineshaft.

"My grandfather found this work difficult. In that region it always rained and snowed, but my grandfather did not stop working. The desert sand absorbed the rain, so very little could grow, and his horse could not find much to eat. He slept alone in a tent, and the mysterious man brought him one meal each evening. Day after day, he dug sand and cleared away layers of clay and rock. And then one morning he finally uncovered the old wooden doors that formed the entry to a cavern. He never went down into the cave. But he felt happy that he had finished his work at last.

"Now the man from the west followed my great-grandfather back to our village. When they arrived, they rode their horses straight to the wells outside of our village. For the first time in two years, water flowed freely from them—enormous volumes of water. Word spread all over the region that a miracle had occurred. You see, our village was once a famous oasis along the ancient caravan trail. But it was rapidly dying. To everyone's amazement, they now had more than enough water to farm and raise livestock for themselves, and even had a surplus."

There was something very familiar about this story. I felt a tingling sensation up and down my spine as the narrative unfolded.

"The man from the Kashi village stayed with my family for a month and showed them how to grow more crops than they had ever grown before. For that reason, we have always called him 'the Gardener.' He is still a hero in my family's town. However, when he left, we never saw him again. In his parting words he told us to always honor our ancient teachings. He said that if we did this, our well would never run dry again."

I resisted the impulse to say that I, too, knew about a man called the Gardener. If the circumstances had been different I would have.

"My great-grandfather said this miracle occurred because of his own great patience," the man went on, "because hour after hour, day after day, week after week, he dug in a desert valley far away from home. He told us repeatedly that it wasn't only the magic powers of the Gardener that saved them. The water would never have returned except for his unquestioning faith and patience."

"Now we know, of course, that magic was not involved." He waved a dismissive hand. "There is a long-forgotten underground cave that links that distant rainy valley to our village miles away. The desert is still filled with these karez irrigation tunnels that have been built over the course of many centuries. So we don't think about this story as a miracle anymore. But my great-grandfather's lesson about patience stayed with us all and has become an enduring vision for our entire village. We know how to be patient."

"It is a wonderful story," I ventured. "Patience is a great virtue." I wondered why he had gone to such lengths to tell me this.

The officer leaned back and lowered his voice. "When the Chinese first came to our village they took our land and tried to teach our children to be ashamed of their Uigher background. Then another miracle happened. After the Soviet Union collapsed, all of the peoples of West Turkestan founded their own countries— Uzbekistan, Kazakhstan, Turkmenistan and Kyrgyzstan. Only the people of East Turkestan remained under Chinese occupation. Many people in this region have tried to advocate for independence—not just the few radicals." He looked at me meaningfully, and said, "They were all shot."

"I hope you believe me when I tell you I have no political interests whatsoever," I said again.

The officer stood and walked to the window. He gazed out at the mountains. "You people in America know all about what happened in Tibet, but almost no one knows about the daily oppression of the Uigher people. It isn't a fashionable cause yet. The Uighers have no political power. But they do have patience. We are all working hard digging out the sand in the desert, just like my great-grandfather. We don't know when equality will come, but we have faith in the power of justice."

The officer turned to face me. I couldn't read his expression.

"I want you to understand I am not advocating for independence. I believe that all of us—Uighers, Chinese, Kazakhs, Kyrgyz, everybody—can forge a great country together. First, the Chinese bosses have to see that they are not so superior. Then maybe they will discover that we of Uigher descent have been around just as long, and have a lot to offer them—and the rest of the world, too."

He walked back to his desk. "I am not going to arrest you, provided you agree to leave Xinjiang right now. You have become a risk to me and to yourself. Do you have your papers with you?"

I showed them to him, along with my open-ended plane ticket.

"I will tell the hotel clerk to make a reservation for you on tonight's flight out of Urumchi bound for Alma-Aty in Kazakhstan. I will call ahead to make sure you are issued a transit visa at the airport. You are on your own once you are out of China." He handed my documents back to me with one last piece of advice: "Please do not forget that you were befriended by a Uigher."

I politely pointed out to him that his suggested departure was in six hours and I had no way to get to Urumchi in time for the flight.

"My man will drive you there in four hours or less. This is for your own good. I suggest you take my offer."

I thanked him and extended my hand to him, but he declined. Instead, he walked abruptly out of the room without looking back.

$\sim$

AND SO I FOUND MYSELF IN ANOTHER CAR, WITH ANOTHER SILENT driver, careening along the rutted, unfinished desert road—back the way I had come earlier. When we had driven away from the town and the farms I started looking off to the left, hoping that I could see where Thod had turned the Land Rover from the main road to get to the village that first day, but I couldn't be sure. Out there somewhere, through red cliffs and a narrow, forested valley was the monastery, and people I cared deeply about. I sent a heartfelt blessing towards them. Almost instantly I felt Gil-Hamesch's presence around me. *There is no separation*, he said, *there is only energy —and the highest energy is love.*

I smiled to myself. Of course . . .

AFTER

BY THE TIME I REACHED HOME, I HAD A ROUGH OUTLINE FOR THE BOOK, plotted out in a succession of hotel rooms and red-eye plane flights.

I had promised I would do my best to tell my story—about my own attempts at spiritual growth and about the people I encountered who so generously helped me. But I knew from the outset that I could never truly describe the effect that Gil-Hamesch had on me. As the months and then years have passed since my journey, I've been surprised by how much I continue to miss him, sometimes to the point of pain and sorrow.

What I now know without a doubt—and I didn't know before—is that there are higher states of awareness, and that it is possible through love and will to awaken to them. That is the great gift that Gil-Hamesch transferred to me. I know that he is aware of my gratitude, wherever he is at this moment. And I do know, in ways that defy explanation, that there is no separation, only energy. And that the highest energy is love.

It was this profound affection in my heart that inspired me to begin my new path once I returned—not the teachings, or even the sacred texts that I was working on, as compelling as they were. As I got deeper into writing this book, I found the desires of my mind to know and understand gradually losing their urgency, and the desires of my heart beginning to flourish.

In time, I have discovered that Thod's assertions—including his comments on my finding my life's companion—were right on target, as they usually were. I've written to him and told him of my progress, and his replies have been brief and typically Thod-like. He tells me that Gil-Hamesch is still alive and well, but becoming more frail. I'm not yet ready to return, but when I do, I hope this time I won't be such a difficult student.

Lately, I've thought a lot about my place in the scheme of things. I am not the first person, and I won't be the last, to travel the ancient Silk Road transporting pieces of wisdom and truth, as well as tangible goods, from one end of the world to another. Warriors, traders and monks have ridden their Mongol horses and Bactrian camels through those same windswept canyons and deserts for longer than we will ever know. With them, new ideas and spiritual beliefs have traveled, forever changing the cultural landscape ahead of them. Maybe it is still true today.

Centuries ago, the great civilization of China was introduced to the Europeans by way of this highway. The trade and cultures that passed along the Silk Road revolutionized the Western perception of the world. This journey across the Gobi Desert changed me, too. I learned that it is all too easy for us in the West to avoid looking deeply inside to find our True Voices. I also learned that the ancient Central Asian views of life possess a wisdom that can greatly enhance our narrowly focused scientific knowledge. In coming together, these two worldviews can make us all more whole.

But most importantly—at least for me personally—I have rediscovered a part of me that is neither of the East nor the West. Whether through the direct connection with Gil-Hamesch, or through the stripping away of layers of inner stories by the solitude of traveling in the desert, I came to experience that subtle power which is inside and surrounds each one of us.

Religion, culture, and economic status are only the masks we wear. When we accept ourselves as unique manifestations of the same eternal essence of life, we will all have the power to create a beautiful world together. This is my dream. I accept that it is possible to achieve.

Glossary of Terms

baxshi
: Shamanic healer who recites epic verses and often uses music for healing.

chakras
: Centers of energy in the body (in yoga philosophy) that correspond approximately to centers in the parasympathetic nervous system.

chang-qobuz
: Metal Uzbek musical instrument similar to a Jew's harp. It is made by attaching a flexible steel strip to a metal hoop. The player vibrates the strip with one hand while inhaling and exhaling on the instrument.

dervish
: Member of a Sufi ascetic order, some of whom perform whirling dances and vigorous chanting as acts of ecstatic devotion.

dhoti
: Traditional Indian cotton loincloth worn by Hindu men.

dombro
: Type of lute with two strings. It is played with arpeggios. Kazakh and Kyrgyz baxshi shamans play it to accompany recital of sacred texts.

dorje
: Tibetan symbol of the life force. It appears in art and ritual objects.

Elán-Puri	Ancient serpent god of Central Asia.
ghat	Broad flight of steps leading down to the edge of a river.
karez	An irrigation tunnel.
karma	A complex concept in Hinduism and Buddhism. In common usage it means the consequence of prior choices, or one's fate or destiny.
kundalini	In yoga philosophy it is the internal energy that activates the chakras.
Kyrgyz	Ethnic group in Western Xinjiang and Eastern Kazakhstan.
madressa	An Islamic theological school.
maya	Indian philosophical concept that states that many of life's certainties are in fact an illusion.
mullah	Muslim religious teacher, leader, or scholar.
Rimpoche	Exalted Tibetan Buddhist teacher.
rishi	Divinely inspired poet or saint.
sadhu	Indian ascetic holy man with no ties to family or society.
Sufi	Member of a mystical order of Islam.
terma	Hidden Tibetan sacred teaching.
Uigher	The primary culture of Xinjiang, China.

Uzbek	Ethnic group found predominantly in Uzbekistan.
Wish-Fulfilling Jewel	Tibetan symbol that looks like an egg with a spiral that circumscribes it.
zikr	Sufi tradition of chanting the divine names of God.

Acknowledgements

I WOULD LIKE TO EXPRESS MY DEEPEST GRATITUDE TO ALL WHO HAVE inspired me and to those who helped with this book. I would like to thank my family, Urai, Jeanine, Vanessa, Bryan and Stephen, for their patience and support; and my friends and teachers, especially Heather Ash, Miguel Ruiz, Ginny Gentry and Kaye Thompson.

There are so many others I would like to thank who have contributed to this life journey: Lisa Andrews, Gae Buckley, Stephanie Bureau, Fu-Ding Cheng, Joya Comeaux, Chuck and Terry Cowgill, David and Linda Dibble, Steven Dorward, Storm Flores, Hal and Maryann Foreman, Ed Fox, JJ Franks, Judy Fruhbauer, George Gorton, Terry Gorton, Susan Gregg, Allan Hardman, Vanessa Henderson, Betty Hillman, Frank Hayhurst, Linda Jacobsen, Gaya and Trey Jenkins, Christinea Johnson, Christine Judal, Robin Karlstedt, Siri Gian Singh Khalsa, Dara and Mersedeh Kheredmand, Audrey Lehman, Jeanie Yee Linden, Skye, Diane and "Merlin," Brandt Morgan, Lisa Navarro, Nicky Orietas, Roberto Paez, Ted and Peggy Raess, Rita Rivera, Sherry Rosenthal, John Ruskell, Mitra Sarkhosh, Valerie Scott, Barbara Simon, Virginia Sease, Dorothy Schlie, Soula Saad, Pitaka Tathagata, Sandra Lee Tatum, Malina Thorpe, Gary and Leo Van Warnerdam, Ramin and Becca Yazdani, and many more of you—you know who you are. Thank you for all you have done for me.

Special thanks are reserved for my editor, Catherine Dees; book designer, Karen Connor; publisher, Paul Kelly, and the dedicated people who helped in the early stages of the book preparation: Nancy Newlin, Ma Mon Mon, Danay Strickwerde, Tracy Audisio and Lynn Riley. Without your exceptional talents and hard work, this book would have been merely a dream.

About the Author

LARRY ANDREWS LEADS CLASSES AND WORKSHOPS IN THE *Song of Eternity*, conducts experiential tours to sacred places throughout the world, and is available for private consultation. He can be reached through his website at www.larryandrews.net

Acknowledgements

I WOULD LIKE TO EXPRESS MY DEEPEST GRATITUDE TO ALL WHO HAVE inspired me and to those who helped with this book. I would like to thank my family, Urai, Jeanine, Vanessa, Bryan and Stephen, for their patience and support; and my friends and teachers, especially Heather Ash, Miguel Ruiz, Ginny Gentry and Kaye Thompson.

There are so many others I would like to thank who have contributed to this life journey: Lisa Andrews, Gae Buckley, Stephanie Bureau, Fu-Ding Cheng, Joya Comeaux, Chuck and Terry Cowgill, David and Linda Dibble, Steven Dorward, Storm Flores, Hal and Maryann Foreman, Ed Fox, JJ Franks, Judy Fruhbauer, George Gorton, Terry Gorton, Susan Gregg, Allan Hardman, Vanessa Henderson, Betty Hillman, Frank Hayhurst, Linda Jacobsen, Gaya and Trey Jenkins, Christinea Johnson, Christine Judal, Robin Karlstedt, Siri Gian Singh Khalsa, Dara and Mersedeh Kheredmand, Audrey Lehman, Jeanie Yee Linden, Skye, Diane and "Merlin," Brandt Morgan, Lisa Navarro, Nicky Orietas, Roberto Paez, Ted and Peggy Raess, Rita Rivera, Sherry Rosenthal, John Ruskell, Mitra Sarkhosh, Valerie Scott, Barbara Simon, Virginia Sease, Dorothy Schlie, Soula Saad, Pitaka Tathagata, Sandra Lee Tatum, Malina Thorpe, Gary and Leo Van Warnerdam, Ramin and Becca Yazdani, and many more of you—you know who you are. Thank you for all you have done for me.

Special thanks are reserved for my editor, Catherine Dees; book designer, Karen Connor; publisher, Paul Kelly, and the dedicated people who helped in the early stages of the book preparation: Nancy Newlin, Ma Mon Mon, Danay Strickwerde, Tracy Audisio and Lynn Riley. Without your exceptional talents and hard work, this book would have been merely a dream.

About the Author

LARRY ANDREWS LEADS CLASSES AND WORKSHOPS IN THE *Song of Eternity*, conducts experiential tours to sacred places throughout the world, and is available for private consultation. He can be reached through his website at www.larryandrews.net